APPOMATTOX COUNTY
HISTORY AND GENEALOGY

by
Nathaniel Ragland Featherston

CLEARFIELD

Originally published
as pages 1–62 and 99–288 of
The History of Appomattox, Virginia:
Also World War II -- I and Spanish American War Service Record
(Appomattox, Virginia, 1948)

Reprinted for
Clearfield Company, Inc. by
Genealogical Publishing Co., Inc.
Baltimore, Maryland
1998, 2003

International Standard Book Number: 0-8063-4760-0

TO

I am dedicating this volume to my father and mother who furnished me a Christian home in which to live, and to those men and women who have served Appomattox County in time of war and in time of peace.

MRS. J. H. FEATHERSTON
1852-1932

Born in Richmond, Virginia, came to Appomattox in early life, spent most of her life in Appomattox County and Roanoke, Virginia.
"MY MOTHER"

JAMES HENRY FEATHERSTON
1845-1901

Confederate Soldier. Reared on a farm, lived in Mississippi 11 years, Roanoke 9 years, Appomattox County most of his life. Taught the first public school in Appomattox County when the public school system was established in the State of Virginia in 1870. School Trustee. Elder in the Presbyterian Church.
"MY FATHER"

FOREWORD

I have undertaken the writing of a History of Appomattox
County with great reluctance, fully realizing my limited
qualifications as a historian, and my limited knowledge of
the facts necessary to make a history of the county worthwhile, but the valuable help given me by the citizens of the
county has made easier its yoke and lighter its burden. I
hope what I have attempted here will be of some help to
the people in tracing up the relationship of the people of
the County.

ACKNOWLEDGEMENTS

I am especially indebted to my friends, Jerry A. Burke, Superintendent of Schools of the County, for his valuable aid and advice in compiling the material; David T. Robertson for his help in the picture line; and Calvin H. Robinson, who in 1931 purchased TIMES-VIRGINIAN, the County paper, for printing.

NATHANIEL RAGLAND FEATHERSTON - 1874

I was also reared in a Christian community. Back in my young days there were seen regularly in old Liberty Chapel Baptist Church, Tyler Pankey, Albert Thornhill, James A. Walker, William A. Thornhill, James A. Agee, D. M. Anderson and S. P. Taylor; and once a month that grand old servant of God, Rev. Thomas N. Johnson, who was pastor of that church from 1851 to 1892, (41 years), would be there to minister to his flock, and only gave up that charge because old age had weighed so heavily upon him he was not able to make the ride from his home, 20 miles down in Buckingham, to the church.

Those old leaders believed in strict obedience to the ten commandments. On the third Saturday in each month they would meet at the church and have their business meeting and a sermon from one preacher. The next morning they would have their regular monthly sermon with no business transacted on Sunday. Thus, under such influences, was the writer brought up, and any short coming that I have cannot be charged to any lack of proper training.

While these old servants of God had to apply their brain and muscle to the resources of the land for an existence, they never failed to take time to trim the lamp of morality sufficiently to make that light so shine that all who came in contact with them could not help but know they were associating with God's servants. Although the last of the above mentioned passed to their glorious reward over a quarter of a century ago, and some over a half century, that good influence was so instilled into the neighborhood that it grew up in the present generation, and shows that influence in its splendid citizenship.

I am giving the above from personal experinece. I do not mean that this is the only neighborhood with a Christian influence. From what I have found out from other sections I think each section had its like leaders and all combined made this a county of which all its citizens can be justly proud.

N. R. F.

TABLE of CONTENTS

In 1845 Virginia needed another star in her crown and she decided to pluck that star from this section which a few years later became one of the historic spots of the world.

From Buckingham such prominent names as Bocock, Flood, Trent, Gills, Thornhill, Walker, Coleman, Nowlin, Jones, Agee, Christian, Anderson, Hix, Johns. Walton, Martin, Moore, and Harding; from Prince Edward, McDearmon, Gilliam, Franklin, Abbitt, and Ligon; from Charlotte, Hannah, Marshall, Wheeler, and Harvey; and from Campbell, Davidson, Stratton, Elliott, Carson, Anderson, McKinney, Shearer, Caldwell, Robertson, Jones, Hunter Cheatham, and Smith, were the leading figures in the new county. With a combination of the above brain, muscle, and character for a foundation, there is no wonder that the structure built thereon was one that rose to the front rank of the old Mother State's galaxy of Sons.

Then arose the task of selecting officers to manage the affairs of this young son of the old Dominion. The task was not to find efficiency, but to choose from the abundance of efficiency. The men selected as officers showed the people's wisdom in their selection.

All State laws having been complied with necessary for the formation of a new county the county officers were picked. The office of Sheriff was the most important in the county, as he was not only the law enforcement officer, but collected all taxes and disbursed them on order from the justices.

No juries were summoned in those days. The Sheriff would go out on the Court Green and find jurors as they were needed at each term of the Court.

Joel Watkins was the first Sheriff and was succeeded by the following: George T. Peers, William Paris, Wilson Hix, W. T. Johnson, William H. Gills, Willis Archer Plunkett, T. B. Bryant, S. P. Coleman, Frank W. McKinney, and the incumbent, H. Winston McKinney.

The Circuit Court Judges were: G. A. Wingfield, J. D. Horsley, Samuel Coleman, George J. Hundley, Robert F. Hutcheson and the incumbent, Judge Joel W. Flood.

After the War Between the States there was a Constitutional Convention held, known as the Underwood Constitution, which established the County Court and the following Judges served: Lewis Daniel Isbel, Henry T. Parrish, and David Alexander Christian. Another Constitutional Convention was held in 1902 and 1903 which abolished the County Courts, effective 1904.

Attorneys for the Commonwealth were: Thomas S. Bocock, Lewis D. Isbel, Crawford Jones, Edward Woodson, Thomas J. Thornhill, David A. Christian, W. C. Franklin, H. D. Flood, Samuel L. Ferguson, Joel W. Flood, and the incumbent, Attorney W. M. Abbitt.

The County and Circuit Court Clerks were: John T. Bocock, Henry F. Bocock, George T. Peers, George W. Abbitt, J. R. Horsley, and the incumbent Clerk C. W. Smith.

Commissioners of the Revenue were: Thomas W. Johns, Isaac Adams, Samuel Walker, William J. Collins, Andrew Baker, John W. Gilliam, George W. Abbitt, Van Gilliam, William Statham, L. E. Smith, H. C. Babcock, E. R. Abbitt, and the incumbent, J. H. O'Brien.

County Treasurers: William H. Gills, Charlie Plunkett, S. R. Franklin, D. Mott Robertson, R. F. Burke, and the incumbent R. L. Burke.

Superintendents of Schools: C. H. Chilton, J. B. Bristow, J. K. Hannah, N. R. Featherston and the incumbent J. A. Burke.

State Senators: Colonel Wyatt Elliott, Colonel Samuel D. McDearmon, Colonel Robert B. Poore, H. D. Flood, Samuel L. Ferguson and incumbent Charles T. Moses.

House of Delegates: Samuel D. McDearmon, Zachariah Cheatham, Colonel Henry DelaWarr Flood, Crawford Jones, R. B. Poore, J. W. Flood, Thomas Bocock, James Watkins, D. Mott Robertson, W. C. Franklin, H. D. Flood, John W. Harwood, Sterling C. Stratton, William H. Ligon, J. R. Horsley, J. C. Jones, A. B. Thornhill, T. J. Stratton, J. W. Cawthorn, and R. L. Burke. Before the convening of the Session of Legislature in 1919, the State was re-districted. The new district has been represented by a man from Buckingham County since this time.

* * * * * *

Back in olden days before the automobile pushed the horse and buggy off the highway, the country store was a center of neighborhood sociability for the men folks. There around the stove many a political platform was formulated and a candidate selected to stand thereon. Often Presidents of the United States have been selected around these little heaters, and occasionally what would come before the Sunday School class the next Sunday would be discussed. There was always a measuring of talent as to who would be entitled to the next Presidency of the Annanias Club. This was a day when the people really enjoyed country life, but, alas! when good roads and the automobile came on the scene they practically put the country merchant out of business, taking all the trade to the cities and small towns and doing away with the social side of life as had been experienced in the country stores.

Then, there was the County Court which convened once a month until the Constitutional Convention met in 1901 and abolished the County Court. Now we have Circuit Courts which convene only four times a year in this county. The County Court was a great day for the people to have social intercourse, and a day for horse trading. Old Appomattox Court House was a large square building with most of the first floor space used as an auditorium; there was a small room on one side for the Clerk's Office, and a long flight of steps leading to an upper porch from which you entered the court room, with two jury rooms to one side. The main road ran in front of the building and circled it, but the road on the one side passing between the Court House and the Hotel was the one traveled. The other was used mostly by horse dealers to

11

stand their horses in the road, tied to the fence that encircled the Court House. The Raine family, who built what is now known as the McLean House, used it as a Tavern, disposing of it several years before the War Between the States. A member of the Raine family, residing in Tennessee, came back about 40 years after the War and built a shaft about 25 feet high, marking the graves of the Raine family. This shaft is near by the Soldiers' Cemetery.

This little village was one of unusual hospitality and quiet sociability until it was practically disbanded when the court house was destroyed by fire in 1892. It was re-built at the Norfolk and Western Station, and the present town has grown to something over 1,000 population.

Between the close of the War Between the States and the time the Court House was destroyed by fire, there lived here George T. Peers, Clerk of the County; Judge H. T. Parris; N. H. Ragland, merchant; the Presbyterian minister; E. G. Hix, hotel keeper who was later succeeded by J. W. McKinney; C. H. Sackett, Lawyer, R. B. Poore, lawyer; William and John Rosser, and E. T. Kindred, and Layne family. All of these were so congenially associated they seemed as one large family.

This county can boast of some unique characters. An old gentleman was so ab-sent-minded that it was said he was riding home one day and his horse blundered, throwing the old man to the ground; getting up, face from his horse, he walked off for-getting he had been riding. Another went out to get wood for the fire, came in, threw the stick of wood on the bed and his hat on the fire. Another kept his table supplied with napkins; when he went visiting he would put the napkin in his pocket thinking it was his handkerchief. An old man would never take an umbrella. He said he had already forgotten and left enough to have the neighborhood supplied. Whenever another old man left home his wife would caution him not to forget to raise his umbrella if it rained. An old man riding down a path came to a fence, dismounted, lowered the fence stepped over, put up the fence before he realized he had not led his horse over, had to lower the fence again to get his horse over. An old gentleman said he had holes in two sides of his room, one to see out and the other to go out, and when his wife's temper reached a certain degree, he used the "go out" hole. An old gentleman, with no children in the home, but with a little friction occasionally, sought refuge in the open air, saying "A man with a house of five rooms and can't stay in narry one." An old gentleman with an unusual amount of wit was in a store, and two drummers, strangers, came in. There was a barrel of cider on the counter, and they, wanting a drink, asked the old gentleman to have one with them. He replied: "Thank you, there are only two classes of people I drink with, those I know and those I do not know." His brother was a merchant and had a fire which destroyed his stock of goods. A neighbor asked the old gentleman what caused the fire. He said: "Fric-tion-a $5,000 insurance policy rubbed up against a $500 stock of goods, and that caused the fire." A lady lost her trunk check, reported it to the baggage agent. He asked her to identify her trunk which she did; he said, "Will you swear that is your trunk?" She said, "Oh, no. It is not right to swear." He repeated, "You cannot have it unless you swear it is your trunk." She insisted it was not right to swear. He told her he was sorry but she could not get it unless she swore it was hers. She said, "I hope the Lord will forgive me, but I be damned if it isn't my trunk." A gentleman who lived on the river would occasionally imbibe too much, and his wife, trying to break him of the habit, when he was out one night, put a cot in the hall, stretched out on it, and had the servant girl cover her up with a sheet. She told her that when her husband came in she should meet him at the door and tell him she was dead. The servant met him and said, "Marse Tom, Miss Ann is dead." He said, "I'm damn glad of it." What happened further was not recorded.

The people were unexcelled in culture, sociability and intellect. Those fortunate enough financially to have their coach and drivers dressed in uniform enjoyed life in the highest, making life in their community all that could be desired in country life; and those coach drivers got great pleasure in feeling their superiority over the servants that had to perform the duties of the field hand.

Then, there was another class of citizens, just as cultured and intelligent but not so fortunate financially as to have the coach and coachman, who had their buggy and surry, drove their own fine horses and had just as high rank in all deliberations of the community.

On the South side of the county, adjoining the counties of Charlotte and Prince Edward, there is an attractive hamlet, the name of which, for years was "Pamplin City", later becoming so widely and favorably known that the "City" part of the name was dropped, and is now the progressive, flourishing "Pamplin". In days long past when the open saloon was in force over the State and Pamplin was one of its distributing points, there was a small segment of the inhabitants who would occasionally imbibe too freely of its products, and thereby feeling their physical superiority, would proceed to demonstrate that fact. But Pamplin is, and always has been, a place in which any one would be proud to reside. It should be, and no doubt is, proud of the fact that it has sent out into the world those ranking high in intellect, strong in character, capable in business, popular in society and prominent in church work. There was Willis H. Ligon, who ably represented this county in the House of Delegates of Virginia; W. Courtney Franklin, one of the political leaders of the day; Rev. James Franklin, efficient in Education and Christian activities, has become a world-wide Statesman. Other good and influential citizens of Pamplin are numerous.

On the Northern border of the county, adjoining the county of Nelson at the foothills of the Blue Ridge mountains where a small stream, Bent Creek, empties into and mingles its crystal waters with the beautiful surging waters of the majestic James is found a hamlet, Bent Creek, which about a century ago was know as Diuguidville. A bridge across the James River at this point was the crossing, before railroad transportation in this section, for those Westerners who drove through the country, cattle, hogs, sheep and turkeys, to the Eastern markets. A few days before the close of the War Between the States, this bridge was burned by Appomattox citizens to keep the Federal cavalry under General Philip H. Sheridan from crossing. From that date until 1922, the people were subjected to the inconvenience of crossing the river in a ferry boat. In 1922 the counties of Appomattox and Nelson and the Cheseapeake and Ohio Railroad appropriated the funds and the bridge was rebuilt. Bent Creek has always been in a class to itself. Anything anyone wishes is available there, religious or worldly. In olden days it was a custom for those who prided themselves on their physical manhood, to gather here on Saturday afternoons to prove their claim, and when the fisticuffs were over, the victor and victim would return to their homes, having fought with no fear and no unfriendliness, ready to return another week-end to have another race for the championship. While these people have a reputation for their fighting qualities, they also have unsurpassed qualities for friendship. If you should pass through Bent Creek and happen to have trouble on the darkest and stormiest night, you would have only to call loud enough to be heard, and immediately help would come, and that help would come wearing a smile that would make you think they were glad you had trouble in order to give them an opportunity to demonstrate their willingness to give help to anyone in need.

Appomattox County furnished leadership that ranked among the highest. Rev. John Bunion Shearer was a large land owner near Spout Spring. He went to North Carolina and for many years was President of Davidson College at Davidson, North Carolina. His descendants and his influence for good are in evidence to this day in the County. McReynolds was born and spent the first few years of his life near Spout Spring. He studied law and rose to the rank of Attorney General of the United States and later was a distinguished member of the United States Supreme Court. He has recently passed to the great beyond.

Colonel Samuel McDearmon, Representative of the Virginia House of Delegates from Prince Edward County when Appomattox was formed in 1845, being a resident of that portion of Prince Edward taken to form Appomattox, was very much interested in the development and success of the new County. Living a few hundred yards from what was called Clover Hill, he donated the land upon which the Court House was built for the new county of Appomattox. He was the first to be elected to the House of Delegates from this County, and also served in the State Senate. Tradition has it that he decided to join the forces that had as their slogan, "Go West", loaded up his wagons, which was the mode of travel in those days, began his journey, and on reaching the present Appomattox Court House, a distance of three miles from his home just abandoned, he, for some unknown reasons, experienced a change of mind, located here, and had the post office at this place named "Nebraska", which in later years was changed to Appomattox. Here ended his Westward journey.

Colonel Willis P. Bocock was one of the intellectual giants of his day. Rev. John H. Bocock was an eminent Presbyterian minister of that day. Thomas S. Bocock was another giant intellectually. Henry Bocock was the Clerk of Appomattox County for a number of years. Charles Bocock took a medical course and was preparing to make a high mark in that profession when he passed away early in life. Nicholas Bocock was a lawyer. He moved to Buckingham Court House and was one of the brilliant lawyers of his day.

Colonel Thomas Flood represented Buckingham County in the House and Senate before that part of Buckingham in which he lived was cut off to help form Appomattox County. Major John Flood took a leading part in the upbuilding of the County. He moved to Lynchburg to spend his last days and became one of the leading tobacconists of the city. Major Joel W. Flood, Confederate soldier, was one of the foremost citizens of the County.

Colonel Robert B. Poore, Confederate soldier and lawyer stood at the top in the practice of law in his day.

Captain William Hannah was an Appomattox Citizen by being in the territory cut off from Charlotte County to help form Appomattox County. Charlotte County thereby lost one of its finist citizens. One of his sons, J. Kirk Hannah, Confederate soldier, was School Trustee and then Superintendent of Schools for sixteen years. Another son, Presley M. Hannah, Confederate soldier, was one of the leading citizens of his neighborhood.

Dr. William Diuguid Christian was one of the best beloved physicians and neighbors in the county.

14

The four Abbitt brothers, George, Ben, Joseph, and William, made the county rich in heritage. George's son, George W. Abbitt, was a Colonel in the Confederate Army. Dr. William (Buck) Abbitt, was a leading physician and formed a Company for Confederate Service.

J. Chap Jones was a gallant Confederate soldier in Pickett's charge at Gettysburg.

Colonel Ben Hunter was a leader in his community. His descendants are valuable assets to the county.

John H. McKinney was a Confederate soldier.

Colonel John Johns, representing the hospitality of the Old South, adopted and reared Captain Thomas W. Johns who was the first Commissioner of Revenue in the County.

Isaac Adams, one of the Commissioners of Revenue of the County, was the father of Duval, Holcomb and Richard Adams, who moved to Lynchburg and were among the leading business men of the city.

Wilson Hix was at one time Sheriff. A son, Dr. Thomas Hix. was a prominent physician. Another son, William Daniel Hix, was a leading citizen in the Hixburg neighborhood and a great help in writing wills, deeds, et cetera for that section.

Squire William Matthews was of Old Virginia stock. His descendents were prominent in State affairs.

Samuel D. Sears was a Confederate soldier.

Van Gilliam, another Confederate soldier.

John Henry Marshall was Justice of the Peace, a leader in church and civic affairs in Hixburg section.

Joel Coleman was a man who could be called a diamond in the rough. Regardless of any faults' he may have had, his heart was always in the right place in all his dealings with mankind.

Colonel Wyatt Elliott was State Senator and Editor of a Richmond paper.

Archer LeGrand's decendants are among the stalwarts of Appomattox.

His cousin, Ethelbert LeGrand, had the first cotton gin in the country. Also, before the War Between the States, he, under direction from Washington, had his land terraced, or ditched as it was called in that day.

Thomas A. Smith was a Confederate soldier.

Charles H. Moses, Supervisor, had many decendants making Appomattox what it is. He was the grandfather of our present representative in the State Senate, Charles T. Moses.

Mr. Lawrence Anderson and his sons were valuable citizens.

Thomas Trent was an officer in the Revolutionary War. His son, Thomas Trent was a veteran of the War of 1812, and grandson, William Henry (Buck) Trent, was a Captain in the Confederate Army.

Cheathams and Caldwells, stalwart citizens, added greatly to the advancement of agriculture and all other worthy projects in their section of the county.

Thomas J. Stratton was a Confederate soldier and one of Appomattox's stalwarts. His brother, Sterling C. Stratton, was one of the leading citizens of the county.

R. F. Burke was for a long time a County Officer.

The names, Taylor, Isbell, Shearer, Horsley, Anderson, Scruggs, Carson and Drinkard, help to make up the list of the splendid citizenship of the old Stonewall neighborhood.

Davidson, Chick, Snapp, Coleman, Smith and McIver were a great asset to their community.

Carnefix, Megginson, Kyle, Lewis, Woodson, Coleman, Harvey and Patteson were leaders in the Rose Bower section.

Abbitt, Covington, Bagby, Torrence, Beasley, and Banton are keeping up a good community around Hollywood Church.

Jones, Elliott, Bates, Overton, Nowlin, Robertson, Caldwell, Cardwell, Thomas, Webb, Tanner, Inge, Dickerson, Burke, Atwood, W. J. (Buck) Trent, Ferguson, Gregory, Purdum, Lee, Morris, Ranson, McDearmon, Pulliam, Baldwin, Franklin, Thornton, Watkins. Morton, Ligon, Gilliam, Swan, Fore, Ford, Rosser, Cawthorn, Hamilton, Farrar, Calhoun, Collins, and Gills are contributors to the splendid name of Appomattox.

Appomattox is an agricultural county, the main crops being wheat, corn and tobacco. The farmers were dependent upon tobacco for their money and unfortunately for a long time they knew of no other source from which to look for revenue. They raised large crops, putting more hard labor on it than any other crop. When the crop was marketed, the profits would go into the hands of the fertilizer manufactures and the tobacconists. There were a few who made a little profit.

A certain portion of the county inhabited mostly by Moores and Martins, experts at curing tobacco, had the reputation, with a section of Bedford County, of raising the finest black wrappers in the world.

Fortunately the people found that tobacco was not the master money crop and they turned their energies to grass and stock.

The people of the county are conservative-progressive, not carried off by every frivolous project. They have to be shown, and keep only one foot on the ground, the other always up ready to the command, "Forward march," into any movement for their betterment.

The first command for a forward march, was given and responded to when Major

16

J. W. Flood was made the first County Agricultural Agent under Mr. T. O. Sandy in 1911 and serving through 1914.

Major Flood fitted well in the job, being an extensive farmer, widely known and very popular over the entire county. He labored under trying circumstances. bad roads and no cars. He had to travel by buggy but he overcame all obstacles and made a success. The people could see from his zeal in the work that he was not only personally interested in farming, but interested in the advancement of his neighbors. He easily won the cooperation of the farmers. He continually impressed upon them the importance of grass and preached that, ''grass is the foundation of good farming.''

Those succeeding Major Flood were men who had graduated from Agricultural Colleges and studied the needs of different soils, which gave them the advantage over those who had to spend most of their life to learn by experience.

B. G. Anderson was the first graduate from an Agricultural College to be made County Agricultural Agent here. He at once won the confidence which made his tenure in office a success. He was for a number of years Superintendent of the Appomattox Experiment Station and has become a permanent and valuable resident of the county. As his years increase, so does his popularity.

Next came E. H. Matheson, a very efficient officer whose services were a great asset to the cause but whose stay was brief.

W. H. Byrne, efficient and popular, served well for several years. He was called to V. P. I. at Blacksburg, a promotion he well deserved.

He was succeeded by R. B. Hudgins who is carrying on the work with the high standard of efficiency set by his predecessors. He, like B. G. Anderson, is growing in popularity.

The late Honorable J. R. Horsley may be considered the pioneer short horn cattle raiser of the county. He, by the help of the county agricultural agent, got his farm which was one of small productive quality, to be one of the best in the county. The farmers of the neighborhood have caught the spirit and you can find in that section beef herds that will compare favorably with those of the blue grass hills of the cattle counties of Southwest Virginia. The farmers are also realizing the value of pure bred stock and have greatly improved their herds in that respect.

One of the greatest assets to the farmers is the lime grinding plant located on Wreck Island Creek, near James River. While this is not a limestone county, there is a vein of that material running through this county that tests by the chemistry department of the Virginia State Department of Agriculture show it to compare favorable with the limestone of the Staunton lime plant.

A few years ago the State located one of its plants in the county, and is supplying the farmers of this and surrounding counties with this very valuable fertilizer for the farms.

The old Jesse Davidson farm, on which for generations its owners labored hard raising tobacco to furnish them money with which to meet expenses, now operated by J. O. Davidson, is watching a nice beef herd of cattle roam its pastures and fur-

17

nishing revenue to take the place of tobacco. This farm was recently recognized by The Progressive Farmer as one of the Master Farms of Virginia.

During 1945 the farmers eagerly responded to another command to advance. Our alert and energetic county agricultural agent, R. B. Hudgins, saw before them the dairy field open for conquest, and he was given the hearty support of R. L. Burke, W. W. Scott, A. R. Harwood, the Lions Club, business people and professional men; and the Coble Dairy Company was induced to open up a receiving plant here for milk. More of the farmers took leave of the laborious tobacco field and established dairy herds, thereby adding to their bank account with much more ease and adding greatly to the fertility of the soil. The plant is furnishing a market not only to Appomattox County, but to many farmers in adjoining counties. This Grade C milk is trucked daily to plants in North Carolina where it is processed and distributed to consumers.

Many modern conveniences have been added to the farmers' surroundings. Electricity is being installed and when this has been consummated the main drudgery of farm life will have been lifted and life on the farm will be made almost as desirable as living in town.

For several years Mr. Wiley M. Morris has been operating a canning factory. Many of the farmers have put some of their labor into raising tomatoes, thus giving them a good return for their labor. This factory is an asset to the Town Appomattox.

In 1943 a community cannery was opened in the basement of the Appomattox High School Dormitory. The outfit was crude and while they labored under many obstacles, the people gave hearty support to the project. The Board of Supervisors, being farsighted and progressive, in 1944 built a community cannery at Appomattox and in 1945 a similar community cannery was built in the Town of Pamplin. The United States Government bore all other expense. The projects are supervised by the Vocational Agriculture and Home Economics Instructors of the High Schools in the county. These canneries are serving about 700 families in the county. The only cost to the people is the cost of the tin cans in which the food is processed. In 1945 the canneries processed approximately 100,000 quart cans of food.

In 1945 the people of Appomattox County brought to the canneries produce sufficient to fill 10,060 cans which they donated to the starving people of Europe through the United Nations Rural Rehabilitation Administration. The cost of these cans was borne by the churches and some individuals in the county.

Mrs. B. G. Anderson, County Home Demonstration Agent, has been very efficiently conducting demonstration clubs over the County. A lady in full possession of ability, diplomacy, and courtesy, she has won the admiration, confidence and cooperation of the people, making success in her project easy.

While Appomattox County stands out prominently in the forefront of the historic spots of the world, she also holds a prominent place in all that makes life. One has only to travel the county over to see the beauty of the crystal waters giving life to vegetation; the rich soil furnishing provisions for the life and nourishment of man and beast. It is also rich in scenery. Lying close to the foot hills of the Blue Ridge Mountains it is a thing of beauty, in the winter time, to gaze upon these snow-capped peaks glistening in the sunlight. As Spring approaches, the bright smiles from the sun cause the snow to drift away, and soon those peaks dress themselves in their coat of green. Another change in the season is due, and the sweltering heat from the Summer sun presses hard upon our heads, but gentle breezes from these mountains relieve that pressure. Another season due, Autumn arrives, and with its artistic hand, decorates those lofty peaks and sun-painted cliffs with golden Autumn leaves, convincing us that there is no need to visit Italy or Switzerland to find scenery upon which to rest our weary eyes.

The farmers' interests and the scenery hunters have been brought up to date, and now let's review some of the sad days leading up to and including the dark days from 1861 to 1865.

Prior to the War Between the States Appomattox had a peaceful, social population and while not lacking in the least courage for war if necessary, they wanted by every honorable means to avoid war. While the older conservative brains over the country, North and South, were doing all in their power for peace, there were those younger whose brains got too hot for their heads, and matters in controversy had to be settled to their notion or war.

As the war clouds grew darker and it seemed inevitable, a Secession Convention was held in Richmond in 1861. Lewis Daniel Isbell was sent as Appomattox County's representative. The decision was made promptly when President Lincoln called on Virginia for troops to suppress the movement of secession in other Southern States, but it was not to join the Federal Army but to join their Sister States of the South that Virginia decided.

The die was cast, the war was on and Appomattox immediately began sending the best of her young manhood on the rough path of war. Companies were organized and drilling was in process at different points in the county. Major Joel W. Flood organized a Cavalry Company, Company H, 2nd Virginia Regiment, and, as their Captain, led them to battle. He was soon incapacitated on account of sickness and was brought home ill. He later returned to service as Major on the staff of General Kemper. He was succeeded as Captain of the Company by Charles E. Webb, who, too, was struck down by sickness. His case was fatal and he passed away in Richmond.

Next in command was Joseph W. Carson who received a bullet wound which shattered his ankle while leading his Company in a charge at Mount Jackson, in the Valley Campaign in 1864 and incapacitated him for further duty.

I can find no records on the subject, but as Lieutenant R. B. Poore was the next in command, I suppose he had charge of the Company from that time on.

Major James E. Robertson marched to battle commanding Company A, 44th Virginia Infantry, Appomattox Invincibles. He was promoted to Major and the next in rank, Samuel H. Overton, was promoted to Captain. In 1862 this Company was changed to heavy artillery.

Company H, 18th Virginia Regiment of the Infantry went into action with Thomas P. Matthews as Captain. Later commanded by Captain W. T. Johnson.

Kyles Company, Heavy Artillery, was commanded by Captain R. R. Kyle, but was soon disbanded and its members joined other commands.

. Company B, 46th Virginia Regiment was led to battle by Dr. William H. Abbitt. Ill health caused him to retire. He was succeeded by his brother, George W. Abbitt, who was later promoted to Colonel.

Colonel T. T. Munford, who commanded the 2nd Virginia Cavalry, some years ago had a very complimentary newspaper article on Company H, in which he said it was the best Company in his Regiment. Those from Appomattox who were under his command were in Company H. I heard my Father and other members of this Company relate the following incident which happened at Mount Jackson.

Captain Joseph W. (Watt) Carson reported to the Colonel for orders. The Colonel said: "You see those Yankees over on that hill, take your company and run them out. I have started a Company over there and they have stopped down in the ravine." Captain Carson ordered his company forward, marching them in column four; the first rank being compased of William A. Thornhill, Dallas Abbitt, William Megginson and J. H. Featherston. When they reached the bridge across the ravine, a soldier, one in the Company that had been sent but stopped in the ravine, was on the bridge and the above named Dallas Abbitt said, "Are you going?" He said: "No." Abbitt, who did not shun a fight, said, "Well get out of our way. We are going." Captain Carson marched his Company up the hill in sight of the Federals, marched parallel to a certain distance, threw his Company of only twenty-six men into Company front and charged in a gallop the whole Regiment of about 500 troops. They opened a volley at the little Company but their aims were poor, and their bullets never found lodgement in any of the Confederates. They beat a hasty retreat, falling back into the Federal lines. The Confederates opened fire with their carbines, each one protected as well as could be, sitting on their horses, behind trees, but there were so many Federals all they could do was fire, ride on and another would come and fire while the previous one went off to load. After a few minutes firing Captain Watt Carson, who was as brave a soldier as ever flashed a sword, rode a few paces ahead and ordered his little Company to charge the whole brigade. Just at that moment William A. Thornhill, who was just as brave as Captain Carson, received a bullet wound in his shin, and called: "Watt, come back. It is no use to get all of us killed and accomplish nothing," The Captain turned and had his ankle shattered as stated above. Then the little Company fell back to the Confederate lines having gained no ground but captured two fine horses from the Federals.

While Captain Carson survived the wound, he wore a limp through life from the effects of it.

The bullet that wounded the above mentioned William Thornhill was for a long time a treasured souvenir in the possession of his daughter, Miss Dora Thornhill, who is at present a resident of Roanoke, Virginia.

The Federal Army started out on a visit, the destination being Surrender, wherever that would be, which in the end turned out to be Appomattox. As the visitors were uninvited and very unwelcome, it turned out to be the most costly and roughest journey they had ever undertaken and the longest, taking them four years to make the journey from Washington to Appomattox. They reached there then because the South had used up all its resources, financial and physical.

When exhaustion of the Southern Army caused a show down and the Northern Army lined up on the South side and the Southern Army on the North side of Appomatox River, the superb General Robert E. Lee struck hands with the magnanimous General Ulysses S. Grant. Immediately all animosity seemed to have mounted the ripples of the Appomattox River and floated down and buried itself in the waves of the Atlantic Ocean. Both armies marched side by side to the tune of Yankee Doodle and Dixie, too; sat down to a peace table from which came the most magnanimous terms ever handed a surrendering army. Unprecedented in human warfare the surrendering General practically wrote the terms of surrender. Then, the two armies which the day before were making desperate efforts to take each others lives, handed each other the glad hand of friendship in a good luck adieu, each starting on their homeward journey to the tune of Home Sweet Home.

In regard to this count's connection with the war the writer thinks it appropriate to insert here the following written by his grandmother in her old age. She was born in 1827 and passed away in 1907.

* * * * * *

Some "During the War" experiences of Mrs. N. H. Ragland.

"When the war commenced my home was in Richmond'. In 1862 I recieved a letter from my brother, who was in the Army, requesting me to go to his farm in Appomattox County, my old home, and take care of his property to the best of my ability. My husband, whose health unfitted him for active service in the field, remained in Richmond. watching for and availing himself of every opportunity to do what he could for the cause. Frequently it was his privilege to help take care of the sick and wounded soldiers, and sometimes he was called into active service when there was any fighting around Richmond.

When I reached Appomattox I found there was no white man on the farm, and the negroes, without any recognized head, were doing little to support themselves, and were very improvident. It would be hard for anyone who never had any experience with slaves to realize what a responsibility it was to own and care for them. They knew very well when I assumed control of my brother's farm that I was inexperienced in my new position, and they were inclined to take advantage of my ignorance; but they were generally very faithful and recognized my authority.

There was one old man, 'Uncle Tom', who had charge of the sheep, and he did not like for anyone to infringe upon his rights. When I wanted a lamb or mutton killed, he was apt to rebel. I was expecting some friends to dinner one day and ordered him to kill a lamb. He obeyed my order, but when the cook saw the lamb she said it was not fit to eat. I sent for Uncle Tom and reproached him for his bad conduct. but he only said, 'Well, it was going to die anyway, and I thought I had just as well kill it so I had to appeal to Jim, the head man. Jim was the carriage driver, and I had noticed that when he drove us to church he never went into the house, though there were seats for the negroes. I spoke to him about it, and his reply was that he had been told that at

21

the judgment day he would be responsible for every sermon he had heard, so he thought he would hear as few as possible.

We had to submit to many privations in those days. Sugar and coffee were very scarce, and many substitutes were used for them, such as sorghum, parched wheat, sassafras, etc. I used these things, though my husband kept me supplied with the real articles, but I kept them locked up, to be used in case of sickness in my own family and among my neighbors.

My husband would frequently buy large bales of scraps from the government that were left in cutting out the soldiers clothes. Sometimes I would get pieces large enough to make the boys suits of clothes by using different colors and having them dyed. Some of the neighbors would utilize the smaller pieces in making slippers and caps, and the smallest were woven into carpets.

Our over-seer was in the army but his family was still on the farm, and his wife would do the spinning and weaving. I had goods woven for my little girls dresses, and we thought they were beautiful, with their bright colors. I remember a dress that I had woven of brown wool mixed with white. I trimmed it with bands of silk, and thought I had a very stylish dress. It was my custom every Spring and Fall to take the children to a shoemaker and have their measures taken and shoes made for them. The shoemaker lived ten miles from us, and this trip was looked forward to as one of the greatest pleasures the children had.

Our church privileges were very much diminished; nearly all of the ministers being in the army. There was a Baptist church about two miles from us, at which there was preaching, but there was no Sunday School, and no men to have one; so I, with several other ladies, determined that we would have one without the men. A day was appointed to begin, but when we arrived at the church we found very few children there, and we were not long in ascertaining the cause of their absence; many of the people were poor, and by reason of the war, their children were without hats and shoes, they had no carriages, and were too proud to allow them to go to Sunday School without these things. I thought I would see what the force of example would do, and the next Sunday my children went barefooted and wore sun bonnets and rode in the ox cart, while I with the governess went in a buggy. My nephew and niece from Big Lick who were with us went as my children did and they all enjoyed it very much. It had a happy effect, and very soon we had a flourishing school.

In the Spring of 1864 I heard that General Sheridan with a considerable army had crossed James River at Bent Creek, about fifteen miles from us, and was marching toward Appomattox Court House. No one who has not had a similar experience can imagine my feelings. With no one to advise me I felt helpless. All was excitement and confusion. But with little time to consider what was to be done I decided to send my oldest boy with his sisters and governess and the 'black mammy' to the house of a neighbor who lived in a very secluded place. After they had gone I was very miserable about them, and after a sleepless night I sent for them, determined that whatever happened I would have my little ones with me. It proved to be a false alarm. The bridge over the river at Bent Creek was burned and they did not cross.

My brother would sometimes get a furlough and come home, and having 'Uncle Henry' at home was always a cause of great rejoicing with the children. He would have his young friends invited and have a big party. It seems strange in looking back that anyone should have felt like indulging in anything of the sort, yet we often had dinner parties and other pleasures, though our hearts were burdened with care and anxiety for our beloved country. But sometimes there was a reaction from the strain, and when the burden was comparatively thrown off, the young people seemed to enjoy themselves with a zest and abandon that I am sure is seldom felt under more favorable circumstances.

These were times of sacrifice and suffering, but sadder days were coming. The terrible Spring of 1865 was approaching. The Winter had passed in unspeakable hardship and in April our lines around Petersburg were broken and the retreat of General Lee's army commenced. In a few days many Confederate soldiers began to pass my house. They were nearly starved, and it was inexpressibly sad to hear their tales of suffering and to see the eagerness with which they devoured their food. For several days I kept women cooking for them. I remained in the dining room and waited on them, giving each one a lunch to take away. At night the house was filled with them, many sleeping on the floor. The Rev. Dr. Lacy passed one night with us and held family worship. His prayers were very comforting and were a great help to us. When he left I gave him my watch and some other articles of value to keep for me, but he had not gone far when he came back and returned them, saying that he thought they would be safer with me. The children buried some silver and jewelry in the woods, and some they hid in a barrel of peas in the pantry. Saturday night, April 8th, my brother, Captain W. H. Trent, and Captain Kindred, who had married my niece at Big Lick, came to my house, but we did not think it was safe for them to stay all night there because the Yankees were so near, and they returned to their respective commands. This seemed to be the most trying hour of my life, my husband away, and I, with my little children, left alone to face a ruthless army of soldiers. I took my burden to my Heavenly Father and received strength and courage to pass through the terrible ordeal before me.

The 9th of April brought with it the sound of artillery and and musketry, but it was of short duration. That day General Lee was compelled to surrender. At first I refused to believe it, but it was only too true, and I bowed in humble submission to the will of my Heavenly Father.

Soon the stragglers from the Northern Army began to arrive. First came a man with an artificial leg, dressed in Gray. He begged me to hide him from the Yankees, but I refused, telling him it would be unsafe for both himself and my family. He became very angry and spoke very roughly to me, and I told him I believed he was a Yankee. I afterwards found that he was a Yankee spy. In a short time a drunken Yankee rode up; my second daughter, a very timid child, was in the yard, and he cursed her and asked where the rebels were hid. She answered that there were none there, and I then met him and told him the same thing. He went away but soon returned. I had sent my little girls to their room; he searched the house, and when he saw the children he cursed them and pointed his pistol at them. It was the first time they had ever heard an oath, and that frightened them as much as the pistol did. Upon reaching the house he told me that I had a watch, and he intended to have it. I did not deny having one, but tried to evade him. My oldest son, twelve years old, was standing by and said, 'O! my dear Mother, how can I see you treated so. The Yankee soldier turned his pistol towards him and said, 'Another word, and I'll blow your brains out.' He then took me by the shoulder, and with his pistol in my face said if I did not get the watch he would tear my clothes from me and kill me. I told him if he would remain in the porch I would get it. He started to follow me, but I told him if he did I would not get the watch. I went to my room and fastened the door. The watch, with fifty dollars in gold, was in a bag tied around my waist. I cut the bag, threw the money under the bed, and went out and gave him the watch. It had been a wedding present from my Mother to my oldest sister, and had been worn by my youngest sister, all of whom were dead.

This man left, and in a little while several more came. One of them said he had been told by the negroes that I had been badly treated by some of the men, and offered to stay and guard us. I had no faith in him, but dared not refuse; so he forged an order from one of his generals appointing him a guard for our house, and really was a great help to us. He acknowledged afterwards that he came to rob, but thought it would be a comfortable place to stay and changed his plans. I believe he was providently sent there, as I am sure that without him we would have all been killed.

The Yankees continued to come in crowds, and declared they would shoot through the house and burn it down, but our guard--so-called--, would manage in some way to drive them off.

Sometimes officers would come and ask for something to eat, and they were usually very polite. The private soldiers were afraid of them and would do the most menial things for them.

Mr. Cunningham, our self-appointed guard, would at night place a negro man at each corner of the yard to help him protect the place. I never felt that I could trust him. Some of the Yankees would send me by a servant a brass ring, or some little trifle to remember them by, or as a keepsake, as if I would ever need a reminder.

Thus matters went on for a week or more. My husband was in Richmond at the time of its fall, and followed the army and came home, but not thinking it best to remain there, returned to Richmond.

After the Yankees had gone, Mr. Cunningham did not seem disposed to leave. He would sometimes tell me that if any of my neighbors had anything that I wanted, I had only to tell him and it should be mine. One day a negro woman was passing the house, and he accused her of having stolen the horse she was riding. She said that her mistress had loaned it to her to go and see her sick child. I begged him to let her go, which he finally did, but made me a present of the saddle. Of course it was returned to the owner after he left.

Many of my neighbors were almost reduced to starvation. I had a cousin whose family consisted of herself, her husband and her mother, all of them old people. Their food was corn picked up where the Yankees fed their horses, washed, toasted and ground. They were wealthy people, but their wealth availed nothing then.

Many people were left without a change of clothing; even their cups, plates, saucers, etc., were destroyed. My husband, not knowing what time he might be cut off from me, had sent me supplies of everything needful during the war, and at its close I had barrels of sugar, molasses, flour, rice, etc., besides dry goods and, in fact, everything that we could need. When I saw the distress of those around me, I realized that I had been permitted to have much, and I felt that Providence had given me these

24

things to use as seemed best for others. Everything was divided, and it was thus my privilege to relieve a great deal of suffering.

In October, 1865, I returned to my home in Richmond to find my husband's store, with all of my furniture, burned, but we were thankful our lives had been spared and that we could be together again.

In 1868, my husband bought the house at Appomattox Court House in which General Lee and General Grant met and drew up and signed the articles of capitulation, at the time of surrender. At the time he bought it it was owned by Major McLean, who also had owned the land on which the first battle of the war was fought. Strange that the first battle of war and the final surrender should both take place on land owned by the same man.

After the death of my husband I sold this property to a Northern man who had the house pulled down with a view of moving it to Washington, but it has never been moved. The bricks are still piled up in the yard, and the woodwork can never be moved now.

I have made this brief record of a few of my experiences during the War Between the States because in the far future I thought it might be of interest to my descendants. If I could see and write as well as I did when I was a young woman, I would add much more, for in those war times every day was filled with incidents full of interest and well worth being remembered. But my children and grandchildren must be content with the little I have been able to do in my old age."

The Union soldiers as a whole must not be judged by the class in the account just given.

Mr. Van Gilliam, whose home was near Hixburg just across the line from Prince Edward County, was captured on the retreat as he stopped at his home to get something to eat, being very hungry as were most of Lee's army. He was taken to Appomattox and liberated the following day.

At Mr. Gilliam's home there was a very nice horse. The war custom, of course, was for such to be confiscated by the enemy but this was left at the home of the owner.

* * * * * *

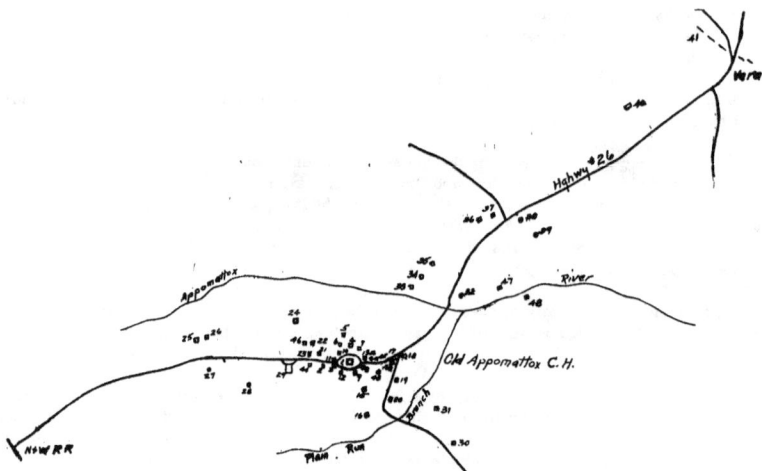

OLD APPOMATTOX COURT HOUSE

No. 1. Old Appomattox Court House, burned about 1892, rebuilt at the present Appomattox Court House.

No. 2. McLean House in which the terms of surrender between Generals Lee and Grant were written April 9th, 1865. Brick building, was torn down about 1894 for removal and re-erection in Washington, but the plans for removal were not carried out and none of the material was moved except pieces carried away by souvenir hunters. Major Wilmer McLean, who owned this property at the time of the surrender was living at Manassas at the outbreak of the War Between the States and the first battle of Manassas was fought on his place. He decided, as he thought, to move out of the danger zone, and came over and bought the above named property, but it turned out that he did not journey far enough before pitching his tent, and the last battle of the war was fought in hearing of his place, and the surrender took place in his house.

No. 3. Frame building on McLean Property. Removed. At the time of the surrender this building stood in the corner of the yard and as the McLean house was built for and used as a tavern by the Raines family, this building was used to help house the guests over night. The McLean property was purchased about two years after the surrender by N. H. Ragland and he had the above mentioned frame building moved.

No. 4. Old Hotel, brick building, used as tavern in stage coach days, still standing.

No. 5. Brick building on hotel property (No. 4) used for guest when hotel was filled. Still standing.

No. 6. Same as No. 5.

No. 7. Brick store house on hotel property. Removed.

No. 8. Old jail, brick, but not used as jail since the Court House was moved to the present Appomattox. Still standing.

No. 9. Frame building, law office of Judge H. T. Parrish. Removed.

No. 10. Frame building, law office of H. T. Parrish, later law office of C. H. Sackett. Removed.

No. 11. Frame house, old home of the Meeks family, later Presbyterian Manse. Still standing.

No. 12. Old brick residence, once occupied by Cornelias Hill, later by Gus Watson, colored. Removed.

26

No. 13. Frame building. Residence and store house of William Rosser. Still standing.

No. 14. Frame building. Law office of R. B. Poore and H. D. Flood.   Removed.

No. 15. Frame building, still standing. At the time of the surrender was occupied by a family of Dixons, later owned by Judge H. T. Parrish.

No. 16. Frame building. Residence of John Rosser. Still standing.

No. 17. Triangle; spot where Confederates stacked arms at the surrender.

No. 18. Frame building. Residence of George T. Peers, who was Clerk of Appomattox County about forty years. Still standing.

No. 19. Frame building. Residence of the Layne family. Removed.

No. 20. Frame building. Old Presbyterian Church. Removed.

No. 21. Frame residence, said to have been occupied at the time of the surrender by the Landons. Later occupied by colored people. House removed, chimney still standing.

No. 22. Frame house, occupied by colored people. Removed.

No. 23. Blacksmith shop of Charles Henry Diuguid, Colored. Removed.

No. 24. Frame residence. Built by the McDearmons; later home of Tibbs, Johns, Tinsley, Kindred, Armes; now owned by the Scotts. Still standing.

No. 25. Frame residence of Doc Coleman. This house was struck by a cannon ball at the time of the surrender 1865. Still standing.

No. 26. Log house in yard of Doc Coleman (25). A colored woman was killed while standing in the doorway of this log house by the cannon ball that struck the Doc Coleman house.

No. 27. Tablet marking the spot where General U. S. Grant's Headquarters were at the time of the surrender.

No. 28. North Carolina Monument, erected in 1906 by North Carolina's U. D. C., claimed by them to have been the spot the North Carolina soldiers reached at the surrender.

No. 29. Soldiers cemetery, where eighteen Confederate soldiers and one Federal soldier were buried. On Memorial Day of each year the graves of these soldiers are decorated and appropriate services held by the U. D. C. of Appomattox. These graves are kept in good condition by the U. D. C., there being no difference in any respect between the one Federal soldier and the eighteen Confederates.

No. 30. Frame building, residence of C. H. Sackett, built about 1882   or 1883 in place of one burned at that time. Still standing.

No. 31. Log cabin in which first public school was taught in Appomattox county, 1870; teacher, J. H. Featherston. Removed.

No. 32. Spot where stood the apple tree under which General R. E. Lee was resting while waiting for answer to message he had sent to General   U. S. Grant in regard to terms of surrender when the Federal Courier delivered the message from General Grant, which led to the surrender that day. Tree cut down and carried away as souvenirs by the Confederate soldiers.

No. 33. Frame residence of Bob Miller Sweeney, musician. Still standing.

No. 34. Said to be the spot where stood the frame residence of old   Joe Sweeney, musician. He went to England and played for the Queen. She presented him with a silk belt containing about $700 in gold, and the belt is now in the possession of D. A. Conner, Deputy Sheriff of Appomattox County. House burned.

No. 35. Frame residence of Charley Sweeney. Still standing.

No. 36. Frame residence of Allen Conner, used for a hospital at the surrender. Removed.

No. 37. Frame residence built on property of No. 36, owned and occupied now by F. A. O'Brien, County Supervisor, and grandson of the above named Allen Conner.

No. 38. Poplar tree under which General R. E. Lee stood and delivered his farewell address to the soldiers of the Army of Northern Virginia.

No. 39. Spot where General Lee had his camp at the time of the surrender.

No. 40. Old Flood home, brick. Home of the late Major Joel W. Flood, now owned by his son, Judge Joel W. Flood. Still standing.

No. 41. Breastworks built by the Confederates on the retreat towards the surrender. Vera Graded School on part of the site.

No. 42. Frame residence. Still standing. Do not know who was the original occupant but later occupied by John Robertson, colored shoemaker.

No. 43. Log cabin. Removed. Occupied by colored people.

No. 44. Brick building. Blacksmith shop. Removed.

No. 45. Blacksmith shop on property of William Rosser. Blacksmith in this shop for a number of years was Gus Watson, colored. Removed.

No. 46. Cabin, occupied by colored people. Removed.

No. 47. Frame tenant house on the Flood farm. Still standing.

No. 48. Frame tenant house on the Flood farm. Still standing.

During the War Between the States when the Southern soldier had left all that was near and dear to him in person and property to fight for his country and his loved ones, heavy clouds hung low and all the future looked dreary. He had the sweet assurance, when he lay down at night, that he had loved ones back home who were sending up petitions to the Heavenly Father for his safety in battle, and divine guidance at all times.

When at Appomattox on April 9, 1865, "Finis" was written on the overpowered Confederacy, and was sadly accepted by the Southern soldier, with sad hearts but unsullied character, courage was still aflame with loyalty and devotion to the cause for which they so stubbornly fought. Apparantly all the unpleasant past had mounted the wings of forgiveness, and flown to parts unknown, never to return, there suddenly was thrust upon the fair South that infamous Carpet-bag, Scallowag rule. The main object of its perpetrators was plunder, and to humiliate the South. Then it was that "God's chosen people" the fair women of the South were looked to for prayers and cheering words to help them face and overcome that gloom which seemed impregnable. Again the noble women gladly responded, and naturally tears were shed by them for their loved ones, but that gentle, sweet smile which was always at their command made those tears sparkle and glisten as dew drops on grass in the bright sunlight of a Spring morning. Whenever there arose trouble for the Southern soldier, the fair women could be counted on the furnish the smiles to fringe the darkest cloud with a silver lining.

April 1865 found Appomattox, like the rest of the South, a country of desolation. It was a land of black-garbed women. There was scarcely a home without an empty chair, a father, husband, brother, or son taken by the war.

The one idea of the women, as always in time of bereavement, was that their loved ones should not be forgotten. They banded together in associations to erect monuments to their memory and to aid the veterans and their families. Practically every county in Virginia has its monument to its Confederate dead, the money for them being raised dollar by dollar and penny by penny, principally through the labor of the women.

In June 1895 a national organization was formed in Nashville, Tennessee, called The Daughters of the Confederacy, the objectives being to preserve the history and ideals of the Confederacy; to aid the veterans and their families. Into this organization were drawn most of the Memorial, Hospital and Sewing societies that had been formed all over the South with same objectives.

Appomattox Chapter No. 11 was chartered in the National organization August 22, 1895, the eleventh in the nation and sixth in Virginia. This chapter was organized by Mrs. Charles W. Hunter who was its first President. Among the many fine women who have served as President of the chapter, Miss M. Anna Jones, sister of Mrs. Hunter, deserves special mention. She served twenty years and under her administration much worthwhile work was done. (Pictures of all the presidents to date are given here.)

MRS. CHARLIE HUNTER,
1st President.
U. D. C.

MRS. J. R. ATWOOD,
2nd President
U. D. C.

MRS. JOEL W. FLOOD,
3rd President,
U. D. C.

MRS. J. B. ABBITT,
4th President.
U. D. C.

MRS. W. B. CALDWELL,
5th President.
U. D. C.

MISS EULA MAY BURKE,
6th President.
U D. C.

MRS. LINDSAY CRAWLEY,
7th President.
U. D. C.

MRS. D. N. TWYMAN,
8th President,
U. D C.

MRS. N. A. WAGERS,
9th President.
U. D. C.

MISS M. ANNA JONES,
10th President.
U. D. C.

MRS. WILLIAM ABBITT COLEMAN,
11th President.
U. D. C.

At the close of the war nineteen soldiers who laid down their lives were buried on the hill overlooking the historic little village of Appomattox. The beautiful little cemetery in which eighteen Confederate soldiers and one Union soldier are buried was and is the work of the chapter. Each year the graves are decorated by the children on Memorial Day.

The lone grave of the Federal soldier, resting far from his home and loved ones, is decorated with flowers and other ceremonies just as it is done for the Confederates. We hope, and believe the day will never come when there will be no gathering on Memorial Day at these graves to show the world our love and appreciation of the service of the Confederate soldier. In 1933 a Mrs. Jamison, a tourist from Illinois, gave to the Chapter $5.00 in appreciation of the care given the unknown Federal soldier's grave.

In 1930 a camp of Confederate Veterans was organized through the efforts of Miss Eula Mae Burke, who has always been untiring in her care of and attention to the veterans.

In 1931 a chapter of Children of the Confederacy was formed with 40 members.

In 1934 we find there were eight living veterans. As this is being written sad news has come that the last surviving veteran, Mr. Charles Wesley Cardwell, has passed away at the age of 99.

The graves of Confederate soldiers have been marked. In 1938 a marker was placed on the grave of "Uncle Frank Green", colored driver of heavy artillery in the Confederate Army.

The Chapter now has on hand necessary funds for a bronze memorial tablet to be erected at the Old Court House, containing the names of all who enlisted from Appomattox and those veterans who helped to develop the County.

Thomas S. Bocock, who for 14 years before the War Between the States, was the distinguished member of the United States House of Representatives was made speaker of the Confederate Congress. During Miss M. Anna Jones term as President of this Chapter of the United Daughters of the Confederacy, she promoted the erection of a tablet to be placed on the wall in the room in which the Confederate Congress held its sessions. The Board of Supervisors of Appomattox County and of Buckingham County appropriated funds for this tablet which was presented to the State of Virginia on June 30, 1947 in honor of Thomas S. Bocock. Members of the United Daughters of the Confederacy from all parts of Virginia were present at the presentation of this tablet. In the absence of the Governor, the Clerk of the Virginia House of Delegates, in a very graceful speech, accepted this.

The efforts of the Daughters were crowned with success by the erection in 1906 of that beautiful Confederate monument of granite which adds such beauty and grandeur to the present Court House Square.

May the United Daughters of the Confederacy, present and future, ever wear that spirit heretofore so pre-eminently displayed on all occasions as to insure the perpetuation of their noble society.

34

The Northern soldier returned to a home which had been kept intact, not having furnished any of the battle ground of the conflict. The Confederate soldier, in contrast, returned to a country ravaged by war; farms depleted for lack of management, sometimes only a chimney to greet him beside which had stood a hospitable old Southern home when he last left it. This was enough to put despair in the stoutest heart, but they had flowing through their veins that same warm Southern blood that was thrilled with the flush of triumph at Manassas, Spotsylvania, and many other battle fields. With unprecedented courage, love of family, and pride in seeing their beloved homeland rebuilt, courageously and successfully began the rebuilding of those homes. Things moved around under a very different regime upon the soldiers' return, for those who furnished the brain and gave orders, now had to furnish the muscle to carry out their own orders, and walked side by side in the field of labor with those to whom they previously had only to give orders. It was indeed a sad occasion; while there were many who missed a bullet; there were many who found a grave on the battle field, and some who trod the rough path of life with a single eye, empty sleeve, or wooden leg. As they began life anew, thinking blood and tears had washed away the Mason and Dixon line forever, they were suddenly chilled by an evil wind which arose in the North, the current being headed for the Southland. Upon its wings were borne the Carpet Bagger of the North and Scalawags of the South which infected the whole of the South. This was not a product of the best people of the North, nor was it sanctioned by them, but they were not interested enough in a matter at that distance to interfere. Thus this evil element whose greed was never satisfied and pillage never ceased as long as there was forage in sight. They only put "right" into use when it would further their power and bulge their money purse. Under such rule the Confederate soldier was put to greater humiliation and heartache that he suffered during the war.

This evil alliance foisted upon Virginia the Underwood Constitution composed of some members who were not natives of the State and whose actions were alien to the best interests of Virginia. Some articles in that Constitution were very obnoxious to the people of the state, but the people labored on under this iniquitous yoke, being encouraged by the hope of a better day, having that hope supported by a Spartan spirit which gave them victory in the Constitutional Convention of 1901 and 1902, which was composed entirely of Virginians who were some of the ablest men of the State. The representative from Appomattox, H. D. Flood, while a member of Congress, took a leading part in the proceedings of this Convention.

With the inauguration of the new Convention, virtually all Carpet Bag rule was obliterated from the map. The able members of this Convnetion re-arranged the map of Virginia with intelligence and good intentions.

H. D. Flood, the member from this county, was one of the most useful men it ever produced.

During the dark days of re-construction this county was one of the political battle grounds of the State and upon its rostrum have stood some of the ablest debaters and most eloquent speakers of the Country. Some few of the debaters from the North sought debates for awhile with the Southerners, hoping to convince them that their way of political thinking was right, but many of them hurriedly returned, regretting that they had chosen that mission.

Some of the greatest orators were not so good in joint debate, but Mr. William Cabell, lawyer of Buckingham County, was gifted in both. A man from the North heard of his reputation and was anxious to meet him, and the opportunity was afforded him at Old Appomattox Court House. The gentleman from the North led off. After delivering some very heavy blows at this opponent, he took his seat with an air of perfect satisfaction that he had delivered himself of a speech of such eloquence and logic that his opponent would stand in ridicule before the audience; but, when Mr. Cabell arose to reply, he opened by saying: ''Fellow citizens, this man has come from the tar North to tell Virginians how to vote. We don't know who he is; we don't know where he came from; we don't know what he represents, we could not tell from anything he said but one thing we do know, he has a bald head and we don't know but that it was skinned in a penitentiary.'' When Mr. Cabell finished his answer to his opponent, he had stripped him of his political hide and left him standing politically naked before the audience, a discredited debater.

On one occasion the silver tongued orator, John W. Daniel, met the little Irishman of wit, Pat McCall, and although McCall's speech was in no way in the class with Major Daniel's oratory, that oratory could not stand against the Irish wit, humerous jokes and sarcastic tongue of McCall and the Major left the stand worsted in the debate.

Colonel Berkley of Farmville and a United States Senator, Riddlebarger of the Valley of Virginia, crossed political swords on the rostrum of Old Appomattox and, both being able debaters and eloquent speakers, the crowd left the court green, having been highly entertained.

In 1881 the brilliant young lawyer, William E. Cameron, one of the candidates for Governor of Virginia, enthusiatic about his success as a debater, came to Appomattox to speak, but there was no one to meet him. Mr. Thomas S. Bocock, although weighted down with age and in feeble health, not having been able to keep himself informed in the political affairs, would not allow the challenge to go unmet, so he agreed upon the terms of debate. In his discourse, Cameron made some statements that kindled anew the smoldering political flames in the old gentleman, and he arose in his old time might. A quick apology came from the young Cameron. If Mr. Bocock had been then as he was a few years earlier, he would have been well the master of the occasion but on account of his condition as above described he left the debate somewhat worsted but he turned for his party what at one time seemed an utter rout, into a graceful retreat. Although Cameron left with the honors of the debate, his ruffled political plumage was evidence of his having been in combat with an antagonist.

John Randolph Tucker met an opponent here but he was a man so gifted in telling jokes and had such an inexhaustable supply that he did not have to touch on the issue at stake but sent his opponent away clothed in ridicule.

Honorable John E. Massey and Judge Paul, (father of the present judge Paul of Rockingham County) came to Appomattox one court day and some of their friends wished a debate between the two. Massey had no claims to oratory but his superior qualities as a debater were well known, not only in Virginia but outside the bounds of the State, and the best debaters never hunted him for a debate. Not being able to have a discussion, Massey spoke to a large crowd in the auditorium of the Court House while Judge Paul addressed his crowd under a locust tree in the Court House yard.

36

Appomattox, like the rest of the South, was partial to its soldiers when the time for election came around. The man with an empty sleeve or a pants leg filled with wood, was given several paces start of his political opponent. The crutch of the brilliant John W. Daniel, which supported his left side, his thigh having been shattered in the service of the Confederacy, gathered him many more votes than his sterling qualities or eloquent tongue.

In the early days of Appomattox the mode of travel was by stage coach, and one of the through state routes ran through the county, passing the Old Court House, known then as Clover Hill. This was the place to stop for meals and to change horses. When the coach driver was approaching the inn, he would give a long blast from the old-time bugle to attract the attention of the inn keeper, then he would give short blasts, the number being governed by the number of passengers for meals.

Later on, the locomotive came upon the scene in Appomattox and pushed the stage coach off the road, as the automobile has done the horse and buggy. The trains and stage coaches had schedules for meeting and it was said sometimes the trainmen would take a delight in pulling out before the coach driver could get to the station. On one occasion the coach driver came in sight as the train was moving off. He lashed down on his team, got them to a gallop, yelling at the trainmen that he had some passengers for his train, but when he saw that the train was not going to stop he yelled: "Well, go on with your damned old tea kittle."

The first passenger train of the Atlantic, Mississippi, and Ohio Railroad, the present Norfolk and Western Railway, that passed here going as far as Roanoke, was in November 1852. As that paralleled to a great extent the old stage line, the stage soon became an unprofitable business and was discontinued.

While the train service revolutionized travel, it was very tame to the present train service. In the first days there was no coal used in this section and wood was used to fire the engines. The writer can remember when there were stacks of wood along the railroad and the trainmen would load up the engine at certain points. The delivering of this wood furnished employment to many Appomattox citizens.

In those days 30 to 40-car trains were considered a load with the old type engine with its large smokestack. Now, with the present day improved engine, they pull 150 or more cars with greater capacity.

PAMPLIN HIGH SCHOOL

APPOMATTOX HIGH SCHOOL
HOME ECONOMICS COTTAGE

APPOMATTOX COUNTY SCHOOL LIBRARY

Built in 1940 at a cost of $16,000.00, and
supplied with 4,780 books, all this an anony-
mous gift, coming from outside of the county.
Miss Violet Ramsey (now Mrs. A. R. Harwood,
Jr.) was first Librarian.

38

APPOMATTOX HIGH SCHOOL, BUILT IN 1809

Lindsay Crawley, 1880, Principal from 1908 to 1947, retiring with the good wishes of all, and wishing for his successor as successful and popular administration as has been their fortune to have administered the school for the last thirty nine years.

Miss Kate Franklin, who has been the very popular and efficient music teacher since 1910; she is still going strong, and we hope she will be filling her present position in the school for many years to come.

Uncle Bob Craig. Efficient and popular janitor since 1909 Retired at the end of the past school session, much to the regret, not only of the school faculty and the pupils, but all who were fortunate to have the acquaintance of this estimable colored citizen.

Professor Peters, who took charge of the school at the beginning of the school term in September, with the best wishes of all.

LINDSAY CRAWLEY 1880

MISS KATE FRANKLIN

ROBERT CRAIG

PROFESSOR JOHN E. PETERS

39

APPOMATTOX HIGH SCHOOL

Built in 1909

Picture of Appomattox County School Board Taken in 1909.

There are three Magisterial Districts in the County, and at the time this picture was taken, there were three school trustees to one district, later the law was changed to one trustee to a district. No. 1, J. Kirk Hannah, Superintendent of Schools from 1897 to 1913. School Trustees as follows: No. 2, Henry Pittman; No. 3, J. F. Dickerson; No. 4, J. C. Jones; No. 5, J. Osborne Davidson; No. 6, Charles E. Lewis; No. 7, John P. Alvis; No. 8, James R. Hamilton; No. 9, S. J. Lee; No. 10, Joel Watkins. J. Osborne Davidson is the oldest trustee in point of service the county has ever had; appointed to the board in 1909, he still holds the office. Of the ten shown in this picture, five have passed away: Nos. 1, 2, 3, 4 and 9.

40

While this county is among the most progressive in all things worth while, perhaps the most notable feature and the one of most importance, is the advancement along the line of education. Prior to 1870 there were no public schools in Virginia and the poor people had no opportunity for education. Those citizens who were able to do so, would employ a private teacher for their homes, or in some cases a few neighbors would combine and employ a teacher for the group.

Under the handicap of being unable financially to give their children an education, many good citizens grew to manhood without being able to read or write.

The first public free school opened its doors and welcomed the children of the rich and the poor alike, which was the opening of a new era in the life of the State.

Education, being free and available to all, has gradually brought closer together the high and low, the rich and poor.

Prior to the period, the pedigree of one's ancestry was an unquestioned pass that admitted him to any society or business and political walk of life; but education has relegated to oblivion those customs so strictly adhered to in the past and now the only credentials one has to present to the public is high character real ability.

In establishing the public school system the leaders in the move were faced with a real problem. Of course taxes had to be levied to carry out the project and the advocating of higher taxes is never a popular move for anyone to make. It required deep thinking and cautious moves to steer it to success.

The first public school in Appomattox County was a log cabin in a field northwest of the Old Court House now in the Appomattox National Park area. The old house has been moved, and the old chimney rocks mark the spot. J. H. Featherston, father of the writer, was the first teacher. C. H. Chilton was the County Superintendent of Schools and retained that position until the Readjusters came into control of the political affairs of the State in 1881. J. B. Bristow was appointed Superintendent and served four years. C. H. Chilton was again appointed and served until 1897. J. K. Hannah succeeded him and served until 1913 when the writer, N. R. Featherston, was appointed and served until 1926, when the present Superintendent, J. A. Burke, was appointed.

Mr. Chilton was heartily in favor of the public school system and his untiring efforts helped greatly in accomplishing the desired results.

As soon as the public schools were opened, the building of school houses was started. The first school house that was built is still standing near Hurtsville and has been turned into a dwelling house.

The lack of finances made the building of school houses progress slowly, but there was enough education spirit in its citizens to keep up the good work, and they soon became used to having their taxes increased for school purposes and of course the schools advanced.

Many of the citizens of the county have had to walk a distance of five miles to get to their nearest school. Now with the school buses conveying the children to school, very few, if any, have to walk over a mile to get to school.

In those days there were no janitors, (I expect Uncle Bob Craig, the present janitor of the Appomattox High School, was the first one of the county employed) and each girl had her day to sweep the school room. Each boy had his day to get wood. The county furnished an axe, but boys were not especially particular to see that the axe went into wood only, therefore, it was soon in about as good condition to cut with as a hoe would be. We boys often had to find dead wood, hit it against a tree to break it up short enough to go into the stove, and then carry it to the school house in our arms.

Thanks to the progressive spirit that has put those hardships in the past, now all a child has to do is to go to school and study, leaving no excuse for any healthy normal child to grow in ignorance.

In the early public school day there was a term of five months and an average monthly salary of about $25.00. At present the term is nine months and minimum annual salary $1,000. In 1926 this county spent $69;274 for school purposes, in 1930, $75,345; in 1935; $100,698; and 1945, $144,507. This is good evidence that its citizens are willing to pay for an education.

In the session of 1908 Professor Lindsay Crawley took charge of the high school here with three teachers and an enrollment of 160 pupils. The school house was a frame building on the lot on which the residence of Mr. T. W. Moses now stands.

The Legislature of that year appropriated funds to help the Congressional Districts establish agricultural schools in each District. H. D. Flood, S. L. Ferguson, and R. F. Burke immediately turned their energies to have the one for this District located here, but it required money outside of public funds, and a liberal contribution was made by many of the citizens, The late Thomas F. Ryan, the millionaire, of Nelson County, being in this Congressional District, contributed $2,000. The funds being assured, the work was begun on a brick building and the school opened this new home in September 1909, as the Tenth Congressional District High School with Professor Lindsay Crawley as Principal.

Any pupils living in this District could attend the school without paying tuition. The school was well patronized but getting boarding places became a problem. Professor Crawley with his fertile brain and unusual business ability, relieved the situation by advocating a dormitory, which was built in 1915. It had a dining room attached and the pupils were comfortably housed and well fed at a very reasonable cost and at a profit to the county.

This school was a great success, but for some reason the Legislature cut off the appropriation for agriculture in these schools and they were operated thereafter as regular four year accredited High Schools. This county continued the Agricultural Department and the same courses are taught in the school as when it was an agricultural school.

The school this year (1946) has thirty teachers and an enrollment of 693. There is a well equipped Domestic Science Department which has been a great benefit to the girl students who have availed themselves of that course.

42

There is also a well equipped, accredited high school doing good work at Pamplin, with twelve teachers and an enrollment of 220. The school is a nice modern brick building and has a splendid auditorium - a school plant which would be a credit to a town much larger than Pamplin.

Mr. W. C. Dudley was the Vocational Agriculture instructor, alternating between Appomattox and the Pamplin High Schools. Mr. Henry B. Pack is now ably filling this position.

Miss Kate M. Franklin, a very talented musician, has been music teacher here since 1910, alternating between the Pamplin and Appomattox schools.

Robert Craig was employed as janitor at the opening of the new school building in 1909. He is a man of intelligence, honest and energetic and interested in doing his duty. He has become so much of a fixture that the returning pupils each Fall look forward as confidently to seeing "Uncle Bob" as they do the school building.

The fact that Professor Crawley has served as Principal since 1908, Miss Kate Franklin as music teacher since 1910, Bob Craig as janitor since 1909, and Mrs. Mozelle Price as Supervisor of Colored Schools since 1918, is sufficient evidence that they are entitled to have efficiency indelibly stamped on their record.

Appomattox can boast of furnishing some teachers with a number of years service in the school room. Misses Deane Johns and Edmonia Hardy taught more than 50 years each; Mr. R. H. Wheeler more than 40 years, and Miss Ida Jones more than 35 years.

The first school year of Appomattox High School there were eleven graduates:

Jamie Gills	Bluefield, West Virginia
George Torrence	Dr. Geo. Torrence, Hot Springs, Virginia
Louis Gills	Appomattox, Virginia
Mary Babcock	Mrs. F. L. Murphy, Appomattox, Virginia
Fannie Pierce Taylor	Mrs. Baker, Richmond, Virginia
Lynolie Atwood	Richmond, Virginia
Jack Atwood	Mrs. Newbill, Richmond, Virginia
Cabell Foster	Mrs. C. W. Smith, Appomattox, Virginia
Venona Sears	Mrs. Bayliss Carson, Wakefield, Virginia
Ethel Abbit	Mrs. J. A. Burke, Appomattox, Virginia
Grace Hancock	(deceased)

The school has flourished to such an extent that it graduates this session 54, but the zenith of its graduation was in 1941-1942, when it graduated 104. The decrease in the number of graduates is partly due to World War II.

Many of the graduates of this school have made high marks in the business world as lawyers, doctors, mechanics, and farmers. While very few failed to fully avail themselves of the opportunity offered them by the public school, there are a few who deserve special mention for their success in overcoming all obstacles, which were numerous, in the path of an education.

43

George Torrence, a product of the farm and of this school, went to a Medical College, graduated in medicine, and for years has been physician for the Hot Springs resort at Hot Springs, Virginia.

Alfred Drinkard, not a graduate of this school but a native of the County, was another who toiled in the hot sun to add to the comforts of his father's household; took a course at Blacksburg and has been one of the efficient members of the Faculty of Virginia Polytechnic Institute for a number of years.

Thomas J. Farrar, a native of this county became a prominent Professor in Washington and Lee University.

The foregoing shows what a young person can accomplish, even though not flushed with finances, if he has the ambition and opportunity.

Many other Appomattox boys and girls have taken advantage of public school education and prepared themselves to secure lucrative positions in many parts of the country.

Appomattox has made fine progress in improving health conditions. Miss Eula May Burke can be given credit for arousing interest and gaining the cooperation of the people in this project. She also, in a great measure was responsible for the success of the Red Cross work in the county.

* * * * * *

Appomattox, though a small town, has many enterprises, giving employment to many of its citizens, male and female, over the county. John E. Sears & Company do a large business in all kinds of lumber and mill work, and in connection with this concern, Miss Lula Irby has a coal and wood yard. Hunter Lumber Company is doing a large lumber business, also W. P. Coleman. All these are within the city limits. Then there are many other mills over the county, giving employment to the citizens of their neighborhood. The Akron Pipe Factory of Pamplin holds the title of manufacturing the finest clay smoking pipes in the world, known as the Powhatan Pipe. The Appomattox Battery Factory ships dry cell batteries to many points in this and adjoining states. The Garment Factory, giving regular employment to a number of ladies, ships ladies' apparel to various sections of the country. An immense amount of railroad cross ties, pulp wood and mine props is being shipped daily from the county.

* * * * * *

Appomattox County was not without its tragedies. In 1876 Dr. John R. McDearmon was called to his front yard in the night and murdered. Of course immediately the officers began a search for the guilty person. A detective of Richmond was employed but he soon gave up the case saying he could get no evidence on anyone. However, there was some manufactured evidence which caused the arrest and trial of John Glover, colored. A track was traced to the McDearmon home, having been made by a man apparently lame, making every other step a short one. John Glover was lame and made tracks in walking as above described, therefore, he was lodged in jail. A great many people felt so sure they had the guilty party that the vigilance committee in existence in that neighborhood at that time met and voted on going to the jail to lynch him. It was a tie vote, the vote being broken by the chairman, the late John Henry Marshall, who voted in the negative, thereby saving from a hideous death a perfectly innocent man.

The manufactured evidence was as follows: A few years ago it was revealed that a man, although not connected in any way with the murder, but in order to help some of the murderers who were his friends, walked to the scene of the murder and acted the part of a lame man, making every other step a short one.

The case, of course, created great excitement and there was interest manifested in a wide area. Honorable Thomas S. Bocock and Colonel R. B. Poore volunteered to defend the negro Glover, free of charge, and Mr. Bocock made the defense speech, upholding well his reputation for oratory and logic in delivering a most brilliant speech, but the manufactured evidence and some false statements of the prosecution's witnesses, which could not be proved false except by a visit to the scene of tragedy, fully convinced the jury of the guilt of the prisoner, outweighed the magnificent defense plea, convicted Glover of first degree murder, and sentenced him to be hanged.

So convinced were the defense lawyers of the innocence of their client that Colonel Poore at once proceeded to gather evidence for a new trial. He visited the scene, found proof of the falsity of some of the prosecution witnesses, and presented it to court. A new trial was granted, also a change of venue, and the second trial was held in Lynchburg. In that trial, Colonel Poore made the defense speech, and, although a young lawyer, his speech was delivered in such a masterly way and with such convincing logic that the jurors at this trial of the case unhesitatingly acquitted the prisoner.

After this poor innocent victim had gone through months of humiliation and heartache, he no doubt felt a great relief when the Lynchburg jury removed from him the prison shackles and humiliation of a murderer and restored to him his rightful status as an American citizen. He also had an everlasting love spot in his heart for those lawyers who so ardently defended him. Colonel Poore left the court room after receiving from the leaders of the Lynchburg bar their hearty congratulations on his magnificent defense of his client.

There was a noted legal battle over a will in the early seventies. The late Jack Johnson, a bachelor, a large landowner, and who in addition had a goodly sum of money for that day, lived near the Buckingham County line in the Tower Hill neighborhood. Mr. Johnson willed the late Thomas S. Bocock, his attorney in legal matters, all his money. The near of kin made a strong attempt to break the will, employing two of the leading lawyers of Richmond. Mr. Bocock employed Major John W. Daniel of Lynchburg. With such an array of talent there was a real legal battle which created interest over a wide territory. When the battle ended, Mr. Bocock was the winner. Before the War Between the States, Mr. Johnson was a large slave owner; he had so many he could not know all the young ones. He would meet them in the road and ask them who they belonged to. They would say: "Belong to you, Mars Jack."

A good portion of his real estate was left to his slaves after the war and many of their descendants own the land now, some of which is located in Appomattox County and some in Buckingham County.

45

Just beyond the Soldiers' Cemetery, near the road leading from the site of the old Court House to Appomattox, there is a monument erected by the citizens of North Carolina to mark the point of the last advance made by the North Carolina troops on the morning of April 9, 1865. The monument was erected and unveiled in 1905. A delegation from North Carolina had charge of the ceremonies. Among them was Governor Glenn, the Governor of North Carolina, who made an excellent address, and Governor Andrew Jackson Montague, Governor of Virginia at that time, accepted the monument in behalf of Virginia.

On June 6, 1906, amid an enthusiastic and cheering crowd, was unveiled that splendid monument erected on the Court Green here to the memory of the County's brave soldiers who rushed to their country's defense in 1861, giving their share in making the Army of Northern Virginia one of the greatest armies that ever marched across a battlefield.

This unveiling was under the auspices of the Appomattox Camp, Confederate Veterans, the committee in charge being five Confederate Veterans, as follows: T. J. Stratton, Dr. W. H. Abbitt, Major J. W. Flood, Captain W. T. Johnson and J. Kirk Hannah.

Committees:

On entertainment, Rev. H. C. Smith, Chairman
On decoration, S. L. Ferguson, Chairman
On invitation, T. J. Stratton, J. R. Horseley, Joseph Button

Chief Marshall:
R. F. Burke

Programme:

1. Formation of parade in front of Presbyterian Church at 10:30 A. M. and march to Monument Square
2. Band concert at Court Square, 11 o'clock A. M.
3. Call to order by prayer
4. Presentation of monument by Judge George Hundley
5. Acceptance of monument by Honorable H. D. Flood
6. Address by Governor Claude A. Swanson

Band concert in the afternoon

In an appropriate and eloquent speech, Comrade James P. L. Fleshman introduced Comrade Judge George J. Hundley, who, in an eloquent speech presented the monument to the County. Honorable W. C. Franklin, in his usual splendid style of speaking, introduced Honorable H. D. Flood, who accepted the monument for the County in a speech of such gifted eloquence as to add honor to the occasion. Honorable S. L. Ferguson, in a few very appropriate remarks, introduced Governor Claude A. Swanson, who sustained his reputation as a high class orator. He received tremendous and prolonged applause as he lavishly praised the old Confederate Soldiers for their valor and achievements from 1861 to 1865.

In the evening, the programme completed, the large crowd, after being served a sumptuous dinner by the noble Daughters of the Confederacy, and having been highly entertained by the gifted orators of the occasion, reluctantly left for their homes, carrying with them pleasant memories which would not be forgotten until their eyes closed in death.

* * * * * *

While the people of Appomattox have a right to be very proud of the achievements in the life of the county, the one thing most important, and of which she is justly proud is, her religious record. You have but to travel into different sections of the county to find nice church buildings with steeples pointing Heavenward.

The Baptist denomination is the strongest numerically and financially. They built here in Appomattox a church building, which in normal times cost $25,000. It has modern conveniences, annex and Sunday School rooms. This building would be a credit to a much larger town than Appomattox.

Appomattox County, while it has only about 9,000 inhabitants, has fourteen Baptist churches, ten Methodist, five Presbyterian and one Episcopalian, and sixteen colored churches.

The denominations are very co-operative, especially in the rural sections where the preaching service is not held at each church each Sunday and each can attent the service of the other church. They gladly work together, believing the way to Heaven does not have to be by any particular denomination.

47

No. 1, log house in which the late Senator S. L. Ferguson grew to manhood. No. 2, Brick residence, old farm home of Robertson, later Martin. Bought by S. L. Ferguson, shortly after reaching manhood. No. 3, frame house built in 1911 by S. L. Ferguson. This last named residence is one of the finest, and the most expensive residences in this county. This is what ambition, energy, determination, combined with high character can accomplish; all these, Senator Ferguson possessed.

FARMERS NATIONAL BANK

Organized in 1918; Presidents as follows: C.
W. Hancock, C. A. Hancock, M. C. Smith, F.
L. Murphey. Vice-Presidents, D. M. Robertson,
M. C. Smith, L. J. Morris, H. W. McKinney, C.
S. McDearmon. Cashiers, A. R. Harwood, Chas.
F. P. Crawley, T. DeWitt Evans. This Bank op-
ened business with a capital stock of $50,000,00.
Surplus $40,000,00.

The McLean House, built in 1848. In this
house, on April 9th, 1865, the terms of surrender were written up between Generals
Robert E. Lee and U. S. Grant. The house was
taken down in 1893 or 1894 to be moved to
Washington, but never moved. The United
States Government having taken over this with
other property adjoining it, making a 900 acre
park, bids have already come in for the rebuilding of this house, and work will begin on
the reconstruction as soon as Spring opens up.

BANK OF APPOMATTOX

Organized in 1901; Presidents as follows: J.
R. Atwood, H. D. Flood, R. F. Burke. Jos. Button,
R. L. Burke Cashiers, R. F. Burke, R. L. Burke,
J. C. Davidson. This bank opened business with
a capital stock of $10,000,00, which has been in-
creased to $40,000,00. Surplus, $60,000,00.

This picture taken at Appomattox Court House May 1, 1945 on the 100th anniversary of the County. At the speaker's stand is United States Senator Harry F. Byrd delivering the address. Seated behind him, left to right, Rev. W. M. Black, Baptist Minister. C. W. Smith, Clerk of the Circuit Court of Appomattox County. N. R. Featherston. Senator Robert Russell of Campbell County. Prof. John G. Fisher.

Residence of the late William Thornhill,
built prior to 1812. Now owned by Dr.
Mosby H. Payne.

Residence of the late Dr. David C. Jones,
built prior to 1812. Now owned by his
grandson, Dr. Mosby H. Payne.

Residence of the late Henry Marshall,
built in 1852. Now owned by Mr. Rush.

Home of the late Captain William Hannah,
built in 1820. Now owned by George Shrieve.

APPOMATTOX COUNTY OFFICE BUILDING

Built in 1934

Appomattox County Jail
Built in 1892

Court House at Appomattox, as it was at
the time of the surrender in April 1865.
Burned in 1892, rebuilt at the railroad station three miles from the old site.

Appomattox County Clerk's Office

Appomattox County Clerks Office, built
in 1892. Confederate Monument in front
of building, erected in 1906.

Appomattox County Court House
Built 1892

This old house built by the Bococks, later owners, Dixons, Judge H. T. Parrish and
S. A. Ferguson.

This old tavern built in 1819 by the
Patteson family, used as a tavern in stage
coach days, later as a country hotel.

Residence of the late George T. Peers,
who for forty years was Clerk of Appomattox County.

HENRY DANIEL JOHNSON, 1861-1943

The colored section of this history is
dedicated to the family, of which this was
the youngest member.

A Brief History of the Splendid Colored Citizenship of
Appomattox County, Virginia.

Even a short history of Appomattox County would be incomplete without some account of its Negro population, who are good citizens and of whom we are proud; in fact, I am sure no county can boast of a higher type of colored citizenship than we have here in our County.

I want to dedicate this colored section of my history of Appomattox County to a family of Johnsons for which I had, not only admiration, but genuine love. Uncle Daniel Johnson was born in 1797 and died in 1900 at the age of 103 years. He was the head hand on my grandfather's place before the War Between the States, and for many years after the war closed in 1865. "Head-Hand" in those days was the leader in the field, and when the overseer was not around, he would give directions to the other hands, and see that they followed his directions. His wife, Aunt Viney, who passed away in 1889 (God bless her dear old soul), was our old Mammy. We loved her and her orders to us were just as strictly obeyed as were those given us by our parents. Children of the above were: Ellis, Sampson, Archer, Frances, Jane, Charlotte, Peter, Catherine and Henry. Sampson died at the age of 65 years and 40 years of his life were spent on the old Agee plantation on which he was born. Henry was the youngest, and the last to pass away, in 1943, in the 82nd year of his life. His picture appears at the head of this section. He was a man of great natural wit and most of the "colored conversations" in this write up are taken from his witty expressions.

While I have taken this particular family for special mention, I do not mean to say that they were the only ones who deserve it, for there are many who can testify to the affection that existed between the white families and the colored ones who had been their slaves. When we take into consideration that at the close of the War Between the States in 1865, the colored people, after all their ancestry had served as slaves, were turned out without homes, except as hired laborers, or renters, not owning any real estate, and now at this date there are 575 colored citizens of Appomattox County who own 19,368 acres of land, valued for taxation at $168,046, and paying taxes to the amount of $2,772.76 on this real estate, in addition to personal property taxes. We think it sufficient evidence that we have a race of colored people who are energetic, honest and progressive. It is a fact that, as in all counties, we have some who are not so desirable, but that can unquestionably be said of some of the whites, and comparing the opportunities of the colored with that of the whites, it can be seen that the colored measure up well with the whites. They have good comfortable school buildings, in a large measure due to their private contributions to supplement the school fund over the county. While they were making progress in the line of education, yet it was rather slow, because of the lack of leadership. In the Fall of 1918, Mrs. Mozelle Price furnished that leadership, taking the colored school situation of Appomattox County in hand as Supervisor of Colored Schools.

At that time there were only six colored schools in the entire county, with a school term of five months, and an average annual salary for the teachers of about $125. Mrs. Price entered into this work with a sincere desire to improve the condition of her people. Having the noble qualities; energy, high ideals, and devotion to duty, and being modest, conservative, and well schooled in business affairs, she has

Carver High School,
Appomattox, Virginia,
Colored

Agricultural Building,
Carver Colored School,
Appomattox, Virginia

MRS. MOZELLA JORDAN PRICE

The efficient Supervisor of colored
schools in Appomattox County.

rightly won the respect and good will of both white and colored. Under her leadership and with the splendid cooperation of the colored people, the schools have advanced from the above mentioned six one-room schools to five one-room, two two-room and one twelve-room schools, requiring twenty-one teachers in addition to the Supervisor. These twenty-one teachers have a nine months term, with an average annual salary of $978.45.

The splendid school plant at Appomattox, a picture of which is shown, with Mrs. Price, is a monument to her and her local co-workers in education, of duty well performed, of which they can justly be proud, for the plant was made possible by the patrons raising by private subscription the sum of $3,000 to supplement the school fund. Credit must also be given to the late Rev. P. W. Price, the husband of Mrs. Price for sponsoring a very worthy cause, the building of a home for the unfortunate. Laboring under many financial difficulties, his courage and faith in the project gave him strength to overcome the difficulties. The work was somewhat checked by the sudden passing of Rev. Price, but it has been taken over by his wife, and is still progressing under her supervision. The colored people all over the county have, under the wise leadership of these two people, caught an inspiration for higher ideals and are making rapid progress toward bettering their conditioning in all respects.

Up to the close of the War Between the States, and in years recent enough for the writer to remember, there was space provided in the rear of the white churches and galleries for the colored. Until they began to build their own churches, the names of those who professed religion were carried on the books of the white church, and when they would succeed in building a church of their own, the members of the white churches would give them a letter in good and regular standing to join their own church. One of the wisest moves that the Negro race ever made was to organize their own separate churches. Otherwise they would never have developed the initiative and leadership that they have today. Now they have good churches in which they praise their Creator. They are noted for their loyalty to their church and their regular attendance at the church services. By their energy and liberality they have built churches in all sections of the County.

The first colored church built in the county was Galilee, a log house; soon the congregation was able to build a frame building, and in 1913, they built the present building, which is a credit to the splendid membership of that church.

The Christian spirit continued to work among their people, and churches sprang up in all sections: Canaan, Springfield, Mt. Airy, Jordan, Mt. Zion, Mt. Obed, one between Stonewall and Concord, one at Concord, Spout Spring, Appomattox, Promise Land, Bethlehem, Bethany, Mt. Pleasant, one across the Appomattox River from Hurtsville, and Morning Star.

"A tree is known by its fruit." The fruit borne by these churches brilliantly shown in the lives of the past and present generation.

The Negroes took as their surname, the name of the white family to which they belonged before "The War." In the old Tower Hill section we find: the Johnsons and Beasleys, thrifty farmers, fine mechanics and carpenters; the Lewises, Craighills, Echols, Thornhills, Agees; and about over the County were: Joneses, Penicks, Trents, Fergusons, McCoys, Isbells, Phelps, Wheelers, Hunters, Sam ("Slick") Payne and his descendants; Christians, Morgans, Scruggs, Pattesons, Floods, Andersons, Bococks, Daniels, Wrights, Sweeneys, Walkers, Marshalls, Saunders, Gilliams, Colemans, Hamlets, Abbitts, Pettys, Gus Watson, the Blacksmith Minister, and his family; Eames, Chiltons, Johns, Connors, McKinneys, Tibbs, Nelson Watson, and his descendants. And who that ever knew them could forget Henry Daughtery and Dave Tibbs.

Now, there is that splendid type of the colored race, almost a thing of the past, known as the "Old Time Darkey" who deserves special mention. Those whites of the younger generation have been deprived of a great privilege, joy and honor by not having lived far enough back in the past to have associated with this type of the colored race. Those of us who enjoyed the privilege look back with great pleasure (and with a tear of regret that that day has forever past) to the time when we were children and would run into their cabins, by a big old time log fire, listen to the stories told by them. We enjoyed our little colored playmates as much as we did our white friends. I think a child's education and training has been sadly neglected who has reached the age of ten years without having had the experience of bare feet, stumped toes, and stone bruises, and who has never played with little negroes.

It was a great treat for the white people to sit in the yard, or on the porch and hear the rich music flow from the crowd of colored people as they would fill the air with music from their splendid voices. No conversation being carried on by the whites was so interesting or so important that it would not be silenced as soon as the tune was raised by the old darkies, ringing out with the old time plantation songs.

Now for a few conversations picked up from the old-times. In relating the following I am casting no reflection whatever on them. It is a dialect belonging strictly to the colored race of that day, and was beyond the power of the whites to immitate. It was music to the ears of us who had the pleasure and the privilege of that association.

A colored boy with a big watch chain (but no watch) was asked by another for the time: "Look here nigger, you go bought you a watch ef you want to 'no the time."

A friend, calling at his house early one morning, finding him in the house said; "Thought I had caught you in bed." He replied, "Or Lord, no sar, I is done did nigh a haf' ur days work."

Uncle Ned had fallen out with his church and had not been to the services for a long time. One of the members passing his house one Sunday morning called to him to come on and go to church; he answered: "Nor, hit is des as nigh from here to hell as hit is from dat church."

Aunt Betsy did not like one of the deacons in her church; one day when there was a communion service, she said: "When dey had Sack'ment he comes to me wid it, but some other deacon had to bring it to me, I wo' gwy take no Sack'ment from him, an old cross-eyed devil."

An old brother who was always thankful for everything, was asked: "How are you feeling?" Uncle Tom replied: "I feeling right poorly, this morning, thank Gard." In discussing one of his neighbors, he said: "He mighty good man, but he is so self-opin-ionified you can't git him ratified."

Uncle Jack said: "I gwy git me a watch, git me a gold watch, I git one for a dollar." Uncle Henry replied: "You can't git no gold watch for a dollar." Uncle Jack said: "Yes I kin." Uncle Henry answered: "If you do hit wo' run." Uncle Jack: "I do' keer ef hit don run, I noa when I gits hongry."

When a certain church member died, Uncle John said: "His pastor wo' sho' dat dat member had lived right, so when he got up to preach his fune'l, he preached him right to de forks uv de road, and dar he lef' him."

Uncle Tom, staring at another of his race, said: "Gard ur Mighty, what a face!" The other man answered: "Look here nigger, do' bother 'bout dis here face, Gard made dis face." Uncle Tom said: "Well, I sho is glad He did not make it on me."

Uncle Tom in taking up collection said: "Now Breren, hit takes three books to get us to heben; de Bible; de him' book and de pocket book, and ef you do' open up dat pocket book, you sho' wo' git dar."

Uncle Tom says: "A boy going down de road met a b'ar he runs and meets a preacher; de preacher says: 'When you meets a b'ar, you jes git down and pray!' De boy he goes back down de road, sees de b'ar coming, he draps down on his 'nees and goes to praying, de b'ar keep acoming, he keep praying 'til de b'ar gits right close to him. He gits up and takes off down the road, runs to the preacher and says: 'Parson, prar may be all right in a prar meeting, but it is damn poor dependence in a b'ar meeting'."

Someone asked Uncle Bill: "How are you feeling these days?" He said: "I hain't feeling well these days: my suggestion is bad; hit is hard for me to suggest anything I eats."

Uncle John, in discussing the war, asked: "Well, what sort o folks is dey 'cross de oshun, is dey like us folks?" Being told they were somewhat like us but spoke a different language, he said: "Well, I thought may be we was us and dey were dem."

Aunt Jane, of powerful physique, went to the Justice of the Peace to get out a warrant against her husband. The justice said: "I do not want to issue a warrant for the arrest of you husband; you go back and settle it with him." She said: "I thanks you for the 'thority, all I wants is de 'thority, I promise you I won't bother you no mo'." She did not bother the Justice after that, but the neighbors pitied her old husband, having to move around under the 'thority of Aunt Jane.

Uncle Tommy joined the church, but could not get enough religion on hand to last him until the next year's protracted meeting, therefore he would re-fess at every fall meeting, and every time he would re-fess they would re-baptize him. After several years of experience in this line, having gone up in one of the meetings, he went down the road and, meeting one of the members of the church, he said: "Good morning Sis Sallie." She said: "Do' call me Sister, I none your sister." He said: "Yes you is, I is done 'fessed 'ligion again and gwy jine your church." She answered: "Nor you ain't, we des ai' gwy sile Gard's Holy Water wid you no mo'." He said:

"Now you jes wiat and let me tell you a dream I had last night. I dreamed I died and went up to St. Peter, and he asked me my name. I says 'my name is Eben'. He say: 'Mr. Eben, whar is you from?' I say 'I is from Oak Grove Church in Buckingham County.' He takes down a big book, de biggest book I uver seed, he looks it through. He could not find nothing from Oak Grove Church. 'Whar you say you from?' I say, from Oak Grove Church, right down here in Buckingham County. He looks all through de book again, den He shot up de book and says: 'You go on in, Eben, dis is de fust time I is uver had anybody to come up from Oak Grove Church.' "

Uncle Joe worked hard, bought a farm and had some money ahead. His brother, Dick, had nothing. Uncle Joe was asked why his brother had nothing ahead, when he was older and had the same opportunity he had had. He said: "Dick, he will scratch a po' man's head long as he lives."

There were two lawyers, one a fine orator, the other not so gifted in that line. Uncle Nick said: "Mr. Tom kno' des as much law as Mr. Frank, but he can't tell it." In speaking of a noted criminal lawyer, Uncle Nick said: "Dat lawyer say he ai' nuber gwy persecute no mo', 'cause he persecuted one man and found he was innocent and he made up his mind he was gwy spend the rest of his life 'fending."

Someone asked Uncle Jim: "What did your boy get fined for?" He said: "Dey kotched him driving dat old car wid no commit."

Uncle Josh had passed his 75th year and had never been more than 40 miles from home. The writer told him to be ready on a certain day and he would take him on a trip; he told him to eat breakfast early, so as to get an early start. He said: "I ai' gwy eat nothing, I gwy fill up on what I sees." He was taken over by Staunton, Harrisonburg, Fredericksburg, Colonial Beach, Richmond and back home, all in one day - a distance of nearly 500 miles. When about half-way round, he said: "You welse to carry me back home now, my eyes done got full, I can't see no mo'." When the Potomac River was reached, it was the first time he had ever been in a salt water section. He was told to taste the water to see if it was salty; he tasted it and then he noticed a crowd of bathers on the beach, a scene he had never witnessed before. When he got home, he related it to his wife. He said: "They told me to taste the water to see if it was salty, and after I had done tasted it, I saw right close by about 50 folks wallowing around in it."

A colored boy was asked by a stranger the direction to Mr. Johnson's. He said: "You go, you des go on down dis here road 'til you gits to whar de road forks, one of dem forks goes to de right, de other fork, hit goes to de lef', you des take dat dar right hand fork and des keep on down dat road about three miles, you will come to two great big gate posts, one of dem gate posts is on de right, de other hit is on the lef'. When you gits to them gate posts, den you know you is on de wrong road, den you comes back and takes dat dar lef' hand road and hit will take you right down to dat man's house."

We, who had the pleasure of associating with those ol-timers, regret that the day is fast coming when we can no more have that pleasure.

The younger generations have many of the qualities of the older ones, but they are more progressive, and are not satisfied to go through life with labor and wit as their only aspiration, but are going ahead and taking a hand in the business but the blessings of the old-timers will never be forgotten until all of us old-timers in the white list have passed on. I feel that the Heavenly Angels are still singing songs of praise over those dear old colored ones for their devotion and loyalty to their masters, and that they will have many bright stars in their crowns when their names are called for them to appear and receive: "Well done good and faithful servants."

Alphabetical List of Families of
Appomattox County

ABBITT, A. B. 1860-1834, married Annie Godwyn
    Father: George W. Abbitt, Mother: Fannie Webb

ABBITT, A. H. 1853-, Married Laura Pankey 1856-
    Father: George W. Abbitt, Mother: Fannie Webb
    Children: Welford C. 1882-1890
                  Frank L., 1883-1910
                  Leslie H. 1885, married Palsie Painter
                  Bertha L. 1887
                  Mattie E. 1889, married Emory O. Martin
                  Ernest P. 1891, married Lottie Finch
                  Ruth P. 1892, married Joe McCormick
                  Ethel W. 1894, married Dewey C. Taylor

ABBITT, AURELIUS WILLIAM
    Father: Dr. Wm. Henry Abbitt, Mother: Sarah Frances Plunkett
    Children: Ethel F., married J. A. Burke
                  Ola Lee, married Luther Throckmorton of Richmond
                  Ann Eleanor, married John M. Scott

ABBITT, BENJAMIN, 1765-1818, married Sallie Flowers, 1765-1855
    Children: Benjamin II, 1799-1874, married Mary Patterson,
                  1803-1883

ABBITT, BENJAMIN II, 1799-1874, Married Mary Patterson, 1803-1883
    Father: Benjamin Abbitt, Mother: Sallie Flowers
    Children: Sara Ann, 1824-1827
                  Benjamin III, 1827-1851
                  Agnes Willie, 1840-1857
                  James C., 1930-1862
                  Adelaide, married Braford, 2nd husband, James Overton
                  Joseph, 1831-1917, married Sarah H. Walker, 1830-
                  Mary Diuguid, 1834-1866
                  George Dallas, 1844-1883, married Bettie Walton
                  William Chatham, 1848-1916, Married Martha West Jones
                  of Campbell County, 1852-1908
                  Josephine, 1842-1914
                  Elizabeth, married Paul Horsley of Nelson County.
                  David, married Miss Payne of Nelson County.
                  Sallie, married John Peryear.

ABBITT, CHARLES A., 1849-1930, married Elvira James LeGrand, 1847-1921.
    Father: Wyatt Abbitt Mother: Sallie Spottswood Jenkins
    Children: Wyatt Alexandria 1871, married Anna B. Coleman
                  William Benjamin, 1873-
                  Mary Katherine, 1875, married Leonard A. Kelly
                  John Luther 1876-1940, married Cornelia M. White
                  Joseph Hunter 1878-1941, married Ruth Edgerton
                  Sallie M 1880-1884

ABBITT, CHARLES A., (continued)
        Nancy Jane, 1882, married James A. Shelton of N.C. 1882
        Lizzie Calhoun, 1883-1946, married Henry E. Jones
        Zaida Elvira, 1888-1907
        Charles James, 1890, married Alenia Massie Irby.

ABBITT, CHARLIE, 1865-1947, Married Mary Elizabeth Hardy, 1863.
    Father,   George W. Abbitt, Mother: Fannie Webb, 1835-1922.
    Children: Thomas Hardy, married Miss Kitchen.
              Charles William, 1899, married Blanch Callahan,
              Jesse Bernard, 1901, married Ethel Newcomb.
              Eddie, married Weakley.

ABBITT, C. N. 1864, Married Mary A. Fleshman 1875-1938
    Father: George Abbitt, Sr.
    Mother: Jane Eleanor Webb
    Children: J. T. Abbitt, 1899, married Gracie E. Mann
              of Bluefield, West Virginia
              George Alfred, 1901, married D. F. Davidson of Nelson
              Elizabeth, 1903

ABBITT, DAVID, Married Miss Payne of Nelson
    Father: Benjamin Abbitt III Mother: Mary Patterson
    Children: James P. II,

ABBITT, EMMETT R., Married Margaret Quisenbury.
    Father: Dr. Wm. Henry Abbitt, Mother: Sarah Frances Plunkett
    Children: Ernest, married Mary Gross
              Russell,
              Katherine,

ABBITT, GEORGE SR. 1801-1878, Married Jane Eleanor Webb
    Father: Benjamin Abbitt, Mother: Sallie Flowers
    Children: George W. Abbitt, Jr. 1828-1912
              Married Fannie Webb, 1835-1922
              Isabel Married Col. Thomas Cheatham
              Dr. W. H. 1832-1907 married Sarah F. Plunkett.
              Eliza married Albert Cheatham.
              Polly married William Coleman
              Benjamin 1859-1926 married Miss Elem of Prince
              Edward County.
              Ellie, 1862-1936 married John W. Paris.
              C. N. 1864, married Mary Fleshman, 1875-1938
              Joseph R. 1866-1916
              I. O. 1869, married Jessie Main, 1944
              Lucy F. 1871-1928 married James Paris
              James,
              Betty T. 1873, married W. H. Clayton of Chesterfield
              Mattie W. 1875, married E. J. Harvey

ABBITT, GEORGE F., 1875, married Otway Moorman of Lynchburg, 1880.
    Father: George W. Abbitt, Mother: Fannie Webb, 1935-1922.
    Children: George F., Jr. 1906, married Josephine Cundif, 1909
                Watkins Moorman, 1908, married Corinne Hancock, 1909
                Dora Otway, 1912, married Lacy Evrod Conner, 1904.
                Herbert Moorman, 1816
                Eloise Frances, 1918, married W. B. Snead of Lynchburg.
                Charles Webb, 1920, married Ann B. Bolyn of Texas.

ABBITT, GEORGE F. JR., 1906, Married Josephine Cundiff 1909
    Father: George F. Abbitt, Sr. Mother: Otway Moorman
    Children: Sarah Peyton, 1941
                Frances Penniton, 1941

ABBITT, GEORGE R., 1882, Married Geneva B. Torrence, 1896
    Father: R. D. Abbitt Mother: Rosa Tweedy
    Children: Hilda, 1917, married George A. Covington of Prince
                Edward County.
                Mildred, 1919, married Robert Gross of Richmond
                Gertrude, 1921, married Robert Ellington of N. C.
                Betty, 1926, married Howard LeWarne of Prince Ed.
                Junius, 1927, married Miss Adams of Charlotte
                June Carroll, 1932, married Spencer St. John of Prince
                Edward
                Susie G., 1938

ABBITT, GEORGE W., 1828-1912, Married Fannie Webb 1835-1922
    Father: George Abbitt, Sr. Mother: Jane Eleanor Webb
    Children: Augustas Henry, 1853 Married Laura Pankey
                R. D. 1855-1927, Married Rosa Tweedy, 1862-1940
                Charlie 1865-1947, Married Mary Elizabeth Hardy 1863
                R. W. 1862-1937, Married Maude Coleman 1880
                Lillie 1858-1933 Married William James Covington
                George F. 1875, Married Otway Moorman, 1880
                Helen, 1872, Married Mark Bernard of Norfolk
                A. B. 1860-1934, Married Annie Godwin
                Colyer, 1868-1890, Married Robert S. Jenkins
                Lizzie, 1870-   Married A. P. White

ABBITT, JAMES B., 1872-1932, married Vara Abbitt.
    Father: Dr. William Henry Abbitt. Mother: Sarah Frances Plunkett.
    Children: Vara W.
                Ann, married Mr. Staples.

ABBITT, JOSEPH, 1831-1917, Married Sarah Heth Walker 1830
    Father: Benjamin Abbitt II Mother: Mary Patterson
    Children: Benjamin Walker, 1857-1907
                Winston, 1861-1924, Married Anna Heth Overton
                Mary Jane, 1865, Married Mr. Nuckols

ABBITT, JOHN D.
  Father: Dr. Wm. Henry Abbitt Mother: Sarah Frances Plunkett
  Children: Edith Frances, married John D. Rose of North Carolina
    Elizabeth
    John D., Jr.
    William Henry

ABBITT, JULIAN, 1870-1905, married Sallie Ballou.
  Father: Dr. William Henry Abbitt, Mother: Sarah Frances Plunkett
  Children: Frances.
    Edward.
    William.
    Julian.

ABBITT, RALEIGH D., 1855-1927, married Rosa Tweedy of Campbell.
  Father: George W. Abbitt. Mother: Fannie Webb.
  Children: Sue, 1880-1945, married George H. Covington of Prince
    Edward.
    George R., married Geneva Torrence.
    Robert, 1890, married Miss Showalter of Prince Edward
    Bettie, married Willie O'Brien.
    Lillie, married_____Casey of Amherst County.
    Walter, 1892.
    Laura, married Holcomb P. Ray, 1899.
    A. Burr, 1898, married Frances Jenkins, 1910.

ABBITT, WATKINS MOORMAN, 1908, Married Corinne Hancock 1909
  Father: George F. Abbitt, Sr.   Mother: Otway Moorman
  Children: Anne Corinne, 1939
    Watkins, M., Jr., 1944

ABBITT, DR. WILLIAM BENJAMIN, 1826-1857

ABBITT, WILLIAM CHATHAM, 1848-1916 Married Martha West Jones
  Father: Benjamin Abbitt II Mother: Mary Patterson D. 1908.
  Children: Wm. J. 1875-1936, Married: Olive Gilliam of Campbell
    County
    Rev. Benjamin, 1876-1940, Married:
    Gertrude Gree of Philadelphia
    Harry W. 1881, Married Margaret Dixon of N. C.
    J. Curry, 1879, Married Mary Frances Moss, 1871
    George Dallas, 1890, Married Bertha Hanson of N. J.
    Lola, 1884, Married Jesse J. Harvey,
    Mary, 1885, Married Henry T. Terry
    Stella Watkins, 1886, married J. B. Wilson.

ABBITT, DR. WILLIAM HENRY, 1832-1907, Married Sarah Frances Plunkett
  Father: George Abbitt, Sr. Mother: Jane Eleanor Webb
  Children: Aurelius William, 1855-1912, Married Nancy Jane
    Tibbs, 1857-1900
    Charles Arthur Plunkett, married Chassie Martin

103

ABBITT, DR. WILLIAM HENRY, (continued)
Rev. George Chapman, married Emma August of Richmond
Jane Eleanor, married George Abbitt Coleman
John David, married Mattie Beale of Southampton
Second wife, Elizabeth Dyer of Southampton, Third
wife, Annie Pretlow
Emmett Robertson, married Margaret Quisenburg
Julian Hamner, married Sallie Ballou
James Benjamin, married Vara Washington Burke
Cynthia Ann Maria, married Thomas B. Pretlow

ABBITT, WYATT, 1818-1865, married Sallie Spottswood Jenkins 1826-1892
Father: William Abbitt
Children: Charles A. 1849-1930, married Elvira James LeGrand,
1847-1921

ABBOTT, B. C., 1854-1902, married Ella Porter, 1856-1925.
Children: Phinizy.
Norman, married Jinnie Hildrup.
Sallie.
B. C., Jr.
Frank, married Willie Cardwell of Campbell.
Nellie, married W. A. Owen.

ADAMS, ISAAC 1800-1857 Married Susan DuVal 1810-1869
Children: Wm. Duval, 1835-1906 Married Betty Mullan
Isaac Holcomb, 1837-1911 Married Mary Ann Patteson
Richard H. T., 1839-1900 Married Sue Scott
Susan, 1833
Sarah, 1849-1920, Married John W. Carroll

AGEE, CLARENCE 1895, Married Margie Cheatham 1900
Father: W.A. Agee Mother: Ella Taylor
Children: Clarence A., Jr., 1921
Kathleen, 1926
Edward E., 1935

AGEE, JAMES Married Lucy Thornhill
Children: Jemina,
Jesse, 1819- Married in Ohio
Sam, 1826-1890
Emily, Married Montgomery Featherston
Sarah, 1821-1896 Married James Alfred Agee
Martha, 1824-1897 Married Rev. Sam Mullan
Katherine, Married Zelotese Adams
Mary,
Frances, 1830-1847
Paulina, -1847
Elizabeth, Married Mr. Walton
Cornelia, -1848

AGEE, JAMES ALFRED, 1819-1896, married Sarah Bransford Agee,
1821-1896.
Father: William Agee, Mother: Susan Walton.
          No Children.

AGEE, WILLIAM   married Susan Walton
    Children: William,   -1876
                 Joseph,
                 James Alfred, 1819-1896, married Sarah Bransford Agee,
                 1821-1896
                 Ann, married Peter Johnson of Buckingham.
                 Mary, married Dr. James R. Pankey, Moved to Ohio.
                 Elizabeth Murray, married Edwin Steger of Buckingham.
                 Henrietta, married Andrew Stratton Wheeler.

AGEE, W. A.   1857-1943 Married Ella Taylor 1853-1936
    Children: Elmo W., Married Lennie Farmer of Buckingham
                 Charles C.
                 Lee, Married Odelle Inge, 2nd Wife of New York
                 Ossie, Married T. M. Rosen of Buckingham
                 John, Married Hallie Tolley of Charlottesville
                 Clarence A., 1895, Married Margie Cheatham 1900
                 Margaret, Married James Alvis
                 Dewey, Married Lillie_____of Front Royal
                 Gladys, Married Douglas Doss

ALMOND, JOHN THOMAS, 1891 .Married Cassie Hudrick 1904
    Children: John Thomas, Jr., 1925
                 Samuel, 1934

ALMOND, WILSON, 1912, Married Evelyn Stewart, 1917

ALVIS, ELWOOD, Married Mildred Eva O'Brien
    Father: J. P. Alvis Mother: Lucy Woodson
    Children: Jacqulyn Walker, 1926
                 Patricia Ann, 1936

ALVIS, GEORGE ANDREW, 1858-1917, Married Addie V. Moore, 1867-1941
    Children: George M. 1891
                 J. E., 1888
                 Marvin M., 1902
                 R. L., 1905
                 Robert Owen

ALVIS, J. DAVID, 1854-1930, Married Ella Worley, 1868-1926
    Children: Harry, 1890, Married Miss Moore of Lynchburg,
                 Ola, 1892, Married S. Spencer
                 Joshua, 1894, Married Miss Cundiff of Lynchburg
                 James, 1896, Married Margaret Agee
                 Elsie, 1898, Married Jack S. Caldwell
                 Ruth, 1900-1910
                 Eloise, 1903, Married Irby Wheeler
                 Virginia, 1908, Married John Gunter

ALVIS, JOHN P. 1865 Married Lucy Woodson, 1875
    Children: Elwood, 1899, Married Mildred O'Brien 1899
              Annie, 1901
              Kenneth, 1903 Married Sarah Timberlake of Powhatan
              J. P., Jr., 1911, Married Katherine Matthews of Orange
              1917
              Ethel, 1913, Married T. DeWitt Evans of Campbell

ALVIS, ROBERT O., 1852-1931, Married Betty Snapp, 1853-1931

ANDERSON, BERNARD GUTHREY, 1882, Married Anna Gay Guthrie
              1885-1921 of Texas
              Second wife, George Ella Smith of Tennessee
    Children: Mandane Ellis
              Willie Guthrey, Married C. Lewis McDearmon

ANDERSON, EDDIE, 1851-1903, Married Cornelia A. Lewis 1852-1935
    Father: Lawrence Anderson Mother: Miss Gilliam
    Children: Edgar, 1876-1935
              Richard A.
              Anna Eliza, Married J. R. Crabtree of Tazewell County
              Dabney William, 1892-1935, married Kate Moorman Carter.

ANDERSON, LAWRENCE, 1801-1870 Married Miss Forbes
                         Second wife, Miss Gilliam
    Children: Alexander F., 1841- Married, Mattie Langhorn 1856-1946
              Dabney M., 1844-1917 Married Mary Susan Thornhill
                                  1845-1922
              Eddie, 1850-1903, Married Cornelia Lewis, 1852-1935

ANDERSON, SAMUEL E., 1869-1943, married Bettie Walker Routen, 1877.
    Father: Sterling Anderson, Mother: Susan Madison.
    Children: George Russell, 1900-1915.
              Nellie Madison, 1906, married Robert Dunkley Gunter, 1906.
                                Second husband, Mr. Krouse.
              Mary Elizabeth, 1916, married John D. Ripley of Lynchburg.
              Jean Aignan, 1918, married John R. Smith of Abingdon.

ANDERSON, SAMUEL G., 1873, married Evie Mae Baker, 1880.

ANDERSON, STERLING, Married Susie Madison of Charlotte County.
    Children: Samuel E., 1869-1943, Married Bettie Walker Routen, 1877.
              Ella, -1889, married William Scruggs.
              Lillie, -1933, married William Scruggs.

ATKINSON, ROBERT, 1836-1903, Married Lucy Fannie Thornhill, 1841-1874
    Children: Wm. Marshall, 1861, Married Berta Bondurant of Prince
              Edward
              Samuel Edgar, 1864, Married Bell Waddell, Isle of Wight
              Jeanette, 1867-1933, Married George Gallup of Kentucky
              Mary Ann, 1871-1944, Married George Brandt of Amherst

ATWOOD, J. R., 1846-1912, Married Florence Chenault 1863-1939
    Children: Edith, 1889- Married R. J. Palmer of West Point
                  Second husband, Dr. L. L. Gayle
                  Virginia, 1891, Married Tom Jones of Alabama
                  Second husband, William Thompson of Tennessee
                  Jacqueline, 1893, Married M. L. Newbill
                  Lynolee, 1894,
                  John, 1896-1898
                  Eloise, 1903 Married Giles Ingledove of Lynchburg
                  Lamar, 1898-1918

AUSTIN, FLOYD, Married Katie Elizabeth Ferguson 1913

AUSTIN, GALLIER of Buckingham
    Children: Tommy, 1937
                  David, 1938

AUSTIN, HENRY, 1896 Married Sadie Austin, 1900
    Children: Charles, 1934

AYERS, WIRT H. 1887, Married Reva E. Rogers, 1893-
    Children: Wm. I., 1917 Married Alma L. Reed
                  Lula May, 1921, Married James M. Burge.

AYERS, WM. I., 1917, Married Alma L. Reed
    Father: Wirt H. Ayers Mother: Reva E. Rogers
    Children: Dorothy Ann, 1943
                  W. A. S., 1944
                  P. J., 1946

BABCOCK, ADELBERT ARTHUR, 1901, Married Annie Laurie Scruggs, 1903
    Father: Homer C. Babcock, Mother: Blanche Moore
    Children: June, 1927
                  William Byron, 1932
                  Rebecca Lou, 1936
                  Bradley Litton, 1939

BABCOCK, FRANK, 1874-1946 Married Annie Collins 1872-
    Father: Bradley Babcock Mother: Miss Cardwell
    Children: Mary Orpha Whitney, 1903, Married Norman Wooldridge
                  May Belle

BABCOCK, HAVILAH, 1899, Married Alice Cheatham
    Father: Homer C. Babcock, Mother: Blanche Moore
    Children: Havilah, Jr., Married Cora Lee Gilliam

BABCOCK, HOMER CURTIS, 1860-1934, Married: Rosa Blanche Moore,
                                         1864-1940
    Father: Bradley Babcock Mother: Miss Cardwell
    Children: Robert W. Babcock, 1885, Married Miss Helen Fay, 1888
                  Mary Hester, 1890, Married, F. L. Murphy
                  Thomas H., Married Lottie Martin

BABCOCK, HOMER CURTIS (continued)
          Havilah, 1899, Married Alice Cheatham
          Rebuh, 1895
          Adelbert Arthur, 1901, Married Annie Laurie Scruggs, 1903
          Carolyn, 1904, Married J. L. Cates
                    Second husband, J. B. Seiginous
          Eddie, 1908-1929
          Bradley W., 1893-1938

BABCOCK, HOWARD WEBSTER, 1917, Married Virginia Moses
     Father: Robert W. Babcock, Mother: Helen Fay
     Children: Webster, Jr.

BABCOCK, ROBERT W., 1885 Married Helen Fay, 1888
     Father: Homer Curtis Babcock Mother: Rosa Blanche Moore 1864-1940
     Children: Homer Curtis, 1910 Married Rachel Dickerson 1940
               Robert Marshall, 1914, Married Mildred Murray of Nelson
               Howard Webster, 1917, Married Virginia Moses
               Margaret Virginia, 1924, Married Howard Saunders
               Fay, married S. Alfred Lawson.

BABCOCK, THOMAS H., Married Lottie Martin of Farmville
     Father: Homer C. Babcock, Mother: Blanche Moore
     Children: Thomas Jr.
               Rosa Etta
               Frances
               Wallace
               Charles
               Walter
               Dwight

BAGBY, CHARLES JAMES, 1895.

BABGY, JOSIAH, 1796-1863 Married Elizabeth_____, 1803-1882
     Children: Wm. G., 1822-1845
               Luke A., 1823-1907
               James, 1826-1872
               Arthur C., 1828-
               Nancy I., 1830-1860 Married Mr. Perrow
               Charles, 1832-1913 Married Betty Lewis, 2nd wife
                                           Emma Coleman
               John H., 1835
               Eliza E., 1837-1882, Married Bead Bryant
               Judiath A. P., 1840-1892, Married Mr. Coleman
               Martha, 1844-1886
               Mary, 1844
               Lucy, 1847

BAKER, ANDREW BERKLEY, 1814-1879 Married Louisa C. Webb,
1822-1904
Children: Mary Elizabeth Trent, 1839-1891 Married John Lawson
Jeanette Frances, 1841
Louivenia Eleanor Watkins, 1843-
Martha Price, 1846
Harriet Eliza Zella Branch, 1848
Samuel Wm., 1853
Lignora, 1855
Alice Maritah, 1857-1940 Married James Moon
Nannie Mosely, 1860
John Robert, 1861
Benjamin Berkley, 1865-1935 Married Miss Foster
Lula Bell, 1868-1946, Married Elantha Drinkard
Louisea Andrew, 1851, married James Lawson

BALDWIN, ALBERT, Born 1850, Married Miss Dickerson

BALDWIN, AUGUST AURELIUS, 1865-1947, Married Edna Young of Prince
Edward
Children: Cassie, 1903.

BALDWIN, JAMES C., 1869, Married Ella Price, 1874-1904
Children: Lacy
Tavil, Married Annie Goin
Edelle, Married Earl Hix
Second wife: Mary Baldwin
Children: Edward
Stanley

BALDWIN, M. J., 1880, Married Wortley J. Lowe, 1884
Children: Chester E., 1907
Marcus R., 1908
Laurence, 1910
Mildred Eloise, 1911
Lucile Mattie, 1914
Frederick J., 1916
Cecil L., 1917
Raymond Leroy, 1919
Myrtle Gladys, 1920
Norwood Kyle, 1922
Stuard Leslie, 1924
Estelle Iris, 1927

BALDWIN, R. D., 1853-1928, Married Mary Davis, 1866-1931
Children: Robert Lewis, 1892
Richard Stanley, 1899-1943, Married Pearl Dunton
Ethel May, 1886, Married J. H. Young of Prince Edward
Marie E., 1903, Married Don Carloc Callejas

BALDWIN, TWYMAN, Married Helen Ware Jenkins

BALDWIN, W. R., 1876, Married Ossie Conner 1876-1917
    Children: Myrtle, 1901, Married P. K. Woodall of Charlotte
                 Lillian, 1903, Married R. B. Ferguson
                 William Alfred, 1906, Married Miss Myter of New Jersey
                 Twyman, 1914, Married Helen Jenkins
                 Harry Deleware, 1917
                                Second wife, Bessie Coleman 1887
    Children: George Ray, 1925

BANTON, CHARLES RICHARD, 1875, Married Lena Ann Smoot, of Amherst
    Father: Sam Banton Mother: Sara Eliz. Thornhill
    Children: Garland Watkins, 1918 Married a Kentuckian
                 Elmo, 1920
                 Carrie Ruth, 1920

BANTON, SAMUEL, 1826-1897 Married Sara Eliz. Thornhill, 1831-1916
    Children: Charles Richard, 1875, Married Lena Ann Smoot of Amherst,
                                                      1891-
                 Wm. LaFayette, 1870-1937

BARLOW, KENNETH, 1893, Married Mattie Pearl Gunter, 1900-
    Father: W.H.S. Barlow Mother: Florence Hamilton
    Children: Warren, 1922
                 Aldah, 1924
                 Alfred, 1929
                 Ninah, 1933

BARLOW, W. H. S., 1868-1945, Married Florence Hamilton 1872
    Children: Kenneth V., 1893, Married Mattie Gunter, 1900
                 Lila, 1895, Married Louis Herncall of Nebraska
                 Alleen, 1898, Married Ira Lucado
                 Louise, 1900-1933, Married H. B. Watts
                 W. C., 1902-1931
                 Helen, 1904, Married Roy Gunter
                 Ralph, 1907
                 Doris, 1909, Married C. A. Brockwell of Clifton Forge
                 Christine, 1911, Married P. F. Staton
                 Neola, 1914, Married Grover Smith

BARNARD, CHARLIE, Married Sarah E. Coleman
    Children: Goldy, Married Joel Inge
                 Annie, Married Joe Tweedy
                 Molly, Married Robert Tweedy
                 Benjamin, Married Betty Sears

BASS, JOHN S., Died 1872, Married Mary Alice Jones, 1831-1866
    Children: Anna Eliza Bass, 1855-1886, Married Mr. Burton.
                 Herbert J., 1857-1911, Married Maude Dillard of Amherst

BASS, WILLIAM C., 1890, Married Emma Doss 1886
   Children: George William, 1915, Married Lucile Jones, 1915
               Mary E. 1918
               Frances G., 1921, Married Bernard Wooten
               Alice Davis, 1923, Married Burton Day
               Richard Lee, 1926, Married Dorothy Williamson 1926
               Lillian C., 1929

BATES, RUFUS H., 1956, Married Edmonia Jones, 1866
   Children: Norman, 1886, Married Emma Childress
                        Second wife, Miss Wiseman of Sebrell
               Macca Virginia, 1888, Married F. O. Jones
               Robert H., 1891-1942
               Eva, 1893, Married Frank Turner of Amherst
                        Second husband, J. McCarthy of Massachusetts
               Arthur, 1895
               Nellie, 1898, Married Clem Morton of Charlotte
               W. Rufus, 1899
               Edward Lemach, 1901, Married Mildred Adams of Brookneal
               Lena, 1902, Married Chap Adams of Charlotte County
               Susie, 1907, Married Ernest Sours of Lynchburg
               Mary Lucile, 1910

BATES, WILLIAM B., 1910 Married Lucy Jane Chick

BEALE, ALBERT THORNHILL 1884 Married Berta May of Buckingham,
                                                 1880-1922
   Children: A.T. Jr., 1908 Married Lula Herring of Richmond
               Thomas Scott, 1910, Married Mamie Beale of Buckingham
               Annie Mae, 1912, Married Robert Clark of Gladys
               David J., 1914, Married Elva Thompson of Baltimore
               Rosa Mae, 1919, Married Al Williams of Baltimore

BEALE, WILLIE BRANCH, 1873, Married Mollie Megginson, 1882-1903
   Children: Clarence
                        Second wife: Lula Walker Megginson, 1883
   Children: Walker
               Bennie, 1908, Married Nellie Mae Hamilton, 1913
               James

BEARD, HENRY MYERS, 1908, Married Mabel Virginia Chick, 1913
   Father: J. H. Beard   Mother: Lottie Thomas, 1887, of Amherst
   Children: Lawrence

BEARD, J. H., 1877, Married Lottie Thomas, 1887, of Amherst

BEASLEY, SYLVESTER, 1867, Married Eliza Webb, 1871
   Children: Mamie, 1896, Married James A. Webb
                        Second husband, Ammon Hancock
               John W., 1898
               Houston, 1900, Married Ruth Dunkum of Buckingham
               Sallie Bet, 1902-1904

BEASLEY, SYLVESTER, (continued)
>Kemper, 1906, Married Ellen Lowe of Buckingham
>Carl, 1908
>Julian, 1910, Married Mrs. Motley
>Frank, 1912
>Earl, 1914
>Ruby Mae, 1916, Married Tommy Motley
>Nannie, 1918

BELL, A. A.   -1933, Married Lelia Wright
>Children: Alpha, 1888, Married Lindwood Crawley of Prince Edward
>Clydia, 1890
>Raymond, 1892, Married Miss Allen of Roanoke
>Ronald, 1894
>S. A. 1896
>W. C., 1898
>Elizabeth, 1900, Married Flethcer Burge, 1908
>Mary, 1902, Married Hazel Campbell, 1912

BELL, BOLLING, Married Lucy Crews

BELL, SAMUEL ANDERSON, 1823-1891, Married Virginia V. North, 1834-1900
>Children: Willie Bolling, 1866-1947
>Walter, 1857-1872
>Albin Augustus, 1859-1933, Married Lelia Wright
>>Second wife, Lula Keen
>James Anderson, 1863-1921 Married Madora Ann Wright
>>1862-1941
>Nannie Lucy, 1870, Married George Zeigler of Cumberland
>Eddie Wyatt, 1873-1941 Married Martha Virginia Crews,
>>1872
>Frank Lesley, 1877, Married Willie Woody
>Mollie, Married Creed Hammersley

BERGMAN, WALTER, 1904, Married Virginia Perdieu, 1904
>Children: Louise, 1926
>Audrey, 1928

BINGHAM, HENRY, Died 1898, Married Florence E. Morris
>Father: John Bingham, Sr.
>Children: Edward Irvin, 1895
>Mary S., 1898, Married Delbert Gordon

BINGHAM, JOHN ALEXANDER, 1890, Married Myrna Sue Childers, 1898-1943.
>Father: John R. Bingham   Mother: Florence Lucado
>Children: Floyd Edward, 1920
>Ruth, 1918, Married Byron B. Cole
>Virginia Florence, 1928
>Marjorie Sue, 1922, Married Cecil Bailey of Prince Edward
>John A., Jr., 1925-1944
>>Second wife, Mrs. Elizabeth Smith Ford

BINGHAM, JOHN ROBERT, 1866-1933, Married Florence Lucado, 1871
    Children: John Alexander, 1890, Married Myrna Sue Childers, 1898-
                  1943
                  Second wife, Elizabeth S. Ford
             Lizzie Bell, 1891-1941
             Nannie Sue, 1892, Married Elmore Wilkerson
             Mary Catherine, 1895-1930, Married John Adamee of
                    Lynchburg
             Robert Elisha, 1898, Married, Mrs. Winnie G. Carter
             Gladys Virginia, 1900, Married Harry T. Woodson 1895-
                  1928
                  Second husband Henry P.
                    Woodson
             Curtis Taylor, 1902, Married Dorothy Burks
             Bernice E., 1904, Married Robert B. Gilbert
             William Albert, 1907-1929
             Sam Wesley, 1909, Married Zetta Perguson of Danville
             Myrtle Madeline, 1911, Married William A. Higgins

BLACKWELL, JAMES LEONARD, 1897 Married Ella Lucinda Fleshman, 1897
    Children: James Leonard Jr., 1923, Married Annie Louise Garrette
                  1927

BLACKWELL, JAMES W.,   -1939 Married Illa Martin   -1932
    Father: George Blackwell   Mother:
    Children: Jesse, 1903-1905
             W. C., 1902, Married Miss Pope of Lynchburg
             Rachel, Married Nichols of Lynchburg
             Jeter, Married Vassar of Lynchburg
             Kitty, Married Hoffman of Lynchburg
             _____, married Casey. of Lynchburg.

BLACKWELL, CURTIS, 1898, Married Virginia Blackwell, 1898
    Father: E. Gilbert Blackwell   Mother: Jennie Wooldridge
    Children: Viola, 1925
             June, 1927, Married James Ray
             Barbary, 1929, Married Lewis Thomas of Nelson
             Fleetwood, 1933

BLACKWELL, E. GILBERT, 1868-1935, Married Jennie Wooldridge, 1878-1946
    Children: Frank, 1896, Married Miss Homer of Pennsylvania
             Curtis, 1898, Married Virginia Blackwell, 1898
             Odell, 1903
             Edward, 1907, Married Edna Chenault
             Lucile, 1915, Married Holland Wright of Nelson

BLACK, W. M., 1872, Married Mattie Eugenia Bowles, 1885, of Fluvanna
Children: Mary Rives, 1917

BLANKS, HARRY L. Married India Colemen, 1880
Children: Henry Edward, 1904
Grace Mae, 1906 Richard Edward Smith
Harry L., Jr., 1908

BLEDSOE, MRS. LOTTIE, 1872

BOCOCK, BENJAMIN WALKER, married Mahala Clark Miller.
Father: Henry Flood Bocock, Mother: Susan Winifred Walker.
Children: Miller.
Harry.
Sarah.
Hulda.
Charles.
Susan.
Madge.
Betty.

BOCOCK, HENRY FLOOD, 1817-1894, married Susan Winifred Walker.
Father: John T. Bocock, Mother: Mary Flood.
Children: Benjamin Walker, married Mahala Clark Miller.
Betty Heath.
James.
Ellen.

BOCOCK, JOHN T., 1773-1845. married Mary Flood, 1788-1850
Children: Amanda Elvira, 1805- married William Megginson.
Willis Perry, 1807-1886, married in Alabama.
Martha Ann, 1809-1842, married Wilson Hix.
Mary Matson, 1811- married John Rice Buchanan.
John Holmes, 1813- married Sarah Margaret Kemper.
Thomas Salem, 1815-1891, married Sarah Patrick Flood,
-1850. 2nd. wife, Annie Holmes Faulkner
Henry Flood, 1817-1894, married Susan Winifred Walker.
William Stevens, 1819-1842, married
Charles Thomas, 1822-1851, married Sarah Ann Spiller.
Nicholas Flood, 1824-1872, married Frances Walker Flood,
-1861. 2nd. Wife Octavia Rosa Gantt.
Mary Fuquer (?), 1827-1852, married _____ Linthicum.
Milton, 1829-1846.

BOCOCK, THOMAS SALEM, 1815-1891, Married Sarah Patrick Flood
Father: John T. Bocock Mother: Mary Flood
Children: Bell, 1849
Second wife, Annie Holmes Faulkner
Children: Mazie, married James Booker of Lynchburg
Second husband, Mr. Hubbal of Baltimore
Thomas Stanley
Willis P., 1861-1947, Married Mattie Baughn of Hanover
Ella, Married Rev. Charles D. Price
Second husband, Rev. Thomas Cary Johnson
Sallié P., Married Charles W. Reynolds
Second husband, W. A. Roberts

BOCOCK, WILLIS P., 1861-1947, married Mattie Baughan of Hanover, 1851-1934.
Father: Thomas Salem Bocock, Mother: Annie Holmes Faulkner.
No children.

BOOKER, HENRY T., Married Theodore Vaughan of Lunenburg
Children: Jessie M., Married N. A. Davis.

BOOKER, JOHN R., 1870, Married, Bertha Coleman, 1879
Children: Susie, 1899, Married Duiguid Christian
Russell Flood, 1900, Married Jean Soderquist of Michigan
Ida, 1902-1918
Olivia, 1906, Married Mr. Ewing of Nelson
George, 1909, Married Martha Harding of Washington
Robert C., 1912, Married Miss Howard of Missouri
Malcolm, 1915, Married Miss Coleman, 1921.
John R., Jr., 1917, Married Miss Roebald of Boston
William A., 1919
Bernice, 1922
Alice, 1927

BONDURANT, J. DAVID, 1853-1938, Married Willie Carter, 1859, died 1931
Father: Joseph S. T. Bondurant, Mother: Louesa S. Seay
Children: Ethel, 1883, Married A. Weakley
Rose, 1884, Married W. H. Robertson
T. J., Married Addie Wooldridge
Ida, 1889, Married Marvin Stratton
Wallace, Married Ruth Wright
Second wife, Rebecca Younger

BONDURANT, JOSEPH S. T., 1830-1924, Married Louesa S. Seay 1835-1903
Children: J. David, 1853-1938, Married Willie Carter of Nelson
Ann Virginia, 1856-1927, Married A. P. Carson
Charles S., 1858-1944, Married Lena Luellen of Missouri
Joseph T., 1864-1924, Married Jennie Stone
Sarah E., 1868-1942, Married Breckenridge Carson
Florence B., 1870-1946, Married Volney Carson
Anna, 1874, Married Tilden Lee
Cora Lee, 1876, Married B. L. Wheeler.

BONDURANT, WALLACE EDWARD, 1897, Married Ruth Wright 1907-1925
Second wife, Rebecca Younger, 1906
Father: J. David Bondurant   Mother: Willie Carter
Children: W. E. Jr., 1925
Virginia Lee, 1934
William, 1935
Carter Thomas, 1937
Richard Hunter, 1938
Madalene, 1940
Eloise, 1941

BRIGHTWELL, W. R., 1881, Married Lizzie Baldwin
    Children: J. W., 1908, Married Miss Boyd of Christiansburg
              Mary, 1910, Married W. D. Ligon
                            Second wife: **Sadie C. Wootton of Burkeville**

BROWN, WILLIAM LAWRENCE, 1868-1943, Married **Mamie H. Evans**, 1978
    Children: Evelyn, 1903, Married James W. Carter
              M. Avis, 1906, Married E. Carroll Smith

BROWNING, ROBERT H., 1852-1926, Married Emiline Lewis, 1848-1926
    Father: William A. Browning   Mother: Elvira Howard
    Children: Grace M., 1873, Married Norman Dawson
              Frank L., 1876-1935, Married Annie Showalter
              Martha E., 1879, Married Nunnally Traylor of Farmville
              William Daniel, 1880, Married Bertha Caldwell, 1881
              Mary Elizabeth, 1883, Married F. L. Martin of Danville
              Robert Aubrey, 1885, Married Evelyn Leg, 1887

BROWNING, WILLIAM A., 1866, Married Elvira Howard of Campbell
    Children: A. McD. 1830-1918, Married Margaret Williamson
              John, 1832-1863
              S., 1837, Married John Laundrum
              Patritia, 1839-1905 married_____Jackson.
              Sue, 1843, Married Samuel Harvey
              Charles P., 1845, Married Miss Allen
                           Second wife --
                           Third wife, Miss Sweeney
              James T., 1847-1932, Married Lula Skidmore of Buchanan
              Mollie, 1850-1924, Married William S. Hamilton
              Robert H., 1852-1926, Married Emiline Lewis, 1848-1926
              William Andrew, 1841-1906, Married_____

BRYANT, JOHN MILES, 1861-1932, Married Mary Sue Jamerson
    Children: Dora
              Allen
              Grace
              Herman, 1916

BRYANT, TIBERIOUS B., 1842-1892, Married Martha W. Bagby, 1844-1888
    Children: Charles L., 1866
              Ruben P., 1870, Married Fannie C. Banton
              R. A., 1872
              Mary L., 1874-1899
              Walker T., 1876-1880
              Thomas B., 1891-1919
              Walter S., 1882, married Verona H. Torrence. 1920
                           2nd. Wife of Tiberious B. Bryant, Martha
                         J. Banton.

BUCHANAN, GEORGE BASKERVILLE, 1891, Married Rosa J. Reynolds 1898
Children: Arlene Virginia, 1919, Married Joseph Tindall of New
                                                                     Jersey
             Ilah Victoria, 1923
             Roslyn D., 1924
             George Baskerville, Jr., 1935

BURCHER, WM. LEWIS, 1911, Married Mary Jane Martin, 1912
Children: Billie Jane, 1933

BURGE, HARRISON M., 1892, Married Willie Stanley, 1892
Father: John William Burge   Mother: Allie Berta Crews
Children: H. M., Jr. 1924-1939
             Catherine

BURGE, HARTWELL, 1901, Married Elizabeth Moore, 1905

BURGE, JAMES E., 1829-1863, Married Frances S. Phelps, 1828-1880
Children: W. F., 1849, 1925 Married Emily F. Coleman, 1854-1928
             James Washington, 1854
             Mary Sue, 1851 Married John D. Gregory
             Frank E., 1856 Married Sue Turner
             Nannie Rebecca, 1858 Married Burge Moore
             Edmonia, 1862, Married Charles Henry Coleman (2nd wife)

BURGE, JAMES M. Married Lula Mae Ayers, 1921-
Children: Shirley, 1942
             Nancy, 1944

BURGE, JOHN WILLIAM, 1852-1916, Married Allie Berta Crews 1858-1940
Children: William Edward, 1877, Married Emma Longfellow of
                                                       Massachusetts
             Hester Elizabeth, 1879, Married W. H. Whitehead
             Mary Ethel, 1882, Married William Mason of Lynchburg
             Thomas Henry, 1884, Married Mary Moore
             Iola, 1886-1888
             Harrison M., 1892, Married Willie Stanley 1892
             Vermont, 1894, Married James Hill of Lynchburg
             Earl, 1897, Married Herman Harding
             Hartwell, 1901, Married Elizabeth Moore
             Ruth Overton, 1889, Married James I. Moore.

BURGE, THOMAS, 1786-1833, Married Rebecca Staples 1797-1871
Children: William Staples, 1819-1846
             Martha Rebecca, 1820-1842
             Thomas Hall, 1822
             Susan Elizabeth, 1824
             Fletcher Benson, 1826-1839
             James Edward, 1829-1863
             Hester Ann, 1832-1904

117

BURGE, W. FLETCHER, 1849-1925, Married Emily F. Coleman, 1854-1928
    Father: James E. Burge   Mother: Frances S. Phelps
    Children: Mary Ocie, 1874, Married Edward W. Moore
               Frances C., 1876, Married C. A. Moore
               Edna W., 1879-1926 Married G. D. Harris
               James W., 1881-1937 Married Berta Harris 1933

BURGE, WILLIAM FLETCHER, 1906, Married Elizabeth Bell 1901
    Children: William Fletcher, Jr., 1927
               Lelia Frances, 1928
               Roberta Lee, 1933
               Richard Alvin, 1936
               Dorothy Ann, 1938
               Lottie Louise, 1941

BURKE, JERRY ALLEN, 1892, Married Ethel Frances Abbitt
    Father: Richard Floyd Burke, Mother: Alice Sears
    Children: Jane Hallowell, 1918, Married J. P. House of Florida
               Jerry Allen, Jr., 1915, Married Helen Bailey of
                                           Massachusetts
               Richard Floyd III, 1920

BURKE, RICHARD FLOYD, 1851-1924, Married Alice Sears, 1852-1928
    Children: Sallie, 1875- Married Walter McGill of Colorado
               William Hallowell, 1876, Married Ella Brown of Roanoke
               Richard Leigh, 1878, Married Roberta Wood of Campbell
               Vara, ·1882, Married Dr. James B. Abbitt 1872-1932
               Alice Floyd, 1884, Married William Taylor Steele 1877-1938
               Martha Elizabeth, 1886-1914, Married B. F. Oden
               Eula May
               Jerry Allen, 1892, Married Ethel Frances Abbitt

BURKE, RICHARD LEIGH, 1878, Married Berta Wood of Campbell County
    Father: Richard Floyd Burke, Mother: Alice Sears
    Children: William Wood, 1905, Married Mary Emily Harvey, 1906
               Richard Leigh, Jr., 1919, Married Elizabeth Megginson

BURKE, RICHARD LEIGH, JR., 1919, Married Elizabeth Megginson
    Father: Richard Leigh Burke, Sr. Mother: Berta Wood
    Children: James Robert

BURKE, WILLIAM WOOD, 1905, Married Mary Emily Harvey, 1906
    Father: Richard Leigh Burke, Sr., Mother: Berta Wood
    Children: Frank Leigh, 1941
               Emily Wood, 1942
               William Allen, 1945
               Margaret Susan, 1947

BURKEY, JUSTIN LAMONT, 1898-1938 Married Mildred Jackson Trent, 1904
    Father: R. W. Burkey Mother:
    Children: Justin Lippincott, 1928
               Mildred Kathryn, 1933
               Robert Lamont, 1935

BURKEY, R. W., married Miss_____of Tenn.
Children: Justin, married Mildred Trent.
             Roscoe.
             Nola.

BURKS, JACK   Married Lucy Riley

BURKS, F. J.,   1917, Married Marye Childress   1913
Children: Joyce, 1936
             Agnes, 1942

BURNETT, JAMES R., ·1860-1946 Married Sarah F. Gills, -1926
Children: Lena Maude, Married T. W. Broadwater.
             O. S. Married Willie Willman
             Elizabeth Cornelia, Married T. C. Stratton
             Sarah Catherine, Married C. S. Spicard
             John E., Married Minnie Maude Carson
             Jimmy Gills, Married C. A. Wiley
             J. Rufus, Married Lucille Lee
             Victor R., Married Evie Drinkard
             William Royal, Married Annie Mae Perry
             Lizzie T., Married Paul Hash
             Alpha Perkins, Married W. L. Thompson

BURNETT, JOHN E., · 1896, Married Minnie Carson, 1898
Father: J. Rush Burnett   Mother: Sarah F. Gills
Children: Maude, 1918, Married, H. F. Braford

BURNETT, J. RUFUS, 1897, Married Lucille Lee, 1901
Father: J. Rush Burnett, Mother: Sarah F. Gills Died 1926
Children: Joseph R., 1921, Married Ruth Pitmore of Lynchburg
             Aubrey L., 1923
             Nadine, 1925
             Thomas R., 1928
             Louise, 1935

BURNETT, REV. OMAR B., Married Eloise O'Brien

CALDWELL, DAVID E., 1879-1914, Married Carrie Harvey, 1881
Father: T. A. Caldwell, Mother: Sallie A. Furbush
Children: Harvey, 1903
             David, 1905, Married Cathline Whittington
             Sarah Saunders, 1907-1908
             Lillian, 1909, Married Walter -Edward Hancock

CALDWELL, DAVID E., JR., Married Cathline Whittington
Father: David E. Caldwell Mother: Carrie Harvey
Children: David Randolph, 1930
             Virginia Carolyn, 1944

119

CALDWELL, HUBERT H., 1899, Married Sarah E. Howerton, 1903
    Father: Mathews C. Caldwell   Mother: Catherine Jones
    Children: Hubert H. Jr., 1925
                 Edward, 1929
                 Edith Ann, 1931
                 Doris A., 1933
                 Fred M., 1939
                 Marvin, 1944

CALDWELL, JACK SEARS, 1890, Married Elsie Alvis, 1898
    Father: William B. Caldwell   Mother: Louvina Clem Crawford
    Children: Jack Sears, Jr., 1920, Married Miss Howard of North Carolina
                 Barbara, 1924

CALDWELL, JACK SEARS, JR., 1920, Married Miss Howard of North Carolina
    Father: Jack Sears Caldwell   Mother: Elsie Alvis
    Children: Katherine Louise, 1947

CALDWELL, JAMES, died 1852, Married Judith Moore 1826-1875

CALDWELL, JAMES WALKER, 1867-1947 married Margaret Smith
    Father: Thomas Caldwell 1812-1894- Mother: Mary Cheatham 1825-1865
    Children: Susie, 1896 married Elliott Marshall
                 Thomas Earl 1898 married Mary Williams
                 Richard Walker 1899 married Evelyn McKenzie
                 Henry Sears, 1901-1940 married Florence Glenn
                 James LeGrande 1902 married Thelma Cawthorn - 2nd wife;
                                                   Margaret Parker.
                 Nannie C. 1904 married F. W. Marshall
                 Margaret S. 1905 married Dewitt Marshall
                 Archer A. 1907
                 Lucy Smith 1910 married H. B. Pack, Jr.
                 Ellis L., 1911-1911

CALDWELL, JOHN CURTIS, 1904, Married Bessie V. Harwood, 1906
    Father: William Benjamin Caldwell Mother: Sarah Taylor
    Children: John Curtis, Jr., 1939
                 William H., 1941

CALDWELL, JOHN RANDOLPH, 1853-1923, Married Adde McFarland Wood,
                                                      1854-1927
    Children: Rachel, 1877-1944, Married Joe O'Brien
                 William Benjamin, 1878, Married Sarah Taylor, 1877
                 Robert E., 1880-1934, Married Fannie Willie Clement
                 Annie Elizabeth, 1881
                 Mattie, 1882, Married Edward H. Hammersley of Charlotte
                 Mary Ursela, 1883, Married W. Pelham Cooke of Norfolk
                 Charles Randolph, 1885, Married Bettie Sue Powell
                 Florence Wood, 1888
                 Emma Lucile, 1894, Married A. J. Bush of Hamton

CALDWELL, LYLE FOSTER, 1896, Married Annie Lillian Carson, 1897
Father: William B. Caldwell   Mother: Louvina Clem Crawford
Children: William Carey, 1920, Married Virginia Donoway of
                                                    Massachusetts
            Robert Elvin, 1922
            Elizabeth Crawford, 1927
            Lina Carson, 1929

CALDWELL, ROBERT EDWIN, 1845-1932, Married Jeanette Blanche Furbush,
                                                    1861-1941
Father: Thomas Caldwell   Mother: Miss Cheatham
Children: Ella Mabel, died 1916
            Janie Belle
            Thomas Jefferson, 1891-1892
            Leonard Harold, 1893-1915
            Florence Estha, Married McCray of Roanoke
            Nannie Elizabeth, Married Schauback
            Grace Married Louis Winters

CALDWELL, T. A., born 1812-1894 married Mary Cheatham 1825-1865
Children: Robert E. 1845-1932 married Blanche Furbush
            Thomas A. 1848-1915 married Sallie Furbush 1847-1908
            Chapman 1850 married Miss Noel of Amherst
            Benjamin 1852
            Mattie Jane 1857- 1945
            William 1854-1914 married Clem Crawford
            Wiley B. 1861 married Alice Cheatham
            Madison C. 1864- 1932 married Susie Jones
2nd Wife: Elizabeth Sears Tweedy (widow of Mr. Tweedy)
Children: James Walker 1867-1942 married Susie Smith 1872-1911

CALDWELL, T. A., 1848-1915, Married Sallie A. Furbush, 1848-1908
Father: Thomas Caldwell   Mother: Cheatham
Children: Lillian C., Married R. C. Jones of South Carolina
            Lacye J., Married R. L. Haycock of Washington, D.C.
            D. E., 1878-1914, Married Carrie Harvey of Campbell
            Bertha U., Married W. D. Browning
            Clara C., Married Harry P. Davis

CALDWELL, WILLIAM B., Died 1922, Married Louvina Clem Crawford 1862
Father: Thomas Caldwell Mother: Cheatham
Children: William Thomas, 1883
            Jack Sears, 1890, Married Elsie Alvis, 1898
            Lyle F., 1896, Married Annie Carson

CALDWELL, WILLIAM BENJAMIN, Married Martha E. Cheatham

CALE, FRANK BROWNLEY, 1895, Married Daisy Burr
Children: Harriett 1925
            George 1922 married

CALHOUN, JAMES DANIEL, died 1883, Married Sarah Elizabeth McDearmon
                                                              died 1894
    Children: Mary Margaret
                 Sidney
                 Sam, Married Miss Carson
                      Second wife: Bessie Rector
                 John
                 James Allen
                 Conelias Corrie, died 1928, Married Rosa A. Ferguson
                                                            1860-1892

CALHOUN, JAMES DANIEL, 1885-1946, Married Venasso Dodd of Lynchburg

CALHOUN, MARY MARGARET, 1888, Married H. G. Basham of Lynchburg

CALHOUN, JUDITH ETHEL, 1890, Married Oscar Cleveland Paulett

CANADA, J. W. D., 1885, Married Maude Elliott, 1887
    Children: Wilsie, 1911, Married I. Randall Irvin
                 Carleton E., 1913, Married Dorothy Bagby
                 Mildred, 1916, Married Morris Calhoun
                 Hazel, 1918, Married John Buslener

CARDWELL, CHARLES W., 1848-1947 Married Sallie Rector, 1850-1912
    Children: Ellen, 1875-1893
                 Clarence, 1877-1946
                 Sue Baylis, 1880
                 Alfred, 1882-1895
                 Ernest, 1883, Married Edna Barksdale of Albemarle
                 Herbert, 1886, Married Florence Barksdale of Albemarle

CARDWELL, WILLIAM L., 1850-1941, Married Berta Martin of Campbell
    Children: Betsy, 1877, Married William Goff of Campbell
                 Alice, 1878, Married Ed Inge of Campbell
                 Elliott, 1880-1902, Married Dora Stahl
                 Andrew, 1882-1920
                 Sarah, 1884, Married Lee Arnbristy of Wythe
                 Lit, 1886-1918
                 Annie, 1890-1945, Married James Johnson
                 Mary, 1893, Married Tom Hagar
                 Mildred, 1896, Married Preston Oliver of Roanoke

CARNEIFX, J. E., 1915, Married Louise Dickerson, 1915
    Father: J. Walker Carnefix   Mother: Eulelia Robertson
    Children: Joel Dickerson, 1943

CARNEFIX, JOHN W., 1868, Married Mary E. Megginson, 1868-1896
    Father: Joel Walker Flood Carnefix Mother: Sarah B. Sharp, 1840-1862
    Children: Joseph Walker, 1888
                 Willie Spencer, 1890-1900
                 Ernest A., 1893-1897
                 Mary Alice, 1896-1896

CARNEFIX, J. WALKER, Married Eulelia Robertson, 1880-1940
    Father: John W. Carnefix   Mother: Mary E. Megginson
    Children: J. E. Carnefix, 1915, Married Louise Dickerson, 1915

CARNEFIX, JOEL WALKER FLOOD, 1830-1908, Married Sarah B. Sharp,
                                        1840-1862 of Tennessee
    Children: John William, 1860-1906, married Mary Lizzie Megginson.
    Joel Walker Flood Carnefix's Second wife: Sarah E. Gordon
                                                1844-1922
    Children: Mary Frances, 1869
                Lucy Walker, 1872, Married Samuel Perkins of Richmond
                George Edward, 1877-1881
                Henry Judson, 1879, Married Eva Wrenn of Richmond
                James Howard, 1882
                Charles Cleveland, 1884
                Thomas Madison, 1887, Married Bettie E. Woodson
                Sallie Ann Gordon, 1890

CARRICO, L. E., 1878,(?)Married Armelia Jones, 1883, of Grayson
    Children: Claude, 1906, Married Elva Almond

CARSON, CHARLES BONDURANT, 1919, Married Mat Marshall
    Father: Ernest Henson Carson   Mother: Emma C. Drinkard
    Children: John Bondurant, 1939

CARSON, CAREY E., 1866-1938, Married Irene E. Chick, 1868-1943
    Father: Joseph Watkins Carson   Mother: Catherine Davidson
    Children: Catherine, Married Thomas L. Christian
                Annie, Married Lyle Caldwell
                Elsie M., Married Robert H. Thornhill
                Mary E., Married D. W. Cawthorn
                Lina D., 1906-1929
                Myrtle
                Eugene W., 1910, Married Ruth Glenn
                Carey E., Jr., 1913, Married Marye Shifflett

CARSON, JR., CAREY E., 1913, Married Marye Shifflett
    Father: Carey E. Carson   Mother: Irene E. Chick
    Children: William D., 1937
                Laura E., 1940
                Carey Ann, 1943

CARSON, CHARLIE LESTER, 1894, Married Agnes Steven Davidson
    Father: Breckenridge Carson   Mother: Sarah Bondurant.
    No Children

CARSON, CLYDE, 1898, Married Ruby Chick, 1902
    Father: William Carson   Mother: Lula B. Taylor
    Children: Louise, 1925
                Ann, 1929

CARSON, EDWIN H., 1858, Married Sallie Owen, 1868
    Children: Owen, 1894, Married Kathleen Drinkard, 1896
                Eula, 1890, Married Melvin Stratton
                John Edwin, 1899, Married Alice Shields, 1904

CARSON, ERNEST HENSON, 1883, Married Emma Catherine Drinkard, 1887
    Children: James Aurelius, 1905, Married Shirley Margerite Bryant
                                          1907
                Crawford Henson, 1908, Married Geraldine Hendricks
                Robert Donald, 1910, Married Hilda Margerite Mays
                Uriel Carter, 1912, Married Gladys Page
                Woodrow Ernest, 1914
                Dolly Virginia, 1916, Married Nelson Hix
                Charles Bondurant, 1919, Married Mat Marshall
                Crote Drinkard, 1921, Married Barbara Hix
                Mildred Catherine, 1923, Married Dr. J. F. Alsop
                William Elantha, 1926
                Jessie Banford, 1930

CARSON, EUGENE W., 1910, Married Ruth Glenn
    Father: Carey E. Carson   Mother: Irene E. Chick
    Children: Dan, 1933
                Gene

CARSON, GEORGE, 1912, Married Katherine Walton, 1919
    Father: Walter O. Carson   Mother: Miss Cheatham
    Children: Frances
                Harriet
                George, Jr.

CARSON, EMMETT, 1870, Married Mattie Wooldridge
    Children: Melvin, 1898, Married Miss Martin of Campbell
                Mary Willie, 1900
                Howard, 1902
                Alcora, 1904
                Esthmus, 1906
                Virginia, 1908, Married Mr. Wood or BuenaVista
                Henry, 1910
                Elridge P., Married Lillie Shearer
                Gesner B. Married Rev. Shearer
                Mary Elizabeth, Married Mr. Roberts
                Ninnie, Married Mr. Lloyd

CARSON, JAMES AURELIUS, 1905, Married Shirley M. Bryant
    Father: Ernest Henson Carson   Mother: Emma C. Drinkard
    Children: Walter Henson, 1932

CARSON, J. OWEN, 1894, Married Kathleen Drinkard, 1895
    Father: E. H. Carson   Mother: Sallie Owen
    Children: Mary Owen, 1922, Married Mr. Roberts of Nelson

CARSON, JOSEPH WATKINS, 1841-1914, Married Catherine Davidson
    Children: Carey E., 1866-1938, Married Irene Chick, 1868-1943
                 Jesse D., 1871-1946
                 Walter O., Married Hattie Cheatham
                 Hubert T.
                 James P., 1884, Married Mary Lou Chick
                 Martha P.

CARSON, MATTHEW, Married Elizabeth Watson
    Children: Matthew J., 1832-1898, Married Katherine Tanner, 1839-1903
                 Lizzie, 1866-1922, Married Alonza Atkinson

CARSON, VOLNEY B., 1872-1936, Married Florence Bondurant, 1870-1946
    No Children

CARSON, WALTER O., 1874, Married Hattie Cheatham
    Father: J.W. Carson   Mother: Kate Davidson
    Children: Eleanor
                 George, Married Katherine Walton
                 Elliott, Married Nannie Harris

CARSON, WILLIAM, 1871-1917, Married Lula B. Taylor, 1876
    Father: Joseph Watkins Carson   Mother: Catherine Davidson
    Children: Clyde, 1898, Married Ruby Chick, 1902
                 Norman Watson, 1902, Married Lillian Martin
                 Wilton Gannaway, Married Virginia Bird Taylor
                 Virginia, 1912, Married Maxwell Davis

CARTER, CARRINGTON L., 1885, Married Laura J. Wright

CARTER, CHARLIE MARYE, 1908, Married Ethel Viola Guill, 1912
    Father: J. W. Carter   Mother: Ella Stanley
    Children: Phyllis Marye, 1929
                 Barbara Jeanette, 1833
                 Charles Dillard, 1934
                 Robert Wayne, 1937
                 Karl Edward, 1941
                 Frederick Carroll, 1945

CARTER, EDDIE, 1894, Married Emma Gray Baber, 1899
    Father: Warner C. Carter   Mother: Mittie Bryant
    Children: Wesley, 1919, Married Catherine McCormick
                 Mary Annie, 1921, Married Leonard McFadden
                 Mobrie, 1923, Married Dorothy Ferguson
                 Harry D., 1925, Married Miss Daniel of New Jersey
                 Eula May, 1927
                 Ada, 1929, Married Amos Cornejoe of New Jersey
                 Cubbie, 1931
                 John Christian, 1933
                 Dale, 1935
                 Ellen Louise, 1937

CARSON, JOHN J. married Elizabeth Stratton

CARTER, JAMES W., Married Evelyn Brown, 1903.
    Children: William Lawrence, 1927
                Jean Carolyn, 1929

CARTER, JESSE, -1866 Married Sarah B. Megginson.
    Children: Willie
                Albion
                Charles E.

CARTER, J. W.,   married Miss Jamerson.
    Father: W. D. Carter, Mother: Virginia Oaks.
    Children: Ada, married Ernest Lee of Lynchburg
                John, married Gladys Harrison of Roanoke
                Annie
                Carrie
    2nd. wife of J. W. Carter, Ella Stanley.
    Children: Rena, married Joseph Austin of Covington
                Judson, married lady from Roanoke
                Florence, married Charles A. Cox of Connecticut
                Pearl, married H. H. Hundley of Roanoke
                Charles M., married Ethel Guill
                Eula Mae, married Lacy Arritt.
                Christian, married Lois Moss, of Gladstone
                Ruth, married Bernard Kennon of Covington

CARTER, LEONARD W., 1896, Married Dillie Morris, 1895
    Father: C. W. Carter   Mother: Peggy Jamerson
    Children: Edwin, 1917, Married Rebecca Richardson, 1921
                Charlie Cabell, 1918, Married Marion Jefferson
                Mildred, 1920, Married Thomas M. Richardson
                Hilda M., 1921, Married Carey Jefferson
                James O., 1923

CARTER, PERCY EDWARD, 1905, Married Rebecca Jennings, 1913
    Father: Andrew Carter   Mother:

CARTER, WARNER C., died 1945, Married Mittie Bryant of Buckingham
    Children: Eddie, 1894, Married Emma Gray Baber, 1899
                Johnnie, 1896-1945, Married Winnie Gobble
                Willie W., 1898-1947, Married Miss Jones of Rural Retreat
                Mobrie, 1900-1942, Married Mildred Webb
                Ada, 1902, Married Harry Ferguson
                Della, 1904, Married Ed Lee Thomas

CARTER, WILLIE WALKER, 1898-1947, Married Katherine Jones, 1905, of
                                            Rural Retreat
    Father: Warner Carter   Mother: Mittie Bryant
    Children: Ellsworth, 1921
                Ila Jean, 1924, Married Mr. Buellner of Ohio
                Ruth, 1926, Married Mr. Johnston of Lynchburg
                Joel, 1928
                David, 1930

CARTER, W. D., 1841-1919, Married Virginia Oaks, 1845-1924
    Children: J. W. , 1866-1938, Married Nannie Jamerson
                                Second wife: Ella Stanley
                C. W., 1871, Married Peggy Jamerson, 1873-1937
                Mary, 1874-1945, Married Walker Davidson
                Alice, 1877, Married Wash Layne
                Bertha, 1880, Married J. T. Guill
                Lou, 1882, Married W. T. Davidson
                Ida, 1884-1896
                Thornton, 1886, Married Ida Davidson
                                Second wife, Bessie Morris

CARY, BERNART T., 1878, Married Lillian Gilliam, 1885

CASEY, JAMES AMMON, 1896, Married Mary S. Simms, 1885

CATES, J. L., Married Carolyn Babcock
    Children: J. L., Jr.
                Eddie Scott

CAWTHORN, CHARLES SAMUEL, 1845-1912, Married Harriet Elizabeth
                                                Clark, 1855-1922
    Father: Rev. John Cawthorn   Mother: Gemima Thornhill
    Children: John Thomas, 1874-1892
                Lillie M. 1880-
                Clinton, Married Sallie Glover Coleman
                Elijah W., 1886, Married Dolly Ann Higgenbotham, 1905

CAWTHORN, CHARLES SAMUEL, 1874, Married Laura Purdum
    Father: Cornelius Cawthorn   Mother: Rosa Phelps
    Children: Rosa Brandenburg, 1899, Married Bascom Lee Price
                Cornelius Philmore, 1901, Married Kathleen Manning
                David Walker, 1903, Married Mary Carson
                Annie Laura, 1905, Married Edgar A. Covington
                Louise Virginia, 1907, Married Walter Dupuy
                Rufus King, 1910, Married Rosa Baker
                Frances Phelps, 1912, Married Duane Barney
                Ida Hewitt, 1912
                Lillie Purdum, 1918-1919
                Charles Samuel, Jr., 1920

CAWTHORN, CLINTON THORNHILL, 1872, Married Sallie G. Coleman, 1883
    Father: Charles Samuel Cawthorn   Mother: Harriett Elizabeth Clark
    Children: Nellie Louise, 1905, Married O. B. Schaubaugh

CAWTHORN, CORNELIUS H., 1851-1914, married Rosa Phelps,
    Children: Charles Samuel, 1874- married Laura Purdum.
                        2nd. Wife, Cora V. Tanner, 1849-1914.
    Children: Thomas Joseph, 1888, married Sallie J. Cawthorn, 1893.

CAWTHORN, EDMOND HUDSON, 1873-1943, Married Nultie McDearmon, 1882
    Father: John D. Cawthorn   Mother: Bettie Phelps
    Children: Howard Duval, 1907, Married Mary Morgan of Campbell
              John Raymond, 1910, Married Dorothy Lindsey

CAWTHORN, ELIJAH W., 1886, Married Dolly Ann Higgenbotham, 1905
    Father: Charles Samuel Cawthorn   Mother: Harriett Elizabeth Clark
    Children: John Samuel, 1931
              Jane Elizabeth, 1937

CAWTHORN, FRANK T., 1887-1937, Married Mary Eva Inge, 1893
    Father: S. W. Cawthorn   Mother: Willie Jenkins
    Children: F. T., Jr.

CAWTHORN, JAMES DANIEL, Married Annie Abbitt Wooldridge, 1900
    Children: Franklin David, 1936

CAWTHORN, JAMES P., Married Martha Conner
    Children: Virginia, Married Col. Thomas Cheatham
              Joel, W., Married Amanda C. Richardson
              C. H., Married Rosa Phelps
                    Second wife: Jennie Tanner
              John D., Married Bettie Phelps
              Elnora, Married E. F. Glover
              S. W., Married Willie Ida Jenkins
              Mollie, Married Richard Foster
              Lottie, Married man from Missouri

CAWTHORN, JAMES W., 1870, Married Lizzie Morris, 1868-1940
    Father: Joseph Wellington   Mother: Amand C. Richardson
    Children: Wellington Ganaway
              Alice, 1895, Married R. C. Simpkins of West Virginia
              Thelma, 1902, Married James L. Caldwell
              Ruth, Married J. A. Tweedy
              Clara, Married Charles Hanenkrat
              Nellie M., 1906, Married William A. Thrasher

CAWTHORN, JOEL T., 1843-1920, Married Mary Louise Coleman, 1847-1916
    Father: Rev. John Cawthorn   Mother: Jemima Thornhill
    No Children.

CAWTHORN, REV. JOHN, Married Gemima Thornhill, 1810-1882
    Children: Bettie Agnes, Married Blass Harvey
                    Second husband: Dick Wooldridge
              Emma Samantha, Married Samuel Watkins Jennings
              Harriett, Married Robert Cheatham
              Joel, Married Lou Coleman
              Samuel, Married Bettie Clark
              Susan, Married Pat Coleman
              Kate, Married John Cheatham

CAWTHORN, JOHN D., 1848-1913, Married Bettie S. Phelps, 1853-1928
    Children: Edmund H., 1873-1943, Married Nultie McDearmon
               Carrie D., 1876-1914, Married J. R. Hamilton
               Heeter P., 1879, Married in Southwest Virginia
               Ella W., 1882, Married Samuel J. Jennings
               Mary Massie, 1884-1940, Married John Jennings
                            Second husband, J.R. Hamilton
               Russell, 1887, Married Miss Ferguson
                         Second wife: W. Earle Farrar
               Rosa Mae, 1889, Married W. S. Farrar
               Myrtice, 1891-1941, Married S. W. Staples

CAWTHORN, JOSEPH WELLINGTON, 1857, Married Amanda C. Richardson
                                                    1855
               Children: James W., 1870, Married Lizzie Morris, 1868-1940
                        Lizzie T., 1868, Married James Gills
                        Martha Bernice, Married Charles Wilkerson
                        Addie P., Married R. S. Jenkins
                        Edna Earle, Married J. R. Trout of Vinton

CAWTHORN, ROBERT W., 1885-1926, Married Annie Tweedy
    Father: Samuel Walker Cawthorn   Mother: Willie Ida Jenkins
    Children: Robert

CAWTHORN, RUSSELL, 1887, Married Miss Ferguson
    Father: John D. Cawthorn   Mother: Bettie S. Phelps
    Children: Dorothy, Married Mr. Simpson
                             Second wife: W. Earle Farrar
    Children: Ann, Married T. I. DeBusk, Jr.,
               Fred

CAWTHORN, SAMUEL   Married Elvira A. Thornhill, 1820-1857
    No Children

CAWTHORN, SAMUEL WALKER, 1860-1928, Married Willie Ida Jenkins,
                                                 1864-1938
    Children: Robert W., 1885-1926-Married Annie Tweedy
                     Frank T., 1886-1937, Married Eva Inge
                     Frances P., 1888, Married James R. Torrence, 1883-1944
                     Sallie J., 1892, Married Tommie Joseph Cawthorn
                     Emma V., 1894, Married William Wesley Wooldridge
                     Silas Paul, 1896, Married Holly Mitchell
                     Samson Dewey, 1898, Married Rachel Perdue, 1904

CAWTHORN, SILAS PAUL, 1896, Married Hallie Mitchell, 1903
    Father: S. W. Cawthorn   Mother: Willie Jenkins
    Children: Harold Grady, 1923, Married Jaunita Wilmer

CAWTHORN, THOMAS JOSEPH, 1888, married Sallie J. Cawthorn, 1893.
    Father: Cornelius H. Cawthorn   Mother: Cora V. Tanner, 1849-1914.
    Children: Mamie Joe, 1914, married C. C. Jennings.
                     Bradley Virginia, 1917, married George L. Jennings.
                     Thomas Jackson, 1920

CHAMBERLAYNE, THOMAS GUALLENDET, 1871-1894

CHANDLER, C. G., 1887, Married Lowis Taylor
    Children: Fred, 1927
               Babarie, 1929

CHANDLER, H. M. 1902, Married Emiline Blackman
    Children: Homer V., 1930
               John H., 1932
               Virginia Lee, 1935
               Richard, 1941
               Nancy Dianna, 1942

CHEATHAM, ELBERT FITZLAND, 1913, married Berta Franklin.
    Father: Oscar Cheatham   Mother: Olive Marshall
    Children: Elbert Larry, 1940

CHEATHAM, ELDRIDGE, 1885, married Annie Marshall
    Father: Samuel Cheatham   Mother: Sallie Nash.
    Children: Susie Bell, 1909, Married Bennie Newman, 1904
               Marshall Winkfield, 1911
               Eldridge Wadell, 1913, married Phoebia Ann Hedrick 1912
               Claude Walker, 1916, married Sue Ellen Carlson, 1916
               Alice Dale, 1923
               Affred Wade, 1923-1923

CHEATHAM, J. H., 1865, married Mollie Evans.
    Children: Annie, married _____Ringham.
               Tucker, married_____
               Alice, married Havilah Babcock.
               Zack, married Mamie Chocklott.

CHEATHAM, MARY   1807

CHEATHAM, NANCY, 1809-1892

CHEATHAM, OSCAR F., 1876, Married Olive Marshall, 1882
    Father: Samuel Cheatham   Mother: Sallie Nash
    Children: Arline, 1905, Married Kennith Carter of Charlotte
               Samuel, 1907, Married Katie Campbell of Amherst
               Margaret, 1909-1940, Married Clyde Fleshman
               William, 1911, Married Frances Miles
               Elbert, 1913, Married Berta Franklin
               Lela, 1915, Married Allen Adams
               Edward, 1917, Married Annie Nash
               Hazel, 1919

CHEATHAM, ROBERT ALEXANDER, 1840-1921, Married Harriett Nelson
                                            Cawthorn, 1847-1916
    Children: Thomas Edwin, 1867-1884
               Lula Jane, 1869, Married Sam E. Howerton, 1894

CHEATHAM, ROBERT ALEXANDER, (continued)

> Mary Catherine, 1871, Married Chancey Babcock
> Jemima Cheatham, Married W. C. Chilton
> R. Elliott, 1877, Married Eltha Caldwell
> Elizabeth, 1887-1936
> Ella, 1874-1915
> Hubbard Robertson, 1873, Married Maude Hunter
> Harriett Agnes, 1880-1899
> Emma Clarkie, 1884
> Elizabeth, 1887-1936
> Russell Aubrey, 1889

CHEATHAM, ROBERTSON, 1798, married Miss Elliott.
    Children: Robertson Beasley, 1808-1855, married Cathrine M. Harris.

CHEATHAM, ROBERTSON BEASLEY, 1808-1855, married Cathrine M. Harris
    Father, Robertson Cheatham   Mother: Miss Elliott
    Children: T. H. Alfred, 1844-1913, married Sarah Emiline Wood.

CHEATHAM, SAMUEL, Married Sallie Nash
    Children: Oscar F., 1876, Married Olive Marshall
               Ada, 1878, Married Wirt W. Woodson
               Norman, 1880, Married Mary Torrence
               Alice, 1882, Married George Thompson
               Eldridge, 1884, Married Annie Marshall
               Elsie, 1886, Married Ed Moses
               Reva M., 1888, Married John Marshall
               Maggie, 1890, Married Clarence Agee

CHEATHAM, SAMUEL BENJAMIN, 1906, Married Kate Camden of Amherst
    Father: Oscar Cheatham   Mother: Olive Marshall
    Children: Mary Alice, 1938
               George Melvin, 1936

CHEATHAM, T. H. ALFRED, 1844-1913, married Sarah Emiline Wood
    Father: Robertson Beasley Cheatham   Mother: Cathrine M. Harris
    Children: John Egbert, 1868-1887
               Walter Beverly, 1870-1917, married Sadie F. Franklin
               Arthur Clayton, 1872-1932, married Grace Dean of Lynchburg
               Jessie May, 1874, married Milton L. Bishop of Campbell
               Cathrine Estelle, 1876, married Rev. George H. Wiley
               Mary M., 1879, married Charlie McKinney
               Alfred, 1884, married Lena West of Roanoke
               Harry H., 1886, married Louise Fisher of Lynchburg
                          Second wife, Brooke McCormick of West
                                       Virginia
               Paul, 1889, married Eunice Gay of Alabama
               Rachel Wood, 1892, married Edward Montgomery Brewer
                                    of N. C.

CHEATHAM, WILLIAM WINKFIELD, 1911, married Frances Miles
    Father: Oscar Cheatham   Mother: Olive Marshall
    Children: William Jean, 1932
                 Hazel Christian, 1934
                 William Richard, 1936
                 Robert Miles, 1938
                 James Edward, 1940

CHEATHAM, ZACH ELLIOTT, 1896, Married Mamie Chocklett, 1901
    Father: J. H. Cheatham   Mother: Mollie Evans
    Children: James Elliott, 1921
                 Jean, 1929

CHENAULT, BENJAMIN C., 1859-1920, Married Emily Morris, 1871
    Children: Raymond, 1893, Married Ura Brightwell
                              Second wife: Thelma Bailey
                 Burleigh C., 1896, Married L. Harris
                 Mary Fannie, 1898, Married Walter Phelps
                 Ethel, 1900, Married Alonzo Martin
                 Stella, 1902, Married Henderson Moore
                 Irma, 1904, Married E. P. Taylor
                 Vernon, 1906, Married Elizabeth Overstreet
                 Emory H., 1908, Married Sarah Ewers
                 Emma Virginia, 1912, Married Charles R. Brown

CHENAULT, JESSE JAMES, 1893, Married Janie B. Coleman, 1896
    Children: Walter David, 1916
                 Edna Frances, 1917, Married Eddie Blackwell
                 Russell Andis, 1919
                 James Braxton, 1920
                 Henry Tyler, 1922
                 Robert Harwood, 1924
                 Maude Uldine, 1927
                 Hallie Clark, 1928
                 Evelyn Claudine, 1931
                 Sallie Lou, 1933
                 Ethel Louise, 1935
                 Margarie Wanda, 1936
                 Lois Jeanette, 1941

CHERNAULT, JAMES L. 1836-1918 married Sue Davenport of Richmond
    Children: Florence 1863-1939

CHENAULT, VERNON B., 1906, Married Elizabeth Overstreet, 1911
    Father: Benjamin C. Chenault   Mother: Emily Morris
    Children: Ralph O., 1933
                 Shirley Mae, 1935
                 Donald Gray, 1942

CHICK, ERWIN LEE, 1881, Married Ruby Drinkard, 1885
Children: Rachel Annie, 1925
Mabel Virginia, Married Henry Beard

CHICK, JAMES EUGENE, 1874, Married Lucy Davis Dawson, 1871
Children: Lucy Jane, Married William Bates

CHILDERS, JAMES EDWARD, 1852-1928, Married Mary Elizabeth Hamilton
1858-1945
Father: Thomas Childers   Mother: Susan Davis
Children: William T., 1883, Married Mary E. Ferguson
Edward, 1885
Ludwell, 1887-1916
Ethel, 1889, Married Littleton Lucado
L. H., 1891, Married Ethel Marsh, 1891
James W., 1893, Married Geneva Horsley
Myrna S., 1895-1942, Married J. A. Bingham
Elizabeth, 1898, Married Thomas H. Marsh

CHILDERS, JAMES WASHINGTON, 1896, Married Geneva Horsley, 1901
Father: James Edward Childers   Mother: Mary Elizabeth Hamilton
Children: Opar Adair, 1930
Bettie Howard, 1935

CHILDERS, JOHN D., 1858-1938, Married Lizzie Scruggs, 1872
Father: Thomas Childers   Mother: Susan Davis
Children: M. Perry, 1895-1946, Married Mrs. Wooldridge
Melvin D., 1897, Married Miss Hancock
John E., 1900, Married Georgie Nettycomb
Lewis B., 1902, Married Violet Nettycomb
Samuel N., 1906, Married Miss Patrick
Bernard, 1908, Married Sue Childers, 1915
Mattie Lucile, 1911, Married M. E. Besody
Addie, married Carroll Ould

CHILDERS, THOMAS, Married Susan Davis of Amherst
Children: James Edward, 1852-1928, Married Mary Elizabeth Hamilton
1858-1945
John D., 1858-1938, Married Lizzie Scruggs, 1872
Thomas

CHILDERS, WILLIAM T., 1883, Married Mary Elizabeth Ferguson, 1883
Father: James E. Childers   Mother: Mollie Hamilton
Children: Otis Mae, 1907, Married Wm. Slusher of Lynchburg
Arnold Thomas, 1909, Married Rachel Ferguson, 1909
Grover, 1912, Married Margaret O'Brien, 1915
William Clinton, 1915, Married Edith Harris, 1922
Minnie Sue, 1917, Married Bernard Childers
Iva Elaine, 1918, Married Roger Pillow
Carol, 1920, Married Virginia Wilmer of Lynchburg

CHILDRESS, THOMAS A., 1846-1902, married Eliza Day of Buckingham
    Children: Sis, married E. W. McCormick
                 B. L., 1864-1930, married Miss Cash of Clifton Forge
                 Mary, 1868, married W. R. Nickels
                 T. P., 1870, married Ida Bryant, 1881
                 Jane, 1872-1915
                 Lou, 1888-1932, married William King

CHILDRESS, THOMAS P., married Ida Bryant
    Father: Thomas A. Childress   Mother: Eliza Day
    Children: Myrtie,   1903, married Leyton McCormick
               Johnny,   1905-1930
               Irene,   1908, married J. E. Martin
               Minnie,   1911
               Marye,   1913, married F. J. Burks
               Thomas A., 1915
               Elmo,   1918
               Robert E., 1920

CHILTON, JOHN B., 1871-1947, Married Laura Rucker, 1873
    Father: Chapman H. Chilton   Mother: Mary Elizabeth Elliott
    Children: Virginia, Married Mr. Samples of West Virginia

(CHILTON, JOHN,   Moved to Bedford)

(CHILTON, JOE   Moved to Bedford)
                                         Brothers
(CHILTON, JACOB   Moved to Texas)

(CHILTON, HENRY Moved to Missouri)

CHILTON, CHAPMAN H., 1832-1914, Married Mary Elizabeth Elliott,
                                                1842-1921
    Children: Raleigh H., 1869-1945, Married Elma Shearer, 1871-1932
                                    Second wife: Bessie Shearer, 1878
                John B., 1871-1947, Married Laura Rucker, 1873
                William C., 1875, Married Jemima Cheatham, 1882
                Maggie
                Lena, married Dr. D. Mott Robertson
                Bessie married Leslie Morris
                Marissa

CHILTON, WILLIAM C., Married Jemima Cheatham
    Father: Chapman H. Chilton   Mother: Mary Elizabeth Elliott
    Children: Nannie Sue, 1909
               Eleanor, 1911
               Harriette, 1912
               Ava, 1914
               Chapman, 1915-1946
               Robert, 1917-1941
               Lois, 1919

CHRISTIAN, DAVID A., 1846-1931, Married Agnes Thornhill, 1858-1947
    Father: William D. Christian   Mother: Lucy Patterson
    Children: David A., Jr., 1880, Married Bessie Stratton, 1896-1944
           Mattie Hamner

           Fannie Lowery, Married G. P. Jennings
           Thomas Lowery, Married Katherine Carson
           Lucy, Married Keeling Sisson
           Agnes, 1889-1943
           Diuguid, Married Susie Booker

CHRISTIAN, JR., DAVID A., 1880, Married Bessie Stratton, 1896-1944
    Father: David A. Christian   Mother: Agnes Thornhill
    Children: Agnes Virginia, 1918, Married George L. Koos of Oregon
           Bessie Stratton, 1919, Married H. E. Thompson of Mass.
           Mildred Collier, 1922
           David A., III, 1923, Married
           Catherine Thornhill, 1925
           Chesley Stratton, 1928
           William Albert, 1930-1947
           Joyce Hamner, 1932
           Charles Edwin, 1934-1946

CHRISTIAN, THOMAS LOWERY, Married Katherine Carson
    Father: David A. Christian   Mother: Agnes Thornhill
    Children: Elsie Lowry

CHRISTIAN, DR. WILLIAM D., 1808-1880, Married Lucy Patteson, 1819-1885
    Children: George, 1843-1867, Married Pocahontas Megginson
           David A., 1846-1931, Married M. Agnes Thornhill
           Willie
           Edwin, died 1885
           Madeline, 1850-1898, Married Rev. L. R. Thornhill
           Mildred

CLAPP, DANIEL A., 1920, Married Hope Cralle 1921
    Father: John A. Clapp
    Children: Sylvia, 1942

CLAYTON, ARTHUR, 1872-1932

CLEMENT, A. H., 1866-1932, Married Pauline Clark Bledsoe, 1867-1916
                                   of Albemarle
    Children: Allen Bledsoe, 1890-1945, Married Adeline Belton of
                                Martinsville
           Russell, 1891-1914
           Pauline, 1895, Married Frank G. Craig of Nelson
           Adam Clark, 1897, Married Josephine Proffitt of Clifton
                                   Forge
           Ruth, 1905, Married C. W. Potts of Dinwiddie

COBBS, JOSEPH M., 1900, Married Grace Richardson, 1907
    Children: Joseph M., Jr., 1930

COLE, BENJAMIN C., Married Miss Anderson of Danville
    Children: Byron B. Cole, Married Ruth Bingham
                 John C. Cole
                 James

COLE, BYRON B., 1911, Married Ruth Bingham, 1918
    Father: B. C. Cole   Mother: Miss Anderson
    Children: Precilla

COLEMAN, BENJAMIN FRANKLIN, 1846-1929, Married Alice Walker
                                                    1849-1904
    Father: Joel Watkins Coleman   Mother: Miss Harris
    Children: James Walker, 1871-1916, Married Estelle Evans

COLEMAN, CHARLES, 1800-1876, Married E. S. Sears, 1802-1891
    Children: J. M., 1822-1894, Married Susan Conner
                 J. S., 1825-
                 S. E., 1827- Married Charlie Barnard
                 A. M., 1829-1888, Married Mosely
                 Albert, 1831-1863
                 E. B., 1834-1906, Mary Ownsberry of Nottaway
                 J. T., 1839-1863
                 M. D., 1847- Married Fetna Tweedy of Campbell
                 Charles Henry, 1836-1905, Married Martha Jane Lewis
                                                    died 1905

COLEMAN, CHARLES HENRY, 1836-1905, Married Martha Jane Lewis
    Father: Charles Coleman   Mother: E. S. Sears
    Children: Roberta, Married Thomas J. Gooding
                 T. E.,   1860- Married Ida B. Megginson, 1861-1881
                 Mary Emma, 1868-1943, Married R. E. Morgan of Buckingham
                 C. Lewis, 1870, Married Florence W. Morgan of Buckingham
                             Second wife: Lilla St. Claire, 1872
                 Anna Belle, 1872-1906, Married Wyatt Abbitt
                 Mattie Walker, 1875, Married John H. Coleman

COLEMAN, CHARLES HENRY, 1843-1945, Married Susie Branch, 1856-1903
    Children: Indiana, 1880, Married Harry Blanks
                             Second husband: William Scott
                 Pearl, 1882-1947
                 Branch M., 1892, Married Mary Goodman, 1879
                 Royal J., 1894, Married Mary Martin
                 Irene, 1893, Married Ottie Rogers
                 Florence, 1895-1945, Married Grover C. Clements
                 Grace, 1896, Married Clarence F. Moore
                 Taylor H., 1898, Married Lois Martin, 1906
    (C. H. Coleman's)------------ Second wife: Edmonia Burge, 1861

COLEMAN, CHARLES SPURGEON, 1859-1936, Married Emma Jane
                                        Ferguson, 1865-1940
    Father: Joseph B. Coleman   Mother: Eliza A. Harris
    Children: Mary Katherine, 1884
                Annie, 1887-1909
                Maggie H., 1888, Married Robert Spiggle
                Preston, 1891, Married Lillian Inge 1898
                Grace B., 1890, Married C. B. Page
                Irvin, 1896, Married T. P. Robertson
                Spurgeon, 1898, Married Mary Inge
                Ruth, 1898, Married North Robertson
                James S., 1900
                Sammie 1905, Married Florence Gilbert
                Joseph P., -1892

COLEMAN, C. LEWIS, 1870, Married Florence W. Morgan
    Father: Charles Henry Coleman   Mother: Martha Jane Lewis
    Children: Jane Elizabeth, 1903, Married Martin Covington
                Ethel, 1904, Married Joseph Baldwin
                Berta, 1905
                C. Lewis Coleman's 2nd. wife Mrs. St. Clair

COLEMAN, DRURY, 1823-1916, Married Sarah Cumby
    Children: William
                Schyler
                James, 1864- Married Miss Bryant
                            Second wife
    Children: Thomas, 1867, Married Agnes Phelps, 1872-1927
                Laura, 1869, Married Robert Phelps

COLEMAN, LESLIE A., 1888, Married Lillie M. Kyle
    Father: Tyler F. Coleman   Mother: Sallie Garrette
    Children: Buford, 1911-1924
                Ruby, 1913, married Kieth Marshall of Charlottesville
                Hazel, 1915-1940
                Kyle, 1921, married Roberta Robertson
                Abbitt, 1923, Married Helen Torrence

COLEMAN, MACE married E. C. Foster
    Children: G. Clement 1871 married Laura Lawson of Lynchburg

COLEMAN, MARTIN B., Married Cleo Reynolds, 1917

COLEMAN, P. WITT, 1871, Married Mildred J. Webb, 1873-1943
    Father: Joel Watkins Coleman   Mother: Sophia Hubbard
    Children: Lois, 1894, Married D. A. Conner
                Inice Lee, 1896, Married L. V. Allen of Prince Edward
                Mildred Sydnor
            Twins(Cassie Carleen, 1911, Married Ernest Farrar
                 (James Calvin, 1911, Married Inez Gregory of Mecklenburg

COLEMAN, SAMUEL HENRY, 1837-1897, Married Amanda H. Abbitt,
1840-1901
    Father: Schuyler P. Coleman   Mother: Sarah L. Glover
    Children: Mary, 1863-1944, Married Robert Irby

COLEMAN, SCHUYLER P., 1804-1884, Married Sarah L. Glover, 1812-1893
    Children: William G., 1830-, Married Mary D. W. Abbitt
               John Robert, 1834-1853
               Samuel H., 1837, Married Annie Abbitt
               Susan A. E., 1839-1891, Married Schuyler Wingfield of
                                     Charlotte
               Josiah E., 1841-1841
               Josiah Ellis, 1844-1865
               Schuyler P., Jr., 1847-1928, Married Elvira Susan
                               Cawthorn, 1849-1918
               George W., 1850- Married Susie Stickley
               Mary Lou, 1853-1938, Married Joel Cawthorn

COLEMAN, JOSEPH B., 1814-1886, Married Eliza A. Harris, 1817-
    Children: Henry H., 1843-1862
               Josiah R., 1846-1893, Married Mary Neister, 1847-1945
               Hiram L., 1848-1893, Married Alice Epps
               George W., 1850-
               Tyler F., 1852-1945, Married Sallie E. Garrett, died 1925
               Rev. James, 1856-1940
               Samuel G., 1857-
               Charles Spurgeon, 1859-1936

COLEMAN, JOSIAH R., 1846-1893, Married Mary Neister, 1847-1945
    Father: Joseph B. Coleman   Mother: Eliza A. Harris
    Children: Mollie E., 1868, Married Willie Hackworth of Lynchburg
               Thomas H., 1870-1944, Married Lula Rapp of Lynchburg
               Alice R., 1872- , Married Thomas Seal of Richmond
               William Edward, 1874-1922
               Mattie C., 1877-1944, Married T. A. Short of Lynchburg
               Samuel Leonard, 1879, Married Miss Martindale of
                                   Philadelphia
               Lelia F., 1881, Married Percy Pugh of Lynchburg
               Walker A., 1883-1919
               Louella, 1886, Married Eddie Phelps of Lynchburg
               James Dillard, 1889-
               Rosa Pearl, 1892, Married Edward Mays of Lynchburg

COLEMAN, JR. JOEL WATKINS, 1863, Married Cassie Maude Webb, 1876
    Father: Joel Watkins Coleman   Mother: Sophia Hubbard
    Children: Jessie, Married Claude East of Prince Edward
                       Second husband, Seldon Hanks of Lunenburg
               Curtis Jackson, 1906, Married Virginia Bernside of
                                   West Virginia
               Gladys Walker, 1911, Married Bernard Wilkerson
               Malcolm Joel, 1919

COLEMAN, JOEL WATKINS, 1822-1915, Married Miss Harris
    Children: Benjamin F., 1846-1930, Married Alice Walker
                             Second wife: Sophia Hubbard, 1830-1917
    Children: Alice, died 1882, Married A. D. Elam of Prince Edward
                 Josephine, 1859-1906, Married James E. Harris of Prince
                                         Edward
                 Joel Watkins, Jr., 1863, Married Cassie Webb, 1876
                 W. T., 1867, Married Ella Webb, 1868-1922
                             Second wife: Mary Sue Plunkett
                 Bascomb, 1869-1873
                 P. Witt, 1871, Married Mildred J. Webb, 1873-1943
                 Hunter, 1874-1894

COLEMAN, JR., SCHUYLER P., 1847-1928, Married Elvira Susan Cawthorn,
                                                  1849-1918
    Father: Schuyler P. Coleman   Mother: Sarah L. Glover
    Children: Robert Ellis, 1868-1888
                 Annie Kate, 1870, Married John Sam Plunkett
                 Jemima Louise, 1872-1902, Married A. Fowlkes
                 Mary Lizzie, 1874, Married T. W. Odor
                 Hubbard Schuyler, 1876
                 Joel Thomas, 1878-1944, Married Bernice Cole
                 Madelen Christian, 1881-1919, Married Ellis Odor
                 Sally Glover, 1883, Married Clinton Cawthorn
                 Samuel Henry, 1886-1918
                 William Patteson, 1888, Married Rebecca Anderson of
                                         Danville
                 Emma Sue, 1892, Married A. J. Zastrow, 1893, of Wisconsin

COLEMAN, SCHUYLER PATTERSON, 1856-1936, Married Mary Elizabeth
                                       Marshall 1863-1900
    Children: Mary Esther, 1884
                 Janna Perreeza, 1886

COLEMAN, TAYLOR H., 1898, Married Lois Martin, 1906
    Father: Charles Henry Coleman   Mother: Susie Branch
    Children: Charles Sidney, 1936
                 Opal Mae, 1939

COLEMAN, THOMAS A., 1845-1908, Married Anna E. Fitzgerald, 1845-1935
    Children: Mattie, 1872, Married Blanch Ferguson
                 Juddie, 1874, Married W. R. Cheadle
                 Joe W., 1876, Married Miss Brown of Lynchburg
                 George, 1876, Married Miss Nicholas of Lynchburg
                                Second wife: Miss Rosser of Lynchburg
                                Third wife: Miss White of Lynchburg
                 Pauline, 1880, Married Robert Holycross
                 Luther, 1882, Married Miss Smith of Lynchburg
                 J. R., 1884, Married Miss Thompson of Lynchburg
                 Bessie, 1887, Married W. R. Baldwin
                 Ella Flood, 1889, Married W. A. Chenault
                 Mace Henry, 1890, Married Miss Daugette of Lynchburg

COLEMAN, THOMAS D., 1867, Married Mary Agnes Phelps, 1872-1927
Father: Drury Coleman   Mother:
Children: Wesley, 1896, Married Dora Wooldridge of Buckingham
            Estelle, 1898-1931, Married Lesley Martin
            Richard, 1900
      Twins(Mary, 1902, Married Clark Moore
           (Thomas, 1902, Married Miss McKay of West Virginia
            Corene, 1904, Married M. F. Catlett of Albemarle
            Edwin Clyde, 1906

COLEMAN, TYLER FRANCIS, 1852-1945, Married Sallie E. Garrett
                                                      1857-1925
Father: Joseph B. Coleman   Mother: Eliza A. Harris
Children: Mazie Allen, 1878, Married Joel Harvey
                         Second husband: Thomas J. Harvey
            Maude E., 1880, Married R. W. Abbitt
            Natlie, 1882, Married T. H. Robertson
            W. T. (Buck), 1884, Married Fannie Patterson
            Leslie A., 1889, Married Lillie Kyle
            Robert H., 1894, Married Ola F. Torrence, 1898
            Janie B., 1897, Married J. J. Chenault

COLEMAN, WILLIAM ABBITT, 1886, Married Helen M. Ferguson, 1886
Father: George A. Coleman   Mother: Janey Abbitt
Children: Helen Abbitt, 1913
            Eleanor Hansen, 1907-1925
            Margaret F., 1909, Married Richard G. Janatka, 1907

COLEMAN, WALTER L., 1876, Married Mittie Nowlin 1884
Father: Pomp Coleman   Mother: Miss Thomas
Children: Hamner, 1908 married J. L. Cook of S. C.
            Allie, 1910
            Helen, 1912, married Lewis Carroll of Concord
            W. Twyman, 1914, married Isabel Marshall 1920
            Lucy, 1916, married S. T. Dodd of Lynchburg
            Mary Ellen, 1925, married H. R. Coates of Lynchburg

COLEMAN, W. T., 1907, Married Anna Robertson, 1908, of Lynchburg
Children: W. T. Jr., 1930
            Dorothea, 1935

COLEMAN, WILLIAM T., 1867, Married Ella V. Webb, 1868-1923
Father: Joel Watkins Coleman   Mother: Sophia Hubbard
Children: Baird, 1890-1911
            Irvin S., 1892-1897
            Pauline, 1894, Married E. R. Glenn
            Willie, 1896
            Frank, 1898
            Bascomb, 1900, Married Miss Eskins of West Virginia
            Wiley, 1902-1931
            Kathleen, 1904, Married Dr. Williamson
                         Second husband, Thomas C. Collins
            Andrew O., 1906
                      Second wife: Mary Sue Plunkett 1888

COLEMAN, W. TWYMAN, 1914, Married Isabel Marshall
    Father: W. L. Coleman   Mother: Mittie Nowlin
    Children: . Ronald, 1938
              Dan, 1940
              Carolyn F., 1946

COLLINS, GEORGE F., 1805-1864, Married Eleanor F. Bishop, 1803-1887
    Children: Robert M., 1832-1850
                 William J., 1837-1923, Married Nannie´P. Clark of Campbell
                 Elizabeth F., 1838-1899, Married Samuel Caldwell of
                 George N., 1841-1842   Campbell
                 Edward F., 1843-1925, Married Harriett Atwood, 1852-1873
                                            Second wife: Martha F. Bates 1854-
                                                                        1939
                 John D., 1847-1853

COLLINS, EDWARD F., 1843-1925, Married Harriett Atwood, 1852-1873
    Father: George F. Collins   Mother: Eleanor F. Bishop
    Children: John A., 1870-1897
                Harriett Annie Eleanor, 1872, Married Frank E. Babcock
                George Robert., 1874, Married Miss Miller of Minnesota
                                                                1878-1941
                                        Second wife: Mary Davidson, 1903
                Edward Randolph, 1876, Married Ella Williams of Lynchburg
                William Daniel, 1877, Married a lady of Roanoke
                Samuel Hill, 1879
                Andrew Nelson, 1881, Married Miss Wilson of New York
                Frank Taylor, 1884-1892
                Thomas Bishop, 1886, Married Ella Collins

COLLINS, WILLIAM JONATHAN, 1837-1923, married Miss Clark of Campbell

CONNER, ALLEN, died 1885, Married Elizabeth Sweeney, 1816-1897
    Children: Mildred Kyle, 1854-1893, Married Robert A. O'Brien

CONNER, DUVAL ADAMS, 1889, Married Lois W. Coleman, 1903
    Father: Jennings Conner   Mother: Lucy J. O'Brien
    Children: Cecil, 1917, Married R. W. Houchens
                J. W. (Sam), 1918
                Sydnor A., 1920

CONNER, J. R., 1875, Married Hassie Harvey, 1890
    Children: J. R., Jr., 1911, Married Virginia Ferguson of Lynchburg

CONNER, JENNINGS, 1839- Married Miss Sweeney
                        Second wife: Lucy J. O'Brien 1857-1939
    Children: Duval Adams, 1889, Married Lois W. Coleman, 1903
                Nettie, 1887, Married J. H. O'Brien

141

CONNER, LACY EVROD, 1904, Married Dora Otway Abbitt, 1912
    Father: Thomas Usher   Mother: Sallie Branch Torrence
    Children: Edna Bolling, 1930
               Dora Otway, 1938

CONNER, RUSSELL, 1912, Married Frances Torrence, 1929
    Father: T. U. Conner   Mother: Sallie B. Torrence
    Children: Mary Carrington, 1938
               Thomas Eugene, 1939

CONNER, SAMUEL, Married Bettie Farrar
    Children: James R., Married Hassie Harvey
               Thomas U., Married Sallie B. Torrence

CONNER, THOMAS U., 1877-1939, Married Sallie B. Torrence, 1876-1947
    Father: Sam Conner   Mother: Bettie Farrar
    Children: William H., 1901, Married Verna Ferguson
               Mabel I., 1902, Married Sam L. Ferguson
               Everod, 1904, Married Dora Abbitt
               Thomas J., 1906
               Walter Samuel, 1908, Married Lucile Chepola
               Vara, 1910, Married Frank Hanenkrat
               Russell C., Married Frances Torrence
               James Abbitt, 1914, Married Thelma Torrence
               John Twyman, 1916

COUSINS, LONNIE, Married Susan Pauline Thornhill, 1832-1857
    Children: Susan, 1858-1858

COVINGTON, ARRIS WALKER, 1894, Married Iva Ferguson, 1904
    Father: William James Covington.   Mother: Lillie Abbitt
    Children: Louise Gwendelyn, 1929
               Arris Beryl, 1930

COVINGTON, EDGAR A., Married Annie Cawthorn
    Father: Edgar F. Covington   Mother: Ida Swan
    Children: Mary Frances, 1927
               Ida Virginia, 1941

COVINGTON, EDGAR F., 1874-1941, Married Ida Swan, 1882-1929
    Children: Edgar A., 1905, Married Annie Cawthorn
               Robert W., 1907, Married Annie Rosser, 1909
               John Howard, 1909-1916
               Henry Judson, 1912, Married Ruby Ferguson, 1911
               Annie Lu Ella, 1913, Married Ernest Rogers
               Samuel Wilson, 1915-1915

COVINGTON, MARTIN, 1827-1913, Married Lucy Jane Davidson, 1831-1904
    Children: ' William James, 1854-1941, Married Lillie Abbitt, 1858-1933
        Thomas F., 1861, Married Emma Jenkins, 1861-1932
        Luther M., 1856-1936, Married Mattie Coleman
        Joe F., 1875

COVINGTON, ROBERT A., Married Miss Covington
    Father: Thomas F. Covington   Mother: Emma Jenkins
    Children: Robert A., Jr., 1922

COVINGTON, ROBERT W., 1907, Married Annie Rosser, 1909
    Father: Edgar F. Covington   Mother: Ida Swan
    Children: R. W., Jr., 1937
        John Howard, 1939
        Estelle, 1942

COVINGTON, THOMAS F., 1861, Married Emma Jenkins, 1861-1932
    Father: Martin L. Covington   Mother: Lucy Jane Davidson
    Children: Lucy, 1886, Married C. R. Woodall
        Joel W., 1887, Married Stella Caldwell
                 Second wife: Annie Tweedy Cawthorn
        Martin L., 1890, Married Gertrude Rooker
                 Second wife: Elizabeth Coleman
        Robert A., 1892, Married Louise Covington
                 Second wife: Helen Covington
        W. T., 1894, Married Edna Torrence, 1897
        Frank O., 1897, Married Jessee Lee Splawn of South
                              Carolina
        Mary V., 1902

COVINGTON, WILLIAM JAMES, 1854-1941, Married Lillie Abbitt, 1858-1933
    Father: Martin L. Covington   Mother: Lucy Jane Davidson
    Children: William James, Jr., 1889, Married Sadie W. Covington
        Abbott B., 1883-1887
        Louise Coyler, 1893-1927, Married Robert A. Covington
        Arris Walker, 1894, Married Iva Ferguson, 1904
        Mary Helen, 1897, Married Robert A. Covington

COVINGTON, JR., WILLIAM JAMES, 1889, Married Sadie Whitehead Covington
    Father: William James Covington   Mother: Lillie Abbitt
    Children: William Judson, 1912, Married Marjory Spicer of Boston
        Dorothy, 1914, Married Joseph Bona of Hampton
        Thelma Rosalyn, 1920, Married Philip Bettole of California
        Lillie Aelise, 1923

COX, WILLIAM F., Married Ollie Mae Dinkins
    Children: Wallace, 1946

CRALLE, CHARLES CRADDOCK, 1885, Married Lucy P. Parker, 1892
        Children: Lucille, 1914
                     Virginia, 1919, Married Benjamin Saunders of Richmond
                     Frances Mae, 1928

CRALLE, HOWARD B., 1898, Married Christine Neill, 1901
        Children: H. B. Cralle, Jr., 1926
                     Hope, Married Daniel A. Clapp

CRALLE, THOMAS H., 1869-1933, Married Mary Pearl Brightwell, 1876
        Children: Gladys, 1900
                     Janette, 1904
                     Ruth, 1906, Married A. V. Weekley of Lynchburg
                     Ida Frances, 1912

CRAWLEY, CHARLES FRANCIS PAYNE, 1914, Married Louise Mildred
                                                   Stratton, 1917
        Father: Lindsay Crawley   Mother: Lucy Marshall Holtzclaw
        Children: Charles Francis Payne, Jr., 1940

CRAWLEY, LINDSAY, 1880, Married Lucy Marshall Holtzclaw, 1887, of
                                                   Fauquier
        Children: Charles Francis Payne, 1914, Married Louise Mildred
                                                   Stratton, 1917
                     Raymond Tinsley, 1923

CREWS, JOHN H., Married Rebecca Moore
        Father: Wrenny Crews   Mother:
        Children: Robert, Married Patricia Knepp
                     Virginia, Married Eddie Bell

CREWS, JOSEPH, Married Hester Martin
        Children: Nannie Patterson, Married John P. Grow
                     Alberta, Married John Burge
                     Thomas H., Married Annie Burge

CREWS, WRENNY, Married widow of his brother Joseph Crews
        Children: Joseph
                     Robert
                     Willie
                     John H., Married Rebecca Moore

CUMBY, MAJOR 1865-1944 Married Lucy Ann Woolridge 1866
        Children: Harry, 1892-1944 married Mattie Wade of Buckingham
                     Mattie 1897 married Ben Garrette
                     Perry 1899 married Myrtle Riley
                     Henry, 1901, married Ethel Almond
                     Nannie, 1904 married Taylor Layne
                     Gracie, 1909 married Herman Johnson

CUNNINGHAM, THOMAS MARSHALL, 1892, Married Harriette E. Powell,
                                                   1912, of Dinwiddie
        Children: Thomas Marshall, Jr., 1939
                     Ann Gay, 1941

CUNNINGHAM, W. C., 1861

DAVIDSON, JAMES M., died 1947, Married Lillie May Simms, 1877-1908
    Children: Clarence Aubrey, 1901, Married Minnie Johnson, died 1946
                Mary Caroline, 1903
                James Robert, 1905, Married Ida Jane Bomar
                Hattie Bell, 1907

DAVIDSON, J. OSBORNE, 1882, Married Annie Thornhill, died 1925
    Father: Thomas Osborne Davidson   Mother: Emma Stratton
    Children: Eleanor, 1914, Married Curtis T. Roach of Surry
                Katherine, 1916, Married Charles N. Judy of West Va.
                Elizabeth, 1917, Married John L. Harrison
                Mary Virginia, 1918, Married Stuart H. Barrell
      Twins (Thomas O., 1921
            (Annie T., 1921
                Lily Bibb, 1925, Married Leighton Haley of Norfolk

DAVIDSON, JESSE T., 1814-1889, Married Martha Osborne
    Father: Samuel Davidson   Mother: Elizabeth Thornhill
    Children: Catherine E., 1841-1894, Married Capt. Watt Carson
                John W., 1843-1916, Married Miss Collins
                Rev. Judson Cary, 1846-1914, Married Miss Diuguid
                Thomas O., 1849-1929, Married Emma M. Stratton
                Emma M., 1852-1917
                Samuel, 1857-1920, Married Elizabeth Howerton
                            Second wife of J. T.: Mrs. Bruce
                                      Robertson Martin
    Children: Ewing, Married Miss Koiner
                Jesse, Married Miss Jeter
                Lizzie, Married Maurice Barnett

DAVIDSON, JOHN W., 1843-1916, Married Carrie B. Collins
    Father: Jesse Davidson   Mother: Martha Osborn
    Children: Robert William
                James Madison, Married Lily B. Simms
                Martha Osborn, Married Robert C. Williams
                Susie Thomas
                John Fowler
                Edward Collins

DAVIDSON, JUDSON CAREY, 1846-1914, Married Elizabeth Diuguid
    Father: Jesse Davidson   Mother: Martha Osborn
    Children: George
                Mabel
                Grace

DAVIDSON, SAMUEL, 1777-1848, Married Elizabeth Thornhill, 1789
    Children: Jesse T., 1815-1889, Married Martha Osborne
                              Second wife: Mrs. Bruce Robertson
                                    Martin

DAVIDSON, SAMUEL, (continued)
     William S., 1816-1897, Married Mattie A. Landrum
             Second wife: Credilla Snap
     Elizabeth S., 1818-, Married George Wheeler
     John Albert, 1820-1834
     Paulina A., 1825-, Married George A. Diuguid
     Samuel S., 1830-1898

DAVIDSON, SAMUEL, 1857-1920, Married Elizabeth Howerton, 1865-1934
 Father: Jesse T. Davidson Mother: Martha Osborne
 Children: Jesse D., 1893
     Thomas B., 1895, Married Terrissa Frazier, 1918 of
                Campbell
    Agnes, Married Lester Carson
    Edith, 1901, Married David Smith

DAVIDSON, THOMAS B., 1895, Married Terrissa Frazier, 1918
 Father: Samuel Davidson Mother: Elizabeth Howerton
 Children: Samuel D., 1933
     Ann Elizabeth, 1935
     Mildred Virginia, 1937
     Joyce Thomas, 1944

DAVIDSON, THOMAS H., 1849-1931, Married Miss Flood of Buckingham
 Children: Annie, Married Dibrel Kyle
     Irene, Married Tom Gilbert
     Kate, Married
     Lee, Married Mrs. Mattie Scruggs North

DAVIDSON, THOMAS OSBORNE, 1849-1929, Married Emma Stratton, 1849-1889
 Father: Jesse T. Davidson Mother: Martha Osborne
 Children: J. Osborne, 1882, Married Annie Thornhill, died, 1925
     Annie, 1884, Married J. Rolfe Horsley
     J. Crawford, 1885
     Kate, 1887

DAVIDSON, WILLIAM BENJAMIN, 1844-1926, Married Rebecca Morris, 1852-1934
 Children: David Nathaniel, 1886, Married Bess Faulconer of Orange

DAVIDSON, W. T., 1872, Married Lou Carter, 1874
 Children: Hester, 1904, Married Floyd Winston Martin
     Evelyn A., 1906, Married Eldridge Martin
     Ollie J., 1910, Married Dorothy Farmer of Lynchburg
     Ida Blanche, 1916, Married Harvey Pulliam
     Nettie H., 1918, Married Walker Hurt of Pamplin

DAVIS, CLEM, 1857-1934, Married Ollie Dickerson, 1863-1937
 Children: Richard B., 1882-1935, Married Jennie Ferguson
     Thomas, 1884, Married Ada Ferguson, 1895

DAVIS, EMBRA, 1916, Married Elizabeth George
 Father: Thomas Davis Mother: Ada Ferguson
 Children: Geane
     Edna Mae
     Perry
     Roger

DAVIS, HURLEY C., 1891, Married Vertie Smith, 1897, of North Carolina

DAVIS, J. D., Married Mary Sears
    Children: Margaret
                  Willie
                  E. J.
                  J. Kent, Married Dorothy Pulliam of Culpeper
                  Mary Kyle, Married Edmund Fields of Culpeper

DAVIS, JAMES T., 1884

DAVIS, JOHN L., 1846-1927, Married Elizabeth Farrar, 1849-1922
    Children: Alma, 1783-1928, Married Nathan Wooldridge
                  Vashti, 1884-1945, Married Floyd Wooldridge

DAVIS, JOSEPH W., 1853-1934, Married Rhoda Anderson Gray, 1845-1927
    Children: A. B., 1880, Married Mabel Douglas of West Virginia
                  J. W., 1882
                  Rosa, 1883, Married Joe Frank of Coleman
                  Shirley, 1884, Married Eilen Hubbard
                  Chalmers, 1886, Married Miss Gordon of Madison
                  H. P., 1888, Married Clara Caldwell

DAVIS, N. A., Married Jessie M. Booker
    Children: Thomas Calvin, 1899, Married Miss Miller of Pennsylvania
                  Myrle, 1901
                  T. Austin, 1907

DAVIS, OTIS, Married Ursula Wooldridge
    Children: James Reginald, 1940

DAVIS, ROBERT R., 1872, Married Della F. Mullin, 1875
    Children: Lucy, 1897, Married Ernest Bateman of Lynchburg
                  Neva, 1899, Married L. P. Inge
                  Robert, 1902-1907
                  Zadie, 1909, Married William Carr of North Carolina
                  E. F., 1905, Married Mary Wood of Prince Edward

DAVIS, THOMAS, 1884, Married Ada Ferguson, 1895
    Father: Clem Davis   Mother: Ollie Dickerson
    Children: Embra, 1916, Married Elizabeth George of Amelia
                  Helen Louise, 1923, Married Harry Yeates of Amelia

DAWSON, ROBERT N., died 1884, Married Miss Portwood of Charlotte
    Children: Nealie, 1852, Married C. Shorter of Charlotte
                  Delie, 1852-1924, Married Thomas Lewis of Buckingham
                  Thomas, 1853-1941
                  Nannie, 1857-1927. Married Joe Dawson
                  Lula, 1861-1920, Married Mr. Harvell of Ivor
                  Addie, 1869-1944
                  Lillie, 1871, Married George Reynolds of Halifax
                  Robert N., Jr., 1873, Married Grace Browning
                  Grace, 1876

147

DAY, JOHN JAMES, 1854-1925, Married Mary E. Wilkerson, 1868-1910
    Children: Patty, 1894, Married Macon Ayers
                Virginia Elizabeth, 1897
                William Andrew, 1897, Married Carrie Harris
                Clementine, 1901, Married Hal Bryant
                Emmet, 1901, Married Blanche Martin
                James, 1904

DAY, LEONARD FRED, Married Rachel Morris
    Children: Wanda Lee, 1935
                Wayne Morris, 1940

DICKERSON, B. D., 1861-1931, Married Anna Farrar 1871-1943
    Children: Alice W., 1889, Married T. R. Richardson
                S. R., 1891, Married Annie Simmons
                Virginia S., 1893, Married Lacy Almond
                Wiley R., 1896, Married Mary Lee Holt of Brookneal
                Lewis E., 1898, Married Flora Goin
                Hutson D., 1901, Married Blanche Holt of Brookneal
                Elsie M., 1905, Married Walter Ranson

DICKERSON, DANIEL, 1809-1900, Married Elizabeth Ann Wade, 1819-1900
    Father: James Dickerson   Mother: Martha Paris
    Children: Martha J., 1835
                William J., 1838
                Sarah Frances, 1840
                Joseph Daniel
                Elijah Thomas
                Mary Elizabeth
                Fletcher Emeline
                Josephine Louise
                Ida Ann
                Laura Viola

DICKERSON, E. THOMAS, 1846-1918

DICKERSON, JAMES, Married Martha (Patty) Paris
    Children: Daniel, 1809-1900, Married Elizabeth Ann Wade, 1819-1900

DICKERSON, H. CAMPMAN, 1895-1920

DICKERSON, JESSE ELIJAH, 1886, Married Vara Agnes Howerton, 1887-1942
    Children: Thomas Hunter, 1913, Married Thelma Gregory Morris, 1916
                Louise, Married J. E. Carnefix
                Ethel Irene, 1919, Married E. L. Martin of Campbell
                Margaret Jeanette, 1923, Married Carlton Wilbun
                Anna B., 1918, Married Wiley Howard Robertson, 1917

DICKERSON, JOHN NATHAN, 1862-1942, Married Bettie Hurt, 1861-1900
                        Second wife: Bunch Jennings
                                  1876-1916
    Children: Margaret, Married Willie Tolly

DICKERSON, L. L., 1892, Married Della Mae Fore, 1896
    Children: Louise, 1914, Married Lloyd Williamson of Lynchburg
        Josie C., 1917, Married Eddie Martin of Farmville
        L. L., Jr., 1919-1942
        Pauline Virginia, 1922, Married Henry Hungate of
                                            Christiansburg
        Braxton L., 1924

DICKERSON, MARTHA ANN, 1831, married Thomas H. Marshall, 1830-1858
    ".   Mary Jane, 1834
    "   Emiline F., 1836
    "   Mary E., 1838
    "   John F., 1841-1920, married Lucy V. Coleman, 1845-1907
    "   Margaret Frances, 1842
    "   Peter F., 1848

DICKERSON, MARY F., 1824-1892

DICKERSON, SALLIE VIRGINIA, 1853-1902

DICKERSON, SIDNEY J., Married Bettie Harvey, 1855-1930

DICKERSON, SAMUEL HENRY, Married Mary Christian Martin, 1895
    Children: Howard, Married Nellie Simms
        Louise, Married Edward Thompson

DICKERSON, W. E., 1878, Married Nannie Morris, 1881
    Children: Estelle, 1905, Married Howlet Martin
        Helen, 1907, Married Richard Lawson
        Sarah Frances, 1910, Married Andrew A. Steele
        Rachel, 1911, Married Homer Babcock
        W. E., Jr., 1912, Married Marcha Viccellio
        Evelyn, 1914, Married Earl H. Frazier
        Erna, 1917
        Claude M., 1918
        Frederick, 1919, Married Christine Caldwell
        Earle Howard, 1923
        Nancy, 1924, Married George M. Turman

DICKERSON, WILLIAM J., 1838-1920, Married Annie P. Webb, 1847-1924
    Children: William J., Jr., 1868, Married Mabel Collins
        Maude, 1870, Married Charlie Carter of Buckingham
        LeVerge, 1872, Married Alsen Franklin Thomas
        Annie, 1874, Married Mr. Anderson
                Second husband, Mr. Bermard
        Albert D., 1875, Married Esther V. Smith of Tennessee
        Edgar W., 1877
        Ernest N., 1878, Married Ida Moore of North Carolina
        Harry H., 1880-1935, Married Gertrude Cook of Roanoke
        Eugene W., 1882, Married Mary Adams of Lynchburg
        Asa A., 1883
        Conrad L., 1884-1943, Married May Sims
        Merdis, 1886
        Aubrey L., 1888, Married Eva Boswell of Lynchburg

DINKINS, DANIEL W., 1886-1944, Married Mattie Kate Ranson, 1893
Children: Merle, married C. E. Richardson
              Elbert, married Louise Williams
              Emmett W.
              James, married Leone McFaden

DINKINS, NEVEL, 1874, Married Lillie Fore
Children: Floyd, 1910, Married Mildred Shaner of Lynchburg
              Thelma, 1912, Married Berkley Rogers
              Twyman, 1915
              Ollie Mae, 1917, Married William P. Cox of Lynchburg
              Murtice, 1921
              Hilda, 1923, Married Watts Gilliam

DIUGUID, SAMPSON, 1795-1856, Married Martha B. Diuguid, 1798-1843

DOSS, AUBREY LaFAYETTE, 1898, Married Gwndelyn Smoot, 1906
Father: James M. Doss   Mother: Mary D. Ferguson
Children: Aubrey L. Jr., 1924, Married Mildred Sheppe of Concord
              Randolph, 1926
              Mabel, 1927, Married James Smith
              Herman, 1929
              Douglas, 1930
              Peggie, 1930
              Samuel, 1931
              Nora, 1933
              William, 1934
              Joseph, 1935
              Harrell, 1936
              Horace, 1936
              Gene, 1940

DOSS, CHARLES ROBERT, died 1879, Married Mollie Frances Doss, died 1934
Children: James M. 1870, Married Everett Ferguson
              Charles H., 1871, Married Maggie Ferguson
              Daisy, 1877, Married J. E. Rogers

DOSS, GEORGE LEWIS, 1900, Married Lougenia Patteson, 1900
Children: LeFern

DOSS, GEORGE THORNHILL, 1860-1940, Married Maggie Bingham, 1860-1933

DOSS, GEORGE W., 1832-1921, Married Martha Tanner, 1850-1927, of
                                                                Charlotte
Children: Sam, 1870, Married Lucy Smith
              Rosa F., 1874, Married Ervin McCollough of Rockbridge
              Buck, 1877
              Broadus A., 1880, Married Elizabeth Tarry of Lynchburg
              Sallie R., 1883, Married Thomas L. Page
              Lillie J., 1889, Married John Pugh of Rockbridge
              Emma S., 1886, Married W. C. Bass

DOSS, HENRY, Married Miss Wright.
    Children: Harry.
                          2nd. Wife, Miss Wright.
    Children: Jesse
                  Mamie
                  David

DOSS, JAMES M., 1870, Married Mary E. Ferguson, 1871
    Father: Charles Robert Doss   Mother: Mollie Frances Doss
    Children: Sadie, 1892, Married F. T. Guill
                  Mattie, 1895-1940, Married Motie Guill
                  James B., 1896, Married Virginia Baldwin of West Va.
                  Aubrey, 1897, Married Guinland Smoot of Lynchburg
                  Victoria, 1899, Married Albert Ferguson
       Twins   (Mazie, 1901, Married John Spiggle
                 (Daisy, 1901, Married Bernard Doss
                  Mary, 1905, Married Bernard Ferguson
                  Robert, 1907, Married Opel Minnis of Richmond
                  Deleware, 1909, Married Lucile Ferguson
                  Elsie, 1911

DOSS, JACOB N., Married Annie Williamson
    Children: Annie, 1870, Married Fielding J. Rogers
                  Luther Scott, Married Fannie Hammersley
                  Thomas Baxter, Married Hattie Marsh
                  Lula Frances, Married Kemper Harris

DOSS, JOSEPH, Married Elizabeth Thomas
    Children: Ella, Married Charlie Powell
                  Edward
                  Walker, Married Sarah Shumaker
                  Manchia
                  John, Married Lizzie McCullough
                        Second wife Elizabeth Coleman
                  Peter, Married Hattie Shumaker
                  Jim, Married Lillie Harris

DOSS, LUTHER SCOTT, Married Fannie Hammersley, 1877-1947
    Father: Jacob N. Doss   Mother: Annie Williamson

DOSS, MARY E., 1848-1929

DOSS, SAMUEL H., 1870, Married Lucy Smith, 1873
    Father: George Doss   Mother: Martha Tanner
    Children: Lewis, 1897, Married Bernice Blackwell
                  Margaret E., 1896
                  Genieve Judson, 1898, Married Herbert Doss
                  Bernard S., 1900, Married Daisy Doss
                  Leona O., 1902, Married Nelson Ferguson
                  Mary Hazel, 1904, Married George W. Baker of Maryland
                  George B., 1906, Married Dot Stanley
                  Thomas A., 1908, Married Alene Ferguson
                  Finley J., 1910, Married Enid Meredith
                  Mamie Virginia, 1913, Married J. I. Kirby of Lynchburg
                  Richard E., 1915-1915

DOSS, W., died 1921

DOSS, WILL, Married Miss Austin

DOSS, WYATT, Married Sallie Perdue of Campbell
    Children: Zerelda
                Mazie
                Mildred
                Floyd

DOVE, WILLIAM B., 1898, Married Annie Lee Nowlin, 1898
    Children: James Lee, 1924

DRESSER, F. C., Married Nettie Moses
    Children: Frank
                Walter

DRINKARD, AUBREY, Married Inez Harding, 1920
    Father: Clarence Drinkard   Mother: Susie Martin
    Children: Dennis, 1941
                Audrey Dale, 1947

DRINKARD, CHARLES M., 1851-1925, Married Mary Ann Martin of Campbell
    Children: Lucile Martin, 1879, Married C. W. Beasley
                Lawrence Marye, 1881, Married Odie Dodson of Chase City
                Alfred W., 1883
                Hattie A., 1884, Married D. Eugene Turnes
                Lula B., 1886, Married W. J. LeGrand
                Sallie Wellington, 1889, Married D. R. Green of N. C.
                Mary Estelle, 1891
                Judith Lobelia, 1893-1917, Married M. P. McNeal of N. C.
                Kathleen M., 1895, Married J. Owen Carson
                Nettie Florine, 1896
                Mollie

DRINKARD, CLAYTON T., 1894, Married Sallie B. Cobb
    Father: William Henry Drinkard   Mother: Lizzie Stone
    Children: Clayton, Jr., 1924
                Tye Cobb, 1930
                William Wade, 1934

DRINKARD, ELANTHA M., 1870, Married Lula Baker, 1868-1946
    Children: James Berkley, 1892 Married Margaret Littell
                Alice H., 1893, Married Joseph C. Tweedy
                Lula Maude, Married Roy Hancock
                Shafter C., 1895
                Lignora, 1899-
                Rheda E., 1901, Married Mr. Watson of Baltimore
                            Second husband, Mr. Milton of Florida
                Edward Crote, 1903, Married Aileen Hill of South Carolina
                Joel Flood, 1906, Married Miss Cobb of North Carolina

DRINKARD, GEORGE E., Married Pattie H. Stratton
    Children: W. A., 1879, Married Mary V. Scruggs, 1880
                 Frank C., 1881, Married Annis Drinkard, 1879
                 Claude, 1884-1947, Married Willie Routen, 1874-1947
                 Etta, Married Henry Routen
                 Harry, 1894-1934

DRINKARD, FRANK C., 1881, Married Annis Drinkard, 1879
    Father: George E. Drinkard   Mother: Pattie H. Stratton
    Children: Frances, 1906, Married Newton Wilkerson of Campbell

DRINKARD, JAMES BERKLEY, 1892, Married Margaret Littelle, 1895
    Father: E. M. Drinkard   Mother: Lula Baker
    Children: Lula Emma, 1914, Married Herbert S. Gibson of Albemarle
                 Margaret Elizabeth, 1917, Married J. H. Robertson of
                                            Albemarle
                 Sara Ina, 1919, Married Carleton Wayne of Prince Edward
                 Willa Jane, 1921, Married Jack Dirben of Lynchburg
                 Elantha Martin II, 1926
                 James Berkley, Jr., 1930
                 Elsie Marion, 1924, Married Charles Martin, 1923

DRINKARD, JOHN B., 1851-1921, Married Mary Lucy Stratton, 1860-1922
    Children: Maurice A., 1881-1888
                 Douglas H., 1883-1884
                 Fannie M., 1885
                 Bessie L., 1887-1894
                 Amine W., 1889
                 Vann O., 1891
                 Mary L., 1893
                 Taylor S., 1895, Married Miss Kent of Amherst
                 Minnie L., 1898-1899
                 John B., Jr., 1900
                 Laura V., 1905

DRINKARD, MARVIN MADISON, 1897, Married Thelma Lee Roberts
    Children: Marvin Lee, 1944
                 Shirley Jean, 1945

DRINKARD, MATTIE)

DRINKARD, T. B.   )

DRINKARD, FRANK)   Brothers and sisters of Mrs. John W. Harwood

DRINKARD, ALICE)

DRINKARD, ELLA)

DRINKARD, MINNIE)

DRINKARD, MELVIN W., Married Alise Martin, 1913

153

DRINKARD, SAMUEL C., 1876-1944, Married Mollie Jane Inge, 1877

DRINKARD, THOMAS AUSTIN, 1858-1945, Married Lucy Annie Stone,
                                                          1863-1938
    Father: William Drinkard   Mother: Jane Moore
    Children: William Micajah, 1888-1940, Married Mabel Willis of Wise
           Mary Moorman, 1890-1906
           Earle Cleveland, 1892
           Thomas Alton, 1902

DRINKARD, WILLIAM, 1832-1914, Married Jane Moore
    Children: William Henry, married Lizzie Stone
          J. B., Married Lucy Stratton
          T. A., Married Lucy Annie Stone
          Fuller, Married Miss Chick
          Sallie, Married S. P. Taylor
          George, Married Pattie H. Stratton
          Jennie Will, Married C. M. Stratton
          One Daughter married Mr. Wright

DRINKARD, WILLIAM ALBERT, 1879, Married Mary Virginia Scruggs, 1880
    Father: George E. Drinkard   Mother: Pattie H. Stratton
    Children: Rosa, 1904, Married H. L. Gough of Campbell
           Thelma, 1906, Married T. W. Booth of Campbell
           Eunice, 1910, Married R. C. Harvey

DRINKARD, WILLIAM EUGENE, 1896, Married Kathleen Drewry Laughan,
                                                          1905-1938
    Children: Phylis Darlyn, 1928

DRINKARD, WILLIAM HENRY, 1848-1930, Married Lizzie Stone, 1860
    Father: William Drinkard   Mother: Jane Moore
    Children: Willie Annis, 1882, Married Frank Clyde Drinkard
           Ruby Moorman, 1885, Married Erwin Lee Chick
           Henry Annis, 1888, Married Lucy Adams Patteson
           Alma Virginia, 1891, Married Frank E. Jennings
           Clayton T., 1894, Married Sallie B. Cobb of Franklin
           Glenn Preston, 1897
           Paul Stone, 1900, Married Jessyln Hancock

DRISKILL, JAMES L., 1854-1944? Married Martha Fitzgerald, 1859-
    Children: Wesley, Married Virginia Lee of Tennessee

DURIE, W. S., 1886, Married Dora Godsey, 1898
    Children: Katie Ella, 1919
           Nellie Annie, 1920
           John William, 1921
           Robert Jackson, 1922
           Charlie Thomas, 1924
           L. Well, 1931
           Evelyn Lee, 1934
           Harvey Obie, 1939

DURRUM, JOHN J., 1843-1919, Married Ann Harvey, 1848-1945
    Children: Emma W., 1867-1923, Married Charles H. Smith
                 Anna, 1870-1925, Married Fields R. Smith
                 Richard F., 1872-19~4, Married Lottie S. Wright
                 James W., 1874-1875
                 Alma S., 1876, Married James A. Spiggle
                 Mildred H., 1878, Married Eddie L. Layne
                 John W., 1880
                 Cora F., 1882, Married Daniel W. Johnson
                 Burnice A., 1890

DURHAM, WILLIAM ARCHER, 1845-1903, Married Ella Fuqua, 1862-1926
    Children: Terry C., 1891, Married Dollie Harnsworth of England
                 Walter E., 1895-1944, Married Helen Mann of Richmond
                 Alpha, 1893, Married J. H. Higgenbotham of Amherst

EAGLE, DAVID W., 1888, Married Lula Godsey, 1900
    Children: David O., 1915, Married Thelma Callaham Glover, 1908
                 Louise, Married Howard Phelps
                 Etna, 1920, Married William Stout
                 Lyle, 1923
                 Elizabeth, 1926
                 Alice, 1927
                 Andrew, 1935)
                 Alfred, 1935) Twins
                 Wiley E., 1938
                 Bobby Ray, 1941

EARMAN, MARTIN LUTHER, 1884, Married Elizabeth E. Roleson, 1889, of
                                                              Pennsylvania

EVANS, CHARLES T., 1872-1943, Married Imogene Clark, 1881
    Children: Ida Bell, 1908-1936
                 Lewis Tucker, 1913-1944, Married Edna Wooldridge
                 Imogene Clarkie, 1915

EVANS, CLARENCE, Married Sallie K. Ranson
    Children: Kathleen
                 Frances
                 Nannie May

EVANS, JOHN W., 1834-1923, Married Pauline M. Wilkes, 1839-1933
    Children: Jesse O., 1859-1933, Married Judie A. Dickerson
                 John W., Jr., 1861-1945, Married Mattie Wingfield
                 Samuel L., 1865-1945, Married Lorena Wooldridge
                 Calvin E., 1866-1945, Married Ella Gilliam
                 Augustus H., 1870-1917, Married Annie E. Gilliam
                 Callie, 1871, Married Walker Coleman
                 Birl Elmo, 1873-1915, Married Wittie Davis
                 W. Carrington, 1875, Married Minnie Foster
                 Mamie H., 1878, Married William Lawrence Brown
                 Thomas T., 1880, Married Emma V. Reed

EVANS, MEREDITH, 1915, Married Elizabeth Cralle, 1917

EVANS, SAMUEL J., 1890, Married Mirtia Johnson, 1899
Children: Carl, 1919, Married Eurline Rosser
Marjorie, 1921, Married C. D. Thomas of Roanoke
William T., 1922
Marion, 1929, Married Ted Almond
Ann, 1939

EVANS, W. CARRINGTON, 1875, Married Minnie Parks Foster
Father: John W. Evans   Mother: Pauline M. Wilkes
Children: Lucy, 1906, Married Cameron Seay of Blackstone
Dorothy, 1909, Married Judge Joel W. Flood

FARMER, WALTER LEE, 1895, Married Oreanna Devin, 1910
Children: Frieda, 1942

FARRAR, CHARLES, Married Virginia Farley
Children: Anna, Married B. D. Dickerson
Maggie, Married Dick Paulette
Ola, Married Callie Tolley
Jeff, Married Bell Daniel of Charlotte
Charlie
Berta, Married Joe Robertson
Price
Willie, Married Edna Berry of Orange
Kate, Married Burruss Williams
Sam, Married Carrie Miller

FARRAR, NORMAN E., 1883, Married Alma G. McDearmon
Children: Kenneth, 1909, Married H. Fizer of Bedford
Stuart, 1913

FARRAR, OMAH PARIS, 1885, Married Maude Pittman, 1886
Children: Omah Paris, Jr., 1916, Married Lottie Land of Mississippi
Maude Elizabeth, 1920
Claude Edward, 1923

FEATHERSTON, JAMES HENRY, 1845-1901, Married Sallie Massie Ragland
1852-1932
Father: Montgomery Featherston   Mother: Emily Agee
Children: Alfra Agee, 1870-1918
Emily Montgomery
Nathaniel Ragland, 1874, Married Anna Marshall, 1870-1934
Mary Elizabeth, Married Warren A. Thornhill
Martha Trent
Lucie Lillie, Married Robert E. Baldwin

FEATHERSTON, MONTGOMERY, 1814-1849, Married Emily Agee, 1823-1859
Children: James Henry, 1845-1901, Married Sallie Massie Ragland
Amanda E., Died 1902

FEATHERSTON, N. R., Married Anna Marshall, 1870-1934
Father: James Henry Featherston   Mother: Sallie Massie Ragland
Children: Mary Elizabeth, 1912, Married Joseph B. Terry

FERGUSON, A. BLANCHE, 1878, Married Mattie Coleman, 1872
Children: Royal Baxter, 1903, Married Lillian Baldwin
Anna, 1905, Married Douglas Harris
Juddie, 1907, Married Howard Glover
Paul Coleman, 1909, Married Emma Gregory 1911-1935.
Second wife: Mrs. Eunice Williams

FERGUSON, ALBERT, 1900, Married Victoria Doss, 1902
Children: Rachel, 1923
Eleanor, 1929

FERGUSON, ANDREW JACKSON, 1896, Married Ellen Smith, 1883
Children: Anna Bell, 1922
Alvin, 1926

FERGUSON, BEN M., 1871, Married Alberta Conner, 1873
Father: C. C. Ferguson   Mother: Sidnor Ferguson
Children: Mary Ethel, 1897, Married C. J. Paulett
Sidney Virginia, 1898, Married R. E. Wooldridge
Flossie Estell, 1900, Married Walter C. Doss
Lucile, 1905, Married Willie T. Puckett
Della Bettie, 1909, Married Oscar Duvall St. Clair
Conner Alvin, 1911, Married Mary Bell Evans
Eva Alberta, 1913, Married A. C. Lerner
Clyde Robert, 1918, Married Elizabeth Violet Rice

FERGUSON, BRYANT DEMARCAS, 1850-1915, Married Louise Bagby, 1846-
1929
Children: Daniel T., 1875, Married Bertha Irene Doss, 1881-1920
Blanche, 1877, Married Mattie Coleman
Mathew, 1880, Married Carrie Beasley
Mary Elizabeth, 1883, Married Willie T. Childers
Minnie Bruce, 1886, Married George E. LeFew
Edward, 1890, Married Mamie Trent

FERGUSON, C. C., 1841-1935, Married Sidnor Ferguson
Children: Puss
Richard, Married Virginia Bingham
Napoleon, Married Lizzie Bingham
Ben, Married Alberta Connor
Daniel, Married Mattie Woodson
Susie
John, Married Alice Woodson
Roland, Married Lelia Smith
Toney, Married Etta Ferguson
Jack
Second wife: Nannie Harris, 1869
Children: Esta, 1890, Married Clifford Wooten
Lee, 1892, Married Elba Baldwin

FERGUSON, C. C., (continued)

        Wade, 1894, Married Tressie Martin
        Nettie, 1896, Married Willie McCormick
        Bertha, 1898, Married Henry Almond
        Alice, 1900, Married Sam Scruggs
        Dewey, 1902, Married Essie Smith
        Evan, 1904, Married Mary Morris
        Minnie, 1906, Married Floyd Martin
        Hattie, 1908, Married Charlie McFadden
        Hopkins, 1910, Married Gladys Bryant
        Hallie, 1912, Married Frances Seay

FERGUSON, CHARLIE L., 1857-1932, Married Jinnie V. Worley
    Children: Turlie, Married Courtney Baldwin
                Dan
                Sam, Married Susie Baldwin
                Frances, Married Herman Richardson
                Bettie, Married Dannie Williams
    Twins   (Pink, Married Richard Davis
            (Preston, Married Bessie Worley
                Ada, Married Thomas Davis
                Laura, Married Cleve Baldwin

FERGUSON, CHARLES JENNINGS, 1876, Married Nannie Simms, 1877
    Father: Daniel P.   Mother: Nancy D. Conner
    Children: Iva Mae, 1904, Married A. Walker Covington
                Idelle M., 1906, Married Jackson King of Montgomery
                Thelma J., 1908, Married Robert E. Lucado
                Hunter Daniel, 1911, Married Grace Burnett
                Addie Lena, 1915, Married Willard T. Paulette

FERGUSON, CLARIPA S., 1841-1864

FERGUSON, DANIEL P., 1844-1938, Married Nancy D. Conner, 1845-1922
    Children: Addie, 1868-1946, Married Charlie H. Morris
                Virgie E., 1870, Married Ben Walker O'Brien
                Tom M., 1873-1936, Married Corris L. Doss, 1875
                Charles Jennings, 1876, Married Nannie Simms, 1877
                Luke A., 1878-1947, Married Ada Lena Wooldridge, 1884
                Robert Hurley, 1883, Married Josie Wright

FERGUSON, DANIEL T., 1875, Married Bertha Irene Doss, 1881-1920
    Father: Bryant Demarcas Ferguson   Mother: Louise Bagby
    Children: Eunice Odell, 1901, Married Mott Perdue
                Carol W., 1903, Married Mary Coleman
                Mary, 1906, Married Realie Fore of Campbell
                Twyman, 1908, Married Luther Moore of Georgia
                William Thomas, 1911, Married Ethel Thompkins of Lynchburg
                Robert, 1914, Married Vivian Flowers of Lynchburg
                David, 1916
                Mabel, 1917, Married Edward Bagby of Lynchburg
                Lula, 1918, Married Sam Fielder of Bedford
                Edith, 1919, Married Cloris Reams of Lynchburg

FERGUSON, DELIA EMMA, 1838-1854

FERGUSON, DAVID BERKLEY, 1917, Married Virginia Trent, 1920

FERGUSON, ELISHA, 1905, Married Hattie Bryant, 1909
    Children: Frances, Married Emmett Harris
                Erma
                Bobby
                Lloyd
                Oral

FERGUSON, GEORGE L., 1843-1912, Married Victoria Lewis
    Children: Samuel L., 1868-1934, Married Adelia Mann, 1872
                Mary E., 1872, Married James M. Doss
                Maggie, 1874, Married Charles H. Doss
                Emma, 1876, Married Harrington Stanley
                Clara, 1880-1918, Married Wilburn Wooldridge
                Leslie F., 1885-1948

FERGUSON, GEORGE LEWIS, 1900, Married Beulah Lee Martin
    Father: Richard Toler   Mother: Margaret Virginia Bingham
    Children: Betty Luvinia, 1932

FERGUSON, HARRY THOMAS, 1899, Married Ada Carter
    Children: Harry, Jr., 1929
                Herbert Wayne, 1938

FERGUSON, HENRY WINSTON, 1873, Married Lillie Morris, 1878
    Children: Mary Frances, 1907
                Rachel Irma, 1909
                Ruby Earle, 1911, Married Henry Covington
                Madeline Oneida, 1914, Married W. E. Inge
                David Winston, 1916
                Nathaniel Lloyd, 1921

FERGUSON, JAMES H., 1911, Married Queenie Myrlene McCormick, 1916
    Children: Terry Gene, 1933
                Nancy Estelle, 1935

FERGUSON, JARRETT, 1802-1862, Married Judith Catherine Paris, 1816-1890
    Children: Daniel Wyatt
                Lucy Joradia
                Elizabeth, Married Alonza Hamilton
                Martha Susan, Married Richard Hamilton
                Josiah Paris, died 1923
                Branch, Married Nannie Dodd of Buckingham
                Samuel A., Married Bessie Rosser
                Rosa Alice, Married C. C. Calhoun

FERGUSON, J. SHELTON, 1882-1922, Married Ossie Morris, 1884
    Children: Bernard Warren, 1904, Married Catherine Turner of
                                              Richmond
                Basil Hubert, 1905-1921
                Morris Enderwood, 1907, Married Evelyn Cullop

FERGUSON, J. SHELTON, (continued)
           Nellie Grey, 1909, Married B. L. Atmore of Richmond
           James Meade, 1912
           Lawrence Nathaniel, 1914, Married Marion Ragsdale of
                      Richmond
           Mary Marjorie, 1918, Married Errall Wynkoop of
                      Pennsylvania
           Henry Westmoreland, 1917
           Naomi W., 1920, Married Joseph Currie of Richmond
           Florence Clemice, 1922
           Bessie Hamner, 1915, Married Wilson Scruggs, 1914
           Lillian Clarice, 1911, Married Hunter Marshall Paris, 1909

FERGUSON, JOHN JAMES, 1830-1857

FERGUSON, JOSEPH D., 1907, Married Sarah T. Morton
    Father: Samuel L. Ferguson   Mother: Adelia Celestia Mann
    Children: Joseph D., Jr., 1926
               Morton, 1928
               Samuel L., III, 1932

FERGUSON, LUKE A., 1878-1947, Married Ada Lena Wooldridge, 1884
    Father: Daniel P. Ferguson   Mother: Nancy D. Conner
    Children: William D., 1906, Married Louise W. Fletcher, 1906

FERGUSON, MARGARET LOUISA, 1835-1855

FERGUSON, MARY JANE 1826-1897, Married William Little

FERGUSON, RICHARD TOLER, died 1923, Married Margaret Virginia Bingham
    Father: C. C. Ferguson   Mother: Sidnor Ferguson
    Children: Pearl, Married N. E. Garrette
               Ernest, Married Lucy Woodson
               Ellie Gertrude, Married J. K. Pulliam, 1892
               Tom Wiley, Married Josie Jamerson
               Richard Bernard, Married Sallie Wingfield
               George Lewis, Married Beulah Martin

FERGUSON, SAMUEL A., 1857-1934, Married Bessie Rosser
    Father: Jarrett Ferguson   Mother: Judith Catherine Paris
    Children: Mary Judy, Married Allen Carter of Buckingham
               Sammie, Married G. L. Furr of Bluefield, West Virginia

FERGUSON, SAMUEL L., 1868-1934, Married Adelia Celestia Mann, 1873
    Father: George L. Ferguson   Mother: Victoria Lewis
    Children: Virginia Victoria, 1895-1943, Married D. B. Henderson, Jr.
                            of Bedford
               Russell Mae, 1899, Married Ned A. Wagers
               Samuel Lewis, Jr., 1901, Married Loretta Hockhart of
                            Richmond
               Harry Gordon, 1903-1903
               Rachel Adelia, 1905, Married J. R. Lawson
               Joseph D., 1907, Married Sarah T. Morton

FERGUSON, SARAH A., 1806-1868

FERGUSON, SARAH E., 1824

FERGUSON, THOMAS M., 1873-1936, Married Corris L. Doss, 1875
    Father: Daniel P. Ferguson Mother: Nancy D. Conner
    Children: Harry Lewis, 1905-1934
               Eleanor Rosa, 1906, Married Penick Harvey
               Elsie Lois, 1908, Married Peyton Shrader of Amherst
               Irene Lillian, 1909, Married John Mann
               Dorothy, 1922, Married Mobrey J. Carter

FERGUSON, "TONEY" WILLIE ALBERT, 1879, Married Mary Etta Ferguson,
                                              1882
    Father: C. C. Ferguson Mother: Sidnor Ferguson
    Children: Obediah Walker, 1902
               Henry Albert, 1900, Married Victoria Doss
               John Robert, 1905, Married Minnie Gilbert
               Jesse Edward, 1908, Married Ola Phelps
               James Herbert, 1911, Married Etta Phelps
                             Second wife, Maralene McCormick
               Lorine, Married Allen Wooldridge
               Second husband: Toney Strict

FERGUSON, WILLIAM ANDREW, 1832-1857

FERGUSON, WILLIAM D., 1906, Married Louise W. Fletcher, 1906
    Father: Luke A. Ferguson Mother: Ada Lena Wooldridge
    Children: Katherine Yvonne, 1938

FERGUSON, WILLIAM W., 1800-1854

FERRELL, W. P., Married Lillian Crouch of Buchanan
    Children: W. E.
               Beulah L.
               Joseph D., Married Alice Goin
               H. P., Married Leona Keller of Baltimore

FISHER, REV. WILLIAM, 1818-1898, Married Matilda Lotz, died 1899, of
                                          Pennsylvania
    Children: T. Howard, 1843-1921
               Annie S., 1844-1922
               Dr. W. Frank, 1849-1930, Married Miss Hoffman of Bedford
                              Second wife: Miss Scott of Halifax
               Mamie S., 1848-1884
               Juddie, 1854-1937, Married Robin Y. Johnson of Boutetort
               John G., 1858-1947
               Dr. E. D., 1867-1938

FITZGERALD, FRANCIS B., 1880, Married Margaret Davel of Scotland
    Children: Mary Hill, 1909, Married Sam Bryant of Zuni

FITZGERALD, FRANCIS B., (continued)
          Francis B., Jr., 1910, Married Edith Smith, 1920
          Jessie, 1912, Married Albert Baird of Buckingham
          Isaac Moon, 1913, Married Christine Smith of Farmville
          Virginia, 1916, Married Norman Spencer of Buckingham
          Thomas E., 1919

FITZGERALD, JR., FRANCIS B., Married Edith Smith
     Father: Francis B. Fitzgerald   Mother: Margaret Davel
     Children: Francis B., III, 1940

FITZGERALD, WESLEY, Married Martha Ann Dowell

FLESHMAN, CLYDE, Married Margaret Bell Cheatham, 1909-1940
     Children: Margeret, 1935

FLESHMAN, DELMA MAE, 1928
          Cornelia Arlene, 1932

FLESHMAN, FLOYD WHITEHEAD, 1869-1907, Married Mattie Pankey,
                                                            1879-1928
     Children: James Thomas, 1903, Married Carrie Frances Carwile
          Aubrey Tyler
          Floyd Walker
          Lowell Donald

FLESHMAN, JAMES PASCHAL, 1847-1923, Married Martha T. Bailey
     Father: Simeon Buford Fleshman   Mother: Annie Leigh
     Children: William Leigh
          Robert Custis, Married Miss Morris
          Thomas Shirley
          Mary Annie, Married C. N. Abbitt
          Randolph Tucker
          Elizabeth Paschal, Married Mr. Cofer of Bluefield
          Lucy Daniel, Married Mr. Frazier of Chilhowie
          Mattie James
          Ethel Terry, Married George Purdum
     Twins   (Maggie, Married Mr. Whitlow of West Virginia
              (Arthur

FLESHMAN, JAMES THOMAS, 1903, Married Carrie Frances Carwile
     Father: Floyd Whitehead Fleshman   Mother: Mattie Pankey
     Children: Lowell Donald
          James Thomas, Jr.
          Shirley Frances
          Wilber Clayton

FLESHMAN, SIMEON BUFORD, Married Annie Leigh
     Children: Sarah J.
          Mary A.
          Fannie A.
          William
          James Paschal, 1847-1923, Married Martha T. Bailey

FLETCHER, J. E., 1858-1936, Married Ame Katherine Watts, 1862-1938
    Children: William Jesse, 1884
                 Louise W., 1906, Married William D. Ferguson

FLOOD, MAJOR HENRY, 1755-1827, Married Mrs. Walker
    Children: Dr. Joel Walker, 1789-1858, Married Eliza Bolling West

FLOOD, COLONEL HENRY, 1816-1872, Married Mary Elizabeth Trent,
                                                              1822-1839
    Father: Dr. Joel Walker Flood   Mother: Eliza Bolling West
    Children: Joel Walker, 1839-1916, Married Ella Faulkner, 1844-1885
                                  Second wife, Mrs. Jennie Pleasants
                                  Third wife, Sallie Delk, 1850-1927

FLOOD, HENRY DELAWARE, 1865-1921, Married Anna Portner
    Father: Joel Walker Flood   Mother: Ella Faulkner
    Children: Bolling Byrd, 1916
                 Eleanor, 1918

FLOOD, DR. JOEL WALKER, 1789-1858, Married Eliza Bolling West
    Father: Major Henry Flood   Mother: Mrs. Walker
    Children: Colonel Henry, 1816-1872, Married Mary Elizabeth Trent,
                                                              1822-1839

FLOOD, JOEL WALKER, 1839-1916, Married Ella Faulkner, 1844-1885
    Father: Colonel Henry Flood   Mother: Mary Elizabeth Trent
    Children: Bolling, Married Richard Evelyn Byrd of Winchester
                 Henry Delaware, 1865-1921, Married Anna Portner of
                                                              Washington
                 Holmes - died young
                          Third wife, Sallie Delk, 1850-1927
    Children: Joel West, 1894, Married Dorothy Evans

FLOOD, JOEL WEST, 1894, Married Dorothy Evans 1909
    Father: Joel Walker Flood   Mother: Sallie Delk
    Children: Henry D., 1943

FORD, JAMES ROBERT, 1898, Married Anna Frances Purdum, 1902
    Father: Thomas H. Ford   Mother: Evy May Marshall
    Children: James R. Ford, Jr.

FORD, THOMAS H., 1872, Married Evy May Marshall, 1872-1938
    Children: J. R., 1898, Married Annie Perdum
                 Ethel, 1901, Married W. T. Jordan, 1896
                 Fettie Harvey, 1903, Married L. B. Laughlon of Bedford
                 Evy Thomas, 1905, Married Carl Ewells of Amherst
                 Bernice, 1910, Married J. L. Pankey

FORD, WILLIAM BOYD, 1875-1946, Married Mary Elizabeth Gilliam, 1882
    Father: William L. Ford
    Children: W. W., 1904, Married Edna Brooks of Lynchburg
                 Frances, 1906, Married J. T. Guilfoil of Fredericksburg
                 W. B., Jr., 1913, Married Vivian Steger of Buckingham
                 Elizabeth, 1918, Married F. E. McCalley of Fredericksburg

FORD, WILLIAM LABON, 1868, Married Carrie Elder of Campbell, 1877
 Children: Frances
             William
             Samuel
             James

FORD, WILLIAM L., Married   Radie Ferguson
 Children: Walter F., 1871-1903, Married Gertrude Gilliam, 1869-1924
             William Boyd, 1875-1946, Married Mary Elizabeth Gilliam
                                                                 1882
             J. Dan, 1878-1947, Married Bessie Zimmerman
             Clara, Married   Crawford

FORD, W. W., Married Mary Elizabeth Smith, 1906
 Father: William Boyd Ford   Mother: Mary Elizabeth Gilliam
 Children: W. W., Jr., 1924, Married Helen Mitchell

FORE, CHARLIE, 1856-1924, Married Iantha Smith, 1861-1939
 Children: Vininka, 1878, Married Hunter Paulette
             Lucy, 1886-1923, Married W. N. Ferguson
             Thornton, 1882
             Lottie, 1890, Married S. T. Paulette
             Mary Ianthia, 1895, Married W. N. Ferguson

FORE, J. J., 1867-1931, Married Jose Booker Inge, 1874-1940
 Children: Bettie Rosa, 1887-1896
             William Henry, 1887-1913
             Lillie Mae, 1889-1930, Married Nevel Dinkins
             Lizzie Frances, 1891, Married Wiley Richardson
             James Allen, 1893, Married Flossie Atkinson
             Della May, 1895, Married L. L. Dickerson
             Grover Cleveland, 1897, Married Margaret Pippins
             Josephine, 1899, Married Arthur Hale
             Lucy Myrtle, 1901, Married William Banton
             Samuel Lawson, 1903, Married Mary Tucker

FORE, JOEL P., 1838- 1925)
             Mary   )
             Ann   )
             Agnes   )
             D. A. P.)
             Stephen)   Brothers and sisters
             Julius   )
             John   )
             James   )
             Judiah   )

FORE, JOEL RICHARD, 1854-1937, Married Iola Gray, 1893-1944
 Children: Hattie Gray, Married Mr. Charlton
             Annie P.
             John James
             R. Edwin, 1898, Married Liddia Rogers
             Rosa Lillian, Married Dr. Pleasants

FORE, PETER WINSTON, Married Mrs. Johnson
Children: Patrick H., Married Miss Agee

FORE, R. EDWIN, 1898, Married Liddia Rogers
Father: Joel Richard   Mother: Iola Gray
Children: R. E. Jr., 1928
             Rosalia Ann, 1938

FORE, R. H., 1884, Married Annie Ramsey, 1896, of Charlotte
Children: Edith, 1918, Married C. C. Hevender of Augusta
             Helen, 1921, Married Clifford Brown of New Jersey
             May, 1925, Married Robert E. Berry of Tennessee

FOSTER, JOSEPH L., 1833-1907, Married Bessie Royster, 1862-1935, of
                                                          Richmond
Children: Minnie, 1880-1913, Married W. C. Evans
             Lucy Cabell, 1890, Married C. W. Smith, 1888

FOX, JOHN ELWOOD, Married Elizabeth P. Trent, 1904
Children: John Elwood, Jr., 1929
             William Trent, 1931
             Betty England, 1935
             Marilyn Frances, 1937

FRANKLIN, ABDALH B., 1875, Married Ella Gobble, 1894
Father: Jesse Franklin   Mother: Mary Etta Gowin
Children: Louetta, 1915-1917
             Etta, 1916-1918
             Beulah, 1917
             Lewis, 1929, Married Piggy Whitten
             Alexander, 1922, Married Miss Hubbard of Amherst
             A. B., Jr., 1924, Married Nellie Bryant
             Benjamin, 1928
             Clarence, 1930
             Cary Junson, 1934
             Thomas Jefferson, 1937

FRANKLIN, CLIFTON E., 1875, Married Margaret Wooten, 1874-1910, of
                                                          Buckingham
Father: Fred Franklin   Mother: Martha Goin
Children: Early, Married Viola Kestner
             Julian, Married Edith Jamison
             Martha Ann, died 1930, Married Richard Baber
             Cliff E., Jr., Married Florence Watson
                          Second wife: Annie Walker Smith
Children: Floris, 1912, Married Clyde White
             James, 1913, Married Connie Carwile
             Wesley, 1916, Married Ruby Goin
             David, 1918, Married Murnice Smith
             Mattie, 1921, Married James Franklin
             Annie Mabel, 1933

FRANKLIN, FREDERICK, Married Martha Goin
    Children: Robert, Married Cora Wootten of Buckingham
                  Sam Dibrel, Married Lou Amos of Buckingham
                  Clifton E., 1875, Married Margaret Wooten, 1874-1910
                              Second wife: Annie Walker Smith
                              Second wife: Bessie Conner
    Children: Courtney, Married Margaret Franklin
                  Lizzie
                  Mary
      Twins   (Jesse, Married Miss Carrico
                  (Witt

FRANKLIN, JAMES, 1797-1873, Married Rhods Thomas, 1807-1873

FRANKLIN, JESSE, 1849-1945, Married Mary Etta Gowen, 1845-1903
    Children: Abdalh B. 1875, Married Ella Gobble, 1894

FRANKLIN, JOHN, 1760-1820, Married Agnes Walker, 1770-1849

FRANKLIN, JOHN ROBERT, Married Martha J. Watson
    Children: Emma Walker, 1856, Married W. D. Thornton
                  W. Courtney, 1858
                  Alice Wyatt, 1860, Married James F. Connelly
                  John A., 1862-1863
                  Samuel Howell, 1864, Married Corrinne Roach
                  Idella Roberta, 1867-1868
                  Robert Leonord, 1868, Married Rosa Hamlet
                  James W., 1870-1935
                  Sallie, 1872, Married C. T. Watkins
                  John R., 1875-1875

FRANKLIN, ROBERT, 1700

FRANKLIN, ROBERT STERLING, 1895, Married Mattie Myrtle Carwile
    Children: Stratton Howard, 1925
                  Catherine Mae, 1928
                  Raymond Sterling, 1930
                  Dillard Leslie, 1943

FRANKLIN, SAMUEL RICE, 1843-1921, Married Mary Jane Burruss, 1849-1919
                          Served as General R. E. Lee's Courier.
    Children: James Henry
                  Kate M.

FURBUSH, CHARLES HENRY, 1856-1918, Married Sarah Ellen Dickerson,
                                        1856-1945
    Father: Jefferson D. Furbush Mother: Matilda Jane Cheatham
    Children: Thomas Jefferson, 1878-1898
                  Frank Irving
                  Nathan H., 1888-1889
                  Lawrence Ellis, Married Ola Sears
                  Kenneth Wilbur, 1893, Married Florence Hancock
                  Eunice Ellen, 1895, Married Herbert S. Jones, 1888

FURBUSH, LAWRENCE ELLIS, Married Ola Sears
    Father: Charles Henry Furbush   Mother: Sarah Ellen Dickerson
    Children: Ellen Ann, Married Mr. Carter of Kentucky
                Ola, Married Jack James

GALLIER, BENJAMIN, 1886-1930, Married Annie Paulette
    Children: Hubert Walker, 1904, Married Hazel Brooks, 1908, of
                                         Campbell
                Clide, 1906, Married Bercha Hamilton of Lynchburg
                Eunice, 1908, Married Herman Maddox of Lynchburg
                Louise, 1911, Married Paul Huston of Lynchburg
                Joseph Carl, 1914, Married Dorothy Cunningham of Buena
                                              Vista
                Maggie, 1918, Married Samuel Almond
                Sterling, 1920
                Shelton, 1925
                Margaret Louise, 1934, Married Calvin McCormick
                Claude Walker

GALLIER, HUBERT WALKER, 1904, Married Hazel Brooks, 1908
    Father: Benjamin Gallier   Mother: Annie Paulette
    Children: Benny Darvis, 1937
                Nancy Lee, 1939
                John Boyd, 1943

GARDNER, EPHRIAM B., 1837-1914, Married Margaret K. Martin, 1846-1929
    Children: William E., 1869-1939
                Charlie, 1871-1932
                Mary Alice, 1877, Married S. B. Phelps
                Thomas J., 1879, Married Eva Moore
                            Second wife: Maggie Phelps
                Robert M., 1882-1946

GARDNER, THOMAS J., 1879, Married Maggie Phelps
    Father: E. B. Gardner   Mother: Margaret K. Martin
    Children: Ethel, 1915
                Elizabeth, 1917
                Emza, Married Walter Cawthorn
                Allen, Married Clara Martin
                Roberta, Married Fleming Drinkard

GARRETT, CALVIN NICHOLAS, 1837-1914, Married Harriet Louellen Bagby,
                                      1848
    Children: Katherine Elizabeth, 1867-1906
                Arthur Sworphy, 1870-1942, Married Emma Maxey of
                                      Buckingham
                Mary Archer, 1872-1935, Married Frank L. Hendricks of
                                      Illinois
                Kendrick Maben, 1874-1938, Married Minta Osborne of
                                      Burkeville
                Lucy Ann, 1877, Married J. M. Watts of Lynchburg
                Harriet Virginia, 1880, Married John Paulette Ranson
                (James Albert, 1882-1947, Married Clara Farmer of Franklin
    Twins   (William Calvin, 1882, Married Beatrice Inge

GARRETT, CALVIN NICHOLAS, (continued)
George Cleveland, 1885, Married Mattie Haley of Meherrin
Second wife: Abbie Ayers of Danville
Helen M., 1887-1889
Janette, 1889, Married Russell Paulette

GARRETT, JAMES ALBERT, 1882-1947, Married Clara Farmer
Father: Calvin Nicholas Garrett   Mother: Harriet Louellen Bagby
Children: Helen Isabel, 1920, Married Toby Inge
Nelson N., 1923
James Melvin, 1925
Ethel L., 1929, Married Kenneth St. John

GARRETTE, JOSEPH H., 1861-1926, Married Clementine Gilbert, 1860-1939
Children: Monroe Lumsden, 1884-1934, Married Mollie S. Bagby
Charles Henry, 1886, Married Georgie Elizabeth Carner
Mary Haskins, 1888, Married John William Scruggs
Mabel Holmes, 1891, Married Leighton Cheatwood Hatcher
Lillian N., 1893, Married Lawrence Jesse Hatcher
Joseph Wiley, 1895, Married Anita Menefee Crobarger
Percy Alton, 1897, Married Ethel Mattie Carson

GARRETT, LEWIS WALKER, 1892, Married Annie Frances Thompson, 1909
Father: William C. Garrett   Mother: Mariah Coleman
Children: Dorothy Lee, 1932
Lewis Christian, 1934
John Ryland, 1936

GARRETTE, MONROE LUMSDEN, 1884-1934, Married Mollie S. Bagby, 1886
Father: Joseph H. Garrette   Mother: Clementine Gilbert
Children: Frances Christine, 1909, Married James F. MacKenzie
Joseph Monroe, 1911-
David Bagby, 1913-1926
Lyle North, 1915, Married Alma Burton Carson
Alfra Josephine, 1917, Married George Hanson
Marshall Jefferson, 1920, Married Ann Hope Walker
Alice Elizabeth, 1922, Married John Moore
Garland Burke, 1924

GARRETTE, PERCY ALTON, 1897, Married Ethel Mattie Carson
Father: Joseph H. Garrette   Mother: Clementine Gilbert
Children: Volney
Frances
David

GARRETT, WILLIAM C., Married Mariah Coleman of Buckingham
Children: Mary Elizabeth, 1878, Married Fitz. L. Martin
Spencer, 1880, Married Annie Harris
Fletcher, Married Queen Victoria Harris
L. Walker, 1892, Married Annie Frances Thompson, 1909
Thomas A., 1895, Married Mary Robertson

GARRETT, WILLIAM CALVIN, 1882-Married Beatrice Inge
    Father: Calvin Nicholas Garrett   Mother: Harriet Louellen Bagby
    Children: Margaret Lina, 1926, Married Melvin Grishaw
              Harriet Louise, 1928, Married Tommy Paulette
      Twins   (David Inge, 1930
             (Doris Marie, 1930

GAYLE, L. L., 1883, Married Edythe Atwood

GILBERT, SEABORN A., 1872-1943, Married Annie Morris, 1871-1941
    Children: Alice, Married Mr. Adamee
              Howard, Married Carrie Pankey
              Ora
              Robert, 1900, Married Bernice Bingham
              Rachel
              Berkeley
              Florence, Married Sam Coleman
              Annie, Married LeGrand Webb
              Estelle

GILES, HARRY BYRD, 1925, Married Sarah Mitchell
    Father: Llewellyn Giles   Mother: Julia Scott Martin
    Children: Katherine Scott, 1946

GILES, LLEWELLYN, 1893, Married Julia Scott Martin, 1896
    Children: Marian Elaine, 1916, Married Pat Godsey
              Llewellyn, Jr., 1920, Married Georgia Hamilton
              Harry Byrd, 1925, Married Sarah Mitchell

GILLIAM, A. SPENCER, 1860-1943, Married Annie E. Gilliam, 1864
    Children: Kathleen

GILLIAM, JR., C. B., Married Nellie Brooks, 1922
    Father: C. Bruce Gilliam   Mother: Mary Reynolds
    Children: Linda B., 1944

GILLIAM, C. BRUCE, 1856-1939, Married Bettie M. Cobb of Charlotte
    Children: Clara, Married F. W. Wilkerson
              Lawrence, Married Miss Anderson of Kentucky
                   Second wife: Mary Reynolds, 1875
    Children: W. E., 1908, Married Viola Woodson of Lynchburg
              Elizabeth, 1910, Married R. A. Campbell of Lynchburg
              C. B., Jr., 1913, Married Nellie Brooks, 1922
              Frank, 1917, Married Euther Brooks, 1919

GILLIAM, HENRY EVANDER, 1845-1899, Married Margaret Alice Sears,
                                        1848-1889
    Father: Spencer Gilliam   Mother: Mary Elizabeth Dupuy
    Children: Harry Edward, 1871, Married Dorothy Turpin of Bedford
              Eugene William, 1873-1931, Married Bessie Perrow
                        Second wife: Lucy D. Marshall

GILLIAM, HENRY EVANDER, (continued)
        Thomas Dupuy, 1877-1945, Married Annie Gwynn, of North
                     Carolina
        Herbert Spencer, 1878, Married Lessie Moore Hill of West
                     Virginia
        Otis Mathew, 1880-1910, Married Lillian Glenn
        Leonard Statham, 1887, Married Marie Moseley of North
                     Carolina
        Gertrude, 1869-1924, Married Walter F. Ford, 1871-1903
                 Second husband: Phil Gilliam
        Elizabeth, 1882, Married William Boyd Ford, 1875-1946
        Alice, 1884, Married Henry Morton Marshall, 1867-1943
        Myrtle, 1885, Married Edward Percy Sears, 1872

GILLIAM, J. J., 1852-1931, Married Delia North of Campbell, 1855-1928
    Children: Lena, Married Alfred Wood
             Chessie, Married E. T. Wright
             Aubrey, 1882, Married Mary Agee
             Morton, 1884, Married Lizzie Agee
             Carney, 1884, Married Fannie Gills of Bedford
             Herman, 1886, Married Rachel May of Lynchburg
             Charles Henry, 1896, Married Lillian Harvey of Lynchburg

GILLIAM, JOHN W., 1860-, Married Fannie D. Cary, 1863, of Prince Edward
    Children: Fannie Lillian, 1885, Married Bernard T. Cary
             William Morton, 1887, Married Miss Moomaw of Roanoke
             Janie Logan, 1889, Married T. J. Ligon

GILLIAM, JOSEPH BARNETT, 1852-1912, Married Sarah Emma Chambers,
                                     1853-1936
    Children: Mary, Married H. P. Gills

GILLIAM, LILLEOUS HERBERT, 1858-1902, Married Lily Christian Harvey,
                                       1860
    Children: William Herbert, 1897, Married Mary Rhodes
             Frank Walker, 1899, Married Mary Burkholder of Roanoke
             Marguerite

GILLIAM, OTIS MATHEWS, 1880-1910, Married Lillian Glenn, 1886
    Father: Henry Evander Gilliam   Mother: Margaret Alice Sears
    Children: Herbert E., 1909, Married Helen Hugelman of Roanoke
             Otis Mathews, Jr., 1910, Married Mary Schwarzelle of
                               Roanoke

GILLIAM, RICHARD HOBSON, 1831-1884, Married Sarah Adalaid Pankey,
                                     1838-1888
    Children: Fleeda, 1861-1931
             Mattie Richard, Married John H. Marshall, Jr.
    Twins   (Lelia Mosley, 1863- Married Hilleary Harvey
          (Laura Elizabeth, 1863, Married George Henry Singleton

GILLIAM, SPENCER, 1805-1879, Married Mary Elizabeth Dupuy, 1810-1890
                                                    of Prince Edward
    Children: Evelyn Dupuy, 1842-1870, Married F. C. Ford of Lynchburg
                 Henry Evander, 1845-1899, Married Margaret Alice Sears,
                                                             1848-1889

GILLIAM, WATTS, Married Hilda Dinkins, 1923
    Children: Gloria, 1941

GILLIAM, W. CARNEY, 1884, Married Fannie Gills
    Father: J. J. Gilliam   Mother: Delia North
    Children: Wilsie, 1902, Married J. D. Allen of Prospect
                 Lee, 1912, Married Cora Via
                 Mary, 1915, Married Preston Elder of Lynchburg
                 Bessie, 1917, Married Charles Ranson
                 Cora Lee, 1919, Married "Huck" Babcock
                 Watt, 1922, Married Hilda Dinkins
                 W. C., Jr., 1925
                 Dabney, 1931

GILLS, DANIEL, 1840-   Married Martha Hix
    Children: Annie, Married Mr. Girkle
                 Edmund, Married
                 Mazie
                 Perry, Married
                 Carrie, Married Tom Payne

GILLS, EDMOND ERNEST, Married Lennice Rosser
    Father: James Thomas Gills   Mother: Cornelia Terrill Pitzer
    Children: Irene Cornelia
                 Ernest Winston
                 Robert Terrill
                 James Pitzer, Married Helena Dillger of Bluefield
                                 Second wife: Lucile Martin of Bluefield
                 Mary Louise
                 Julian Braxton
                 Edmond Theodore, Married Marion Wagner
                 Archibald Alexander

GILLS, GEORGE, Married Mary E. Hurt, -1878
    Children: Elizabeth, 1857, Married Frank P. Brightwell of Prince
                                                             Edward

GILLS, JAMES THOMAS, Married Cornelia Terrill Pitzer of Botetourt
    Father: William Perkins Gills, Sr.   Mother: Mary Wright
    Children: Edmond Ernest, Married Lennice Rosser
                 James, Married Miss Cawthorn
                 William Pitzer, Married Ella Agnes Pittman
                                 Second wife: Bertha O'Brien

GILLS, SR., WILLIAM PERKINS, Married Mary Wright
    Children: William Perkins, Jr., Married Mary Elizabeth Hix
                James Thomas, Married Cornelia Terrill Pitzer of Botetourt
                William Henry, Married Mary Ranson of Buckingham

GILLS, WILLIAM PITZER, 1859-1941, Married Ella Agnes Pittman, 1862-1896
    Father: James Thomas Gills Mother: Cornelia Terrill Pitzer
    Children: Elizabeth, 1883-1885
             Henry Pitzer, 1884, Married Mary Gilliam, 1887
             Lucy M., 1890, Married Luther B. Pittman of Halifax
                      Second wife: Bertha O'Brien, 1876
    Children: Cornelia Kyle, 1901, Married James A. Conner of Halifax
             Mary Taylor, 1903, Married W. H. Copenhaver of Smyth
             William James, 1904-1906
             Joseph Allen, 1906, Married Miss Wood of Lynchburg
             S. Kennard, 1907, Married Miss L. Atkins of King William
             Catherine, 1909, Married R. B. Frazier of North Carolina

GLENN, ERIE R., 1882, Married Pauline Coleman
    Father: Luther R. Glenn Mother: Nannie Wheeler
    Children: Virginia
             Maxine

GLENN, LUTHER R., 1861-1932, Married Nannie Wheeler
    Children: Erie R., 1882, Married Pauline Coleman
                    Second wife: Mollie B. Wheeler, 1860-1942
    Children: Herman A., 1884, Married Amy Lecompte of Maryland
             Lillian B., 1886, Married Otis Mathews Gilliam
             Earl, 1887-1888
             Lee R., 1889
             S. Myrle, 1891, Married Clara Jennings of Roanoke
             Joe B., 1893, Married Mavis Mitchell of Charlottesville
             Thomas Henry, 1894, Married Mildred Bell of Rockbridge
             (Bessie, 1900, Married Charles O. Calhoun of Roanoke
      Twins (Bertha, 1900, Married Melvin Beauchamp of Baltimore
             Lenwood B., 1904, Married Evely Shorter of Roanoke

GLOVER, ELIJAH FRANK, 1853-1939, Married Elnora Dabney Cawthorn
                                      1856-1933
    Children: George W. Glover, 1881, Married Bessie Williamson

GLOVER, ELIZABETH A., 1846-1906

GLOVER, GEORGE W., 1881 Married Bessie Williamson, 1884, of Charlotte
    Father: Elijah F. Glover

GLOVER, MARVIN A., 1893, Married Reva Roberts, 1894
    Children: Marvin A., Jr., 1928
             Carl M., 1931
             Fred C., 1937

GOBBLE, ALEX, 1875, Married Etta Layne of Washington County
Children: Ella, 1898, Married Abdahla Franklin
             Gilbert, 1900, Married Louise Nichols of Roanoke
             Beulah, 1902, Married D. L. Smith
             Ambrose, 1904, Married Evelyn Montgomery of Richmond
             Winnie, 1906, Married Johnnie Carter
                       Second husband: R. E. Bingham
             Georgia, 1908, Married Chap Garrette
             Summers, 1910, Married Lorine Handy
             Clarence H., 1913, Married Carrie Guill 1917
             Pauline, 1915, Married Joe Thompson
             Defrone, 1918, Married Hurbert Lucado
             Abraham, 1924, Married Dorothy Goff

GODSEY, GROVER CLEVELAND, (Pat), 1907, Married Marion Giles
Children: Leo, 1936
             Ted, 1938

GODSEY, ROBERT LEE, 1868-1932, Married Hattie R. Powell, 1870-1939
Children: Cliff, 1889
             Annie, 1890, Married Joseph Jamison
             Wiley, 1894, Married Maude Guthrie
             Willie, 1898
             Taylor, 1900-1932
             Berkley, 1903-1928
             Otha, 1909, Married Ardlin Godsey
             Harry, 1912
             Kermit, 1915
             Bessie, 1917, Married Thomas LeGrand

GOIN, DeWITT T., 1895, Married Katie C. Grebb, 1899-1926
Father: Joseph M. Goin   Mother: Mary E. Gunter
Children: Frank A., 1918
             John H., 1919
             Evie C., 1922
             DeWitt T., Jr., 1924-1926
             Conrad J., 1926
                    Second wife: Alice R. Brown   1912
Children: Joseph W., 1930
             Kate R., 1932
             Rachal A., 1934
             Hunter J., 1936
             Nannie B., 1939
             Marshall D., 1941
             Lester M., 1943
             Mary F., 1944
             Barbara L., 1946

GOIN, HENRY NELSON, 1875- Married Ella Franklin, 1876
Children: David

GOIN, JOSEPH M., 1832-1911, Married Mary E. Gunter, 1871
Children: Samuel H., 1893
             DeWitt T., 1895, Married Katie C. Grebb
                          Second wife: Alice R. Brown
             Susie M., 1897
             Cassie O., 1899
             Annie B., 1901
             Bessie, 1903
             Otis W., 1905
             Emit J., 1907

GOIN, RUBEN, Married Virginia Taylor
Children: Carrie, Married Paul Irvin
             Mary, Married Roy Price
             Frances, Married Peyton Seay
             Joel
             Rosa
             Barbara
             Elnora

GOODMAN, ALONZO M., 1855, Married Carrie Dickerson, 1848-1917
Children: Mary, 1879, Married Branch Coleman
             William D., 1881, Married Alice Spencer, 1880
             Lula Bell, 1883, Married Otha Martin
             Mittie A., 1885, Married W. B. Harvey, 1863-1934
             Charlie A., 1888, Married Myrtle Martin, died 1938

GOODWIN, THOMAS JACKSON, 1862-1911, Married Miss Coleman
                          Second wife: Josie B. Beal, 1867-
                                                    1905
                          Third wife: Alma Virginia Beale
Children: Mary Ellen, 1897
             John Thomas, 1899
             Etta, 1888, Married Mr. Harris

GORDON, EDWARD, Married Harriet Howard of Campbell
Children: Mary Elizabeth
             Sarah Ann, Married Joel W. F. Carnefix
             Nancy Clark, Married William Colvin
             Sam Howard
             Thomas
             Henry
             Elvira Campbell, Married Thomas Marsh
             James Edward, Married Mary Calhoun
                          Second wife: Rachel Harvey

GORDON, JAMES EDWARD, 1858-1924, Married Mary Calhoun
Father: Edward Gordon   Mother: Harriet Howard
                 Second wife: Rachel Harvey, 1872-1899
Children: Elsie

GORDON, JAMES LESLIE, 1896, Married Jessie Morris, 1897
   Children: James Leslie, Jr., 1918
              Maurice Elliott, 1919, Married Ella B. Lewis
              Frances Lobelia, 1922, Married Carmon Hilton of Wytheville
              Alfred Ray, 1931

GRAVES, F. P., 1864, Married Mary Jefferson of Pittsylvania, 1864
   Children: Mary C., 1891

GRAY, G. E., 1830- Married Rhoda Anderson, 1845-1929
   Children: J. E., 1868-1947, Married Ada Gordon
              Iola, 1870- Married J. R. Fore
              W. R., 1872, Married Mary Hayne of Buckingham

GREGORY, ABNER H., 1878-1924, Married Lillie Hancock, 1880
   Father: Nathaniel H. Gregory   Mother: Pattie Ellett
   Children: Florence, Married T. M. Trent
              Emma, Married P. C. Ferguson
              Charles

GREGORY, NATHANIEL H., 1841-1919, Married Pattie Ellett of Nottoway
                                           1856-1922
   Children: Abner, 1878-1924, Married Lillie Hancock, 1880
              Maude, 1880-1946, Married R. C. Moore
              Helen, 1883, Married J. Dillard Morris
              Leonard, 1888, Married Lucile Doley of Ohio

GRESHAW, L. L., 1844-1928

GRINELS, J. S., 1904, Married Ida H. Hoppich, 1915, of Pennsylvania

GROW, CHARLIE, 1872-1920, Married Alice Megginson, 1879
   Children: Julian B., 1907, Married Mary Elizabeth Hamilton, 1908
              Ida Florence, 1910, Married J. W. Mustain of Richmond

GROW, JOSEPH, Married Annie Moore
   Children: Samuel, Married Estell Grow
              Esmonia, Married Walker Martin
              James, Married Laura Whitehead

GROW, JOHN B., Married Miss Crews
   Children: Charlie, Married Alice Megginson
              Estelle, Married Samuel Grow
              Mallie B., Married Elridge Martin
                        Second husband, Hiram Martin
              Virgie,B., Married Jennie Childress of Lynchburg
              Abner
              Grover
              Pearl, Married Thomas M. Martin
              John, Married Olive Kerford of Roanoke
              Sidney
              Ida, Married Marvin Moore

GUILL, EDWARD T., 1903, Married Lula Iola Layne, 1907
    Father: Joel L. Guill   Mother: Bertha E. Carter
    Children: Doris Elizabeth, 1924, Married Alfred N. Luck of Lynchburg
                 Merlie Frances, 1927

GUILL, JAMES A., 1915, Married Elmana Barlow, 1920
    Children: Edward D., 1938
                 Linda, 1940

GUILL, FLETCHER T., 1892, Married Sadie Doss, 1892
    Father: N. F. Guill   Mother: Willie Viar
    Children: Jesse, 1910, Married Hilda McGuire of Amherst
                 Wilson, 1912, Married Nellie Tarsell
                 James Alfred, 1914, Married Elmana Barlow
                 Charlie, 1916, Married Mae Brawnings of Washington
                 Berkley, 1919
                 Thomas R., 1921, Married Martha Martin
                 Hal Flood, 1928

GUILL, JOEL L., 1881-1941, Married Bertha E. Carter, 1880
    Father: N. F. Guill   Mother: Willie Viar
    Children: Joel Taylor, 1901, Married Annie Maude Slemp of Tennessee
                 Edwart T., 1903, Married Lula Iola Layne
                 Clara Viola, 1905, Married Floyd Mitchell
                 Bertha Hester, 1907, Married Roy B. Witt of Lynchburg
                 Willie V., 1909, Married Robert Younger of Lynchburg
                 Ada Isabell, 1911, Married Zach Collins of South Boston
                 Rachel M., 1913, Married Fred Robertson
                 James Delaware, 1915, Married Margaret Jordon of Concord
                 Hattie Cornelia, 1917, Married Percy George of Chatham
                 Julian Crafton, 1919
                 Dan Twyman, 1920

GUILL, MOTY SIMS, 1890, Married Mattie Viola Doss, 1895-1940
    Children: James Middleton, 1920
                 William Rudolph, 1930
                 Ethel, Married C. M. Carter
                 Alice Virginia, 1924, Married B. C. Phelps

GUILL, N. F., 1861-1916, Married Willie Viar, 1859-1944
    Children: Joel, 1881-1943, Married Bertha Carter
                 Thomas, 1883, Married Cleo Drinkard
                              Second wife: Miss Morris
                 Virginia, 1885, Married T. Goodman
                 Annie, 1887-1932, Married Holmsey Smith
                 Herman, 1888, Married Myrtle McCormick
                 Octavia, 1890-1946, Married George Iverson Smith
                 Fletcher T., 1892, Married Sadie Doss, 1892
                 Samuel, 1896, Married Ida Dove

GUILL, WILLIAM HERMAN, 1888, Married Myrtle McCormick 1890
    Father: N. F. Guill   Mother: Willie Viar
    Children: Gertie Virginia, 1910, Married Thomas Jamerson
                 Maggie
                 Elsie, 1911, Married Kit Thomas
                 Willie Elmo, 1913, Married Maude Coleman
                 Carrie Myrtle, 1917, Married Clarence Gobble
                 Randolph Deleware, 1920, Married Gladys Franklin
                 Rachel Lee, 1922, Married Olof Waddell of Charlotte
                 Myrna Christian, 1925, Married Richard Nash
                 Robert Allen, 1927
                 Ruth Annie, 1930
                 Mollie Jaunita, 1932

GUNTER, B. F., 1867, Married Bettie S. Thornton, 1863
    No Children

GUNTER, C. C., 1870-1943, Married Mary Catherine Wooten, 1871-1917
    Children: Lelia Ann, 1891, Married L. E. Mann
    Twins   (Emily, Frances, 1894, Married E. T. Mitchell
             (Eddie, 1894-1942, Married Eva Stone of Norfolk
                 William Walter, 1897, Married Mirna Stahl of Lynchburg
                 Mattie Pearl, 1900, Married K. T. Barlow
                 C. C., Jr., 1902, Married Hazel Roberts of Lynchburg
                 Robert Dunkley, 1905, Married Foy Tillery

GUNTER, JOHN R., 1871-1927, Married Alice O. Gunter, 1871-1927
    Children: Oswell U., 1896, Married Kate Harvey, 1897

GUNTER, OSWELL U., 1896, Married Kate Harvey, 1897
    Father: John R. Gunter   Mother: Alice O. Gunter
    Children: Phoebe Kester
                 William
                 Alice E.   1937

GUNTER, WILLIAM THOMAS, 1862-1946, Married Willie Ann McFadden,
                                                      1871-1944
    Children: Mattie Lillian, Married F. Lee Thornhill
                 Samuel Thomas, Married Laura Virginia Moore
                 Wyatt Hamner, Married Mary Crouch of Lynchburg
                 Esther, died in infancy
                 Edward Beacon, 1895-1918
                 Julia Blanche, Married Walter R. Saunders of Halifax
                 John Whitcomb, Married Virginia Alvis
                 Roy Washington, Married Helen Barlow
                 Aubrey Alfred, died young
                 Bessie, Married William D. O'Brien
                 Annie Ruth, died young
                 Thelma Christine, Married Robert Emmert of Pennsylvania

GUTHRIE, W., 1913, Married Margaret Estelle Pote, 1925, of Lynchburg

HALEY, ROBERT BRUCE, 1896, Married Goldie Marie Brown, 1905
    Children: Robert Bruce, Jr., 1926
                Wallace Greer, 1928
                Gayle

HALL, CHARLIE, 1913, Married Louise Stinson, 1918
    Children: Ruby, 1936

HALL, CLYDE RANDOLPH, 1940

HALL, DOROTHY, 1938

HALL, JOHNNIE, 1911

HALL, KATIE, 1917

HAMLIN, STEPHEN VIRGIL, 1888, Married Verdie Ponder, 1890

HAMMERSLEY, CHRISTOPHER CREED, 1856-1939, Married Mary Virginia
                                           Bell, 1868-1947
    Children: Thelma, 1898, Married Eugene Budd of Farmville

HAMMERSLEY, JAMES HARDY, 1853-1932, Married Nannie Scruggs, 1866-1939
    Children: Hazel V., Married Herbert Carrico
                Bessie, 1896, Married W. R. Raborg of Richmond
                James Andrew, 1882-1944
                Emmett Royal, Married Miss Saunders
                          Second wife, Mrs. Waymack
                Irvin
                Floyd, died 1921

HAMMERSLEY, JOSEPH DELBERT, 1851-1908, Married Agnes Bell Howard,
                                           1850-1919
    Children: Fannie, Married Luther Doss
                        Second husband: Mr. Ward
                Elwood Howard, 1878, Married Elizabeth Feather
                Henry Carrington, 1882-1943, Married Nannie Murrell
                Laura Bell, 1884-1919
                Lena Bernice, 1886, Married C. W. Bishop of Albemarle

HAMILTON, ALONZA, 1837-1914, Married Bettie Ferguson, 1845-1899
    Children: John D., 1863-1938, Married Virginia Inge, 1869
                Beulah, 1870-1947, Married W. H. Lucado
                Annie Judith, 1873-1908, Married Elbert Smith
                Samuel J., 1876-1890
                Mary Rose, 1879, Married Holmsey Inge
                William J., 1881-1942

HAMILTON, J. D., Married Fannie Burge
    Children: Venice Hazel, Married Harry Lucado
                  Raymond H., Married Virginia Moore
                  Elva, Married Warren Harris
                  Frances, Married R. L. Glover
                  Floyd, Married Nannie Sue Watson

HAMILTON, JAMES R., 1872, Married Carrie Cawthorn, 1876-1914
    Children: Lonelle, 1906, Married James T. Inge, 1906
                  John Kent, 1908, Married Ruby Wooldridge, 1913
                        Second wife of J.R., Mary Massie Cawthorn,
                                        1884-1940

HAMILTON, JOHN D., Married Virginia L. Inge, 1869
    Father: Alonza Hamilton   Mother: Bettie Ferguson
    Children: E. N., Married Emiline Shupe
                  W. A., Married Neva Morris
                  Harry
                  Russell

HAMILTON, JOHN KENT, 1908, Married Ruby Wooldridge, 1913
    Father: James R. Hamilton   Mother: Carrie Cawthorn
    Children: Richard Floyd, 1944
                  Donald K., 1946

HAMILTON, RICHARD ALVIN, 1874, Married Bessie.Patteson, 1876
    Father: William Hamilton   Mother: Mollie Browning
    Children: Kervin Vain, 1898, Married Clara Routen of Bedford
                  Mabel Kathleen, 1900
                  Robert St Clair, 1902, Married Ruperta Bailey of Lynchburg
                  Richard Alvin, Jr., 1904, Married Verna Morris, 1902
                  Lloyd Raymond, 1906, Married Miss Watts of Lynchburg
                        Second wife: Daisy Robertson, 1910
                  John William, 1910
                  Virginia Christian, 1915-1933
                  Hunt Patteson, 1923

HAMILTON, JR., RICHARD ALVIN, 1904, Married Verna Morris, 1902
    Father: Richard Alvin Hamilton   Mother: Bessie Patteson
    Children: Carolyn Ann, 1933
                  Julia Bell, 1939

HAMILTON, ROBERT, 1875
    Children: Raymond

HAMILTON, WILLIAM S., 1848-1918, Married Mary L. Browning, 1849-1930
    Children: R. A., 1874, Married Bessie Patteson
                  Alma, Married Cabel Moore
                  Florence, Married W. H. S. Barlow
                  Mabel, Married Mr. Jones
                  Winonah, Married E. J. Marsh
                  Reva, Married Mr. Gravely
                  J. D., Married Fannie Moore

HANCOCK, C. A., Married Ella Rosser
    Father: Charles W. Hancock   Mother: Emma C. LeGrand
    Children: Virginia, Married Mr. White
                Marguerite, Married Mr. Gimble
                Elizabeth
                Braxton, Married

HANCOCK, CHARLES W., 1853-1928, Married Emma Chessman LeGrand,
                                            1852-1921
    Children: Pete, Married
                C. A., Married Ella Rosser
                Lily, Married Abner H. Gregory
                Naomi

HANCOCK, THOMAS HARVEY, 1845-1928, Married Sallie Morgan
    Children: A Daughter married Mr. Campbell
                A Son married Maude Drinkard

HANCOCK, WALTER E., 1905, Married Lillian Caldwell, 1909
    Father: Walter M. Hancock   Mother: Matilda LeGrand
    Children: W. E., Jr., 1941

HANCOCK, WALTER M., 1864-1935, Married Matilda LeGrand, 1867
    Children: Grace LeGrand, 1892-1916
                Nannie Sue, 1895, Married W. W. Scott
                Emma Matilda, 1897, Married W. F. Woolfolk
                Annie Martin, 1899
                Jessalyn, 1902, Married P. S. Drinkard
                Walter E., 1905, Married Lillian Caldwell
                Corinne, 1909, Married Watkins M. Abbitt
                Nathan A., 1914-1915

HANDY, JAMES EMETT, 1888, Married Cassie Mays, 1892
    Children: Lessie, Married Jesse Mayberry
                Herbert
                Eugene
                Emmett

HANENKRAT, CHARLES F., 1894, Married Clara Cawthorn, 1904
    Father: F. W. Hanenkrat   Mother: Lena Wilhelm Rider
    Children: Fred, 1923
                Thomas, 1926
                Dorothy, 1928
                Inez, 1932
                Elizabeth, 1934

HANENKRAT, FRANKLIN WILHELM, 1872, Married Lena Wilhelm Rider,
                                        1875, of Ohio
    Children: Charles F., Married Clara Cawthorn
                F. W., Jr., Married Vara Conner

HARDING, BENNETT, 1896, Married Annie Martin, 1900
    Father: Howard Harding   Mother: Bessie Chick
    Children: Inez, 1920, Married Aubrey Drinkard
              Allyne, 1922, Married Otho Wells

HARDING, CHARLES J., 1862-1945, Married Mary Jane Crews, 1866-1945
    Father: Nicholas Harding   Mother: Angeline Chick
    Children: W. R., 1888, Married Susie Kesley of Amherst
              Wiley, 1894, Married Vara Henley of Michigan
              Walker, 1897, Married Alice Cheatham
                          Second wife: Bessie Wright
              Lyle M., 1899, Married Sarah Herrick of Norfolk
              Verna W.
              Jesse, 1908, Married Lizzie Helly of Greensville

HARDING, HERMAN, 1889, Married Earl M. Burge, 1898
    Father: H. G. Harding   Mother: Bessie Chick
    Children: Garland W., 1916
              I. M., 1920
              Bessie Jeane, 1931

HARDING, H. G., 1865-1929, Married Bessie Chick, 1867-1923
    Father: Nicholas Harding   Mother: Angeline Chick
    Children: Bennett, 1896
              Herman, 1889

HARDING, NICHOLAS C., 1816-1893, Married Angeline Chick, 1830-1898
    Children: H. G., 1865-1929, Married Bessie Chick, 1867-1923
              Charles J., 1862-1945, Married Mary Jane Crews, 1866-1945

HARDING, W. R., 1888, Married Susie Kesley of Amherst
    Father: Charles J. Harding   Mother: Mary Jane Crews
    Children: W. R., Jr., 1918
              Robert Lee, 1919

HARDY, THOMAS JOHNSON, 1819-1885, Married Lucy Elizabeth Cheadle,
                                      1835-1884
    Children: Edmonia Virginia, 1857-1939
              Thomas T., 1856-1940, Married Lucy Gills of Bedford
              John W., 1868- Married Hattie McFadden
              Kemper S., 1873-1941, Married Lucy Wilkerson
              Lucy, Married J. T. Hubbard
              Mary, Married C. W. Abbitt

HARRIS, CALVIN, 1929

HARRIS, D. MOSBY, 1894, Married Lela Walton, 1894
    Children: Richard, 1914, Married Lorine Gilliam
              Nannie, 1918, Married Elliott Carson

HARRIS, JOHN A., Married Mary E. Harris
    Children: Kemper L., Married Lula F. Doss
                  Harry H., Married Margaret M. Burge
                  Robert L., Married Ruby L. Harris
                  Frank C., Married Evely N. Whitehead

HARRIS, JOHN C., 1857-1939, Married Sallie Slagel, 1869-1927
    Children: J. S., 1888-1888
                  W. B., 1890, Married Pearl Thornhill
                  D. P., 1892
                  L. M., 1894
                  L. E., 1896
                  C. E., 1899
                  S. R., 1902
                  L. A., 1904
                  E. W., 1907-1908
                  E. O., 1910-1928

HARRIS, LEWIS MOSES, 1894, Married Alma Estelle Spiggle, 1905
    Children: Lewis H., 1924, Married Mary Lucile Boswell
                  Alice Gertrude, 1926, Married D. A. Allen of Nelson
                  Crawford Watts, 1931
                  Douglas Ray, 1946

HARRIS, MARSHALL, 1933

HARRIS, RICHARD, 1914, Married Lorine Gilliam
    Father: D. M. Harris   Mother: Lela Walton
    Children: Richard, Jr., 1943
                  Earle, 1945

HARRIS, W. BRANCH, 1890, Married Pearl Thornhill, 1893
    Father: John C. Harris   Mother: Sallie Slagel
    Children: Olivia Pearl, 1912
                  John Branch, 1918
                  Warren Newman, 1933
                  Sheby Jean, 1938

HARVEY, COURTNEY C., 1893, Married Elizabeth Harvey, 1890
    Father: William B. Harvey   Mother: Sallie B. Penick
    Children: Courtney Frances, Married B. H. Paulette

HARVEY, CORNELIUS, 1869, Married Mary Sue Kidd, 1870

HARVEY, BENNIE W., 1888, Married Margaret Lee Norfleet, 1890, of Suffolk
    Children: Edward Newton, 1918
                  Jessie Frances, 1920, Married Hubert Martin, 1900
                  Millard Vernon, 1921, Married Joan Lawson, 1929
                  Herman Wilson, 1922
                  Margaret Virginia, 1925, Married Eddie Lucado
                  Vivian Ann, 1927

HARVEY, EDWARD B., 1825, Married Elizabeth Cawthorn, 1839
Children: Elvira

HARVEY, EDWARD LARKIN, 1884, Married Mannie Pearl Clark, 1898
Children: Nettie Mae, 1920, Married Hubert Deadman
             Martha, 1922
             James Edward, 1924
             Willie Henry, 1925
             Mary Jane, 1927, Married Twyman Phelps
             Lewis Glover, 1932
             Ida Roberta, 1937

HARVEY, HILLIARY RICHARDSON, 1851-1910, Married Lelia Gilliam,
                                                         1863-1900
Father: Thomas Harvey   Mother: Frances Jennings
Children: Herman, Married Miss Woodall
             Thomas

HARVEY, JAMES FRANKLIN, 1872, Married Maggie Susan Johnson, 1881, of
                                                         North Carolina
Children: Emily, Married W. W. Burke
             Nell, Married Oscar Cole
                 Second husband: L. A. Young
             Willie Rebecca, 1910

HARVEY, JAMES WALTER, Married Roberta Phelps, 1875
Children: Percy

HARVEY, JAMES W., 1867-1947, Married Geneva Lewis, 1876-1934
Father: Thomas Harvey   Mother: Elvira Woodson
Children: Mae, 1900
             Lewis, 1899
             Mildred, 1903, Married L. W. Waters of Amherst
             Davis, 1908, Married Irwin J. Mack
             Willie, 1900-1912
             Ada, 1911
             James H., 1916, Married Mary Bell of Campbell

HARVEY, JESSE J., 1877, Married Lola Abbitt, 1884
Father: William Clifton Harvey   Mother: Mildred Walker
Children: Virginia, Married Houston Crowder
             Jesse J., Jr.
             B. Curry, Married Frances Plunkett

HARVEY, JOHN, Married Susie Abbitt Marshall Nash, 1896
Children: Joseph, 1917, Married Frances Widemer
             Dorris Isabelle, 1918, Married Elmer Miller

HARVEY, JOSEPH MOTT, 1888, Married Mattie Lou Clark, 1890
    Children: Fay Netta, 1919, Married Wiley Richardson
                 Thelia, 1924
                 Josephine, 1925

HARVEY, LYTTON, 1884, Married Etta F. Martin
    Father: William Clifton Harvey   Mother: Mildred Walker
    Children: John Clifton, 1912, Married Annie Robertson
                 Winifred, 1913, Married Charlie Martin
                 Edgar, 1916
                 Rachel, 1918, Married Norman H. Jones
                 Lathan, 1921
                 H. T., 1923
                 Leon, 1926-1934
                 Bertie, 1932

HARVEY, NATHAN TANNY, Married Harker Hutcheson Wooldridge

HARVEY, SAMUEL GLOVER, 1858-1939, Married Kate Arrington, 1866-1915
    Children: Homer Hutson, 1888, Married Lois Eunice Harvey, 1895
                 Elizabeth, Married Courtney C. Harvey

HARVEY, THOMAS, 1836-1928, Married Elvira Woodson, died 1927
    Father: Thomas Harvey   Mother: Frances Jennings
    Children: James W., 1867-1947, Married Geneva Lewis, 1876-1934
                 Louella, 1869-1944, Married B. W. Morris
                 Ida, 1872
                 Joel, 1878-1907, Married Mazie Coleman

HARVEY, THOMAS, 1806-1891, Married Frances Jennings, 1813-1891
    Children: Mary Frances, 1832-1909
                 Jesse Tipton, 1834-1904
                 Thomas, 1836-1928, Married Elvira Woodson, died 1927
                 James Glover, 1838-1863
                 Holcomb P., 1840-1921
                 Annie Rebecca, 1842-1845
                 Samuel Mullan, 1844-1918, Married Sue Browning
                 John S., 1846-1935, Married Jane Cunningham
                 William Clifton, 1848-1923, Married Mildred Walker
                 Joel Watkins, 1849-1862
                 Hilliary Richardson, 1851-1910, Married Lelia Gilliam,
                                             1863-1900
                 Frank Walker, 1853-1915
                 Lily Christian, 1860, Married Lilleous H. Gilliam,
                                             1858-1902

HARVEY, THOMAS C., 1900, Married Hazel Leysay, 1907, of Alleghany
    Father: Joel Harvey   Mother: Mazie Coleman
    Children: T. C., Jr., 1926, Married Peggy Moses
                 Gerald, 1927
                 Charlie, 1932
                 Mazie, 1936
                 Harriet, 1945

HARVEY, THOMAS W., 1890, Married Josephine C. Marshall, 1902
    Children: Emma Katherine, 1922
                 Jessie Lucille, 1924
                 Thomas W., Jr., 1927

HARVEY, WILLIAM B., 1863-1934, Married Sallie B. Penick, 1863-1925
    Children: Walter Watts, 1891-1936
                 Courtney C., 1893, Married Elizabeth Harvey, 1890
                 Lois E., 1895, Married H. H. Harvey
                 Collier B., 1897
                 W. D., 1899, Married Mattie Nash
                 Naomi, 1901, Married Hunter Harvey
                 Robert P., 1903, Married Miss May
                 Linwood Irvin, 1905, Married Ella Maxwell
                                    Second wife of W.B., Mittie Goodman

HARVEY, WILLIAM CLIFTON, 1848-1923, Married Mildred Walker, 1848-1924
    Father: Thomas Harvey   Mother: Frances Jennings
    Children: Rachel, 1872-1899, Married James Gordon
                 John T., 1873, Married B. Smith of Norfolk
                 Alice, 1875-1926, Married J. Edgar Martin
                 Jesse J., 1877, Married Lola Abbitt, 1884
                 William C., Jr., 1880, Married Belle Moss
                 Lytton, 1884, Married Etta Martin, 1890
                 Lester B., 1886, Married Helen Morris Welch, 1899
                 Frances, 1890, Married William J. Walton

HARVEY, JR., WILLIAM C., 1880, Married Belle Moss
    Father: William Clifton Harvey   Mother: Mildred Walker
    Children: Richard C., 1908, Married Eunice Drinkard
                 Alfred
                 William Eston, 1913, Married Lucile Akers

HARVEY, ZEBULON VANCE, 1895, Married Gladys Saunders Jennings, 1907
    Children: Phyllis J., 1932

HARWOOD, ALFRED RICE, 1880, Married Bessie Hamner Sears
    Father: John William Harwood   Mother: Alice Newton Drinkard
    Children: Bessie Virginia, 1906, Married John C. Caldwell
                 Alice, 1909
                 Eleanor, 1911, Married Barry Dahl
                                Second husband: Harold Caudle
                 Kathrine Wilsie
                 Alfred Rice, Jr., 1913, Married Violet Ramsey 1915

HARWOOD, JOSEPH U., 1867-1918, Married Mattie Rudd Marshall, 1863-1938
    Father: John W. Harwood   Mother: Ellen Culley
    Children: Joseph M., 1900-1918

HARWOOD, JOHN WILLIAM, 1844-1909, Married Ellen Culley, 1833-1878
     Children: Joseph Unwin, 1868-1918, Married Mattie Rudd Marshall
                    William Henry, 1870-1881
                    Elizabeth Ann, 1872-1878
                    Ellen Holmden, 1875, Married Rev. B. C. James
                                  Second Husband: W. K. Graves
                                  Second Wife of J.W.: Alice Newton
                                  Drinkard, 1855-1933, of Prince Edward
     Children: Alfred Rice, 1880, Married Bessie Hamner Sears
                    Annie, Married John Broadus Abraham
                    Bessie Newton, 1884-1884
                    Samuel Gladstone, 1885, Married Ione Reniff
                    Janie Stuart, 1887, Married Jackson W. Haden
                    John Prentiss, 1889, Married Fennell Crawley
                    Frank Spurgeon, 1892, Married Blanche Fleming
                    Ruth Haverge, 1894-1943, Married Wilson Hix
                    Ernest Wightman, 1896, Married Clara Jones
                    Edith Alice, 1899, Married John Thomas Hix

HATCHER, LAWRENCE J., 1891, Married Mabel Garrette, 1893
     Children: Harold Burke, 1925

HATCHER, LEIGHTON C., 1884, Married Mabel Holmes Garrette, 1890-1943
     Children: Marguerette Hopkins, 1922

HAYCOCK, WILLIAM HARRISON, Married Margaret Ann Washington LeGrand,
                                                              1845

HENDERSON, JR., D. B., Married Virginia V. Ferguson
     Children: Catherine Adelia, 1928

HEWITT, ALBERT WILBER, 1866-1946, Married Gertrude Colvill, 1876, of Ohio

HIGGINBOTHAM, J. H., 1891-1934, Married Alpha Durham, 1893
     Children: Alpha, 1920, Married M. D. Pruitt of Baltimore
                    Betsy, 1928

HILLMAN, EDMOND JAMES, 1909, Married Margaret Marsh, 1910
     Children: Cecil Kay, 1936
                    Gail, 1937
                    Norma Ray, 1940

HIX, E. G., Married Birta Tibbs
                    Second wife: Eva Tibbs
                    Third wife: Miss Cobbs of Franklin
                    Fourth wife: Miss Cobbs of Franklin
     Children: Arthur

HIX, JOHN THOMAS, Married Edith Alice Harwood
     Father: William Daniel Hix   Mother: Fannie Sears
     Children: Barbara Alice, 1925, Married Crote Carson
                    John Thomas, 1926-1931
            Twins   (Frances Elizabeth, 1928
                       (Un-named twin, 1928-1928

HIX, JOHN, Married Miss Payne of Nelson
    Father: Wilson Hix   Mother: Martha Ann Bocock
    Children: Charlie, Married Maude Nelms
               Dan
               Winston, Married Miss Elam
               A Daughter Married Mr. Smith

HIX, DR. THOMAS WILSON, 1828-1884, Married Bettie Stephens Gough,
                                          1834-1916
    Children: William Gough, 1854-1929
               Virginia Thomas, died 1886, Married W. R. Bracey of Miss.
               Mary Agnes, 1861-1926, Married B. A. Hooper
               Thomas Bocock, 1864-1946, Married Susie Garnet
               John Wilson, 1867, Married Kate Thurman of Russell
                          Second wife: Mrs. Doss of Craig
               Lizzie S., 1868-1902
               Lucy, 1870-1913, Married C. A. Garden of Prince Edward

HIX, WILLIAM DANIEL, 1836-1911, Married Fannie Elizabeth Sears,
                                        1842-1923
    Father: Wilson Hix   Mother: Martha A. Bocock
    Children: Mattie Bocock, 1862-1867
               Sarah Mathews, 1864- Married Walter Chamberlain
               Mary Margaret, 1866
               Fannie B., 1871-1890
               William Daniel, 1874
               Wilson, 1875, Married Ruth Harwood
               John Thomas, 1878-1931, Married Edith Harwood
               Carrie Virginia
               James Sears, 1884, Married Mary Pierce of North Carolina
               Florence Augesta, 1886, Married William Erwin of North
                                        Carolina

HIX, WILSON, 1795-1875, Married Martha A. Bocock
    Children: William Daniel, Married Fannie Sears
               Thomas, Married Betty Gough of Campbell County
               Martha, Married Daniel Gills
               Mary
               Carrie
               John, Married Miss Payne of Nelson County
                     2nd. wife of Wilson Hix, Lucy H. Goldman
    Children: E. G., Married Berta Tibbs, 2nd. Wife Eva Tibbs, 3rd. Wife
                     Miss Cobbs of Franklin, 4th. Wife Miss Cobbs of
                                        Franklin
               Daughter Married Cogen

HIX, WILSON, 1875, Married Ruth Harwood, 1894-1944
   Father: William Daniel Hix   Mother: Fannie Sears
   Children: John Wilson, 1928
                Harwood Sears, 1929
                William Daniel, 1931
                Ruth H., 1932
                Joseph Thomas, 1934

HOFFMAN, L. W., Married Minnie Lee Thornton, 1892

HOLLAND, RICHARD, 1755-1803, Capt. in Revolutionary War, Married
                     Martha Jones Walker, 1762-1820, widow of Capt.
                     Henry Walker
   Children: Nancy
                Henry Walker
                William
                Elizabeth Arter, Married Mr. Stewart
                Dick

HOLTZCLAW, CHARLES E., Married Catherine Elizabeth Payne, 1852-1944
   Children: Lucy, Married Lindsay Crawley

HORSLEY, BENJAMIN ABBITT, 1849-1898, Married Virginia Thomas, 1859-1934
   Children: Benjamin Abbitt, Jr., 1883, Married Lillian H. Marsh, 1882
                Geneva H., 1901, Married James Childers
                Thomas Abbitt, 1903, Married Ruth Taylor of Amherst
                Hazel Virginia, 1907, Married L. P. Elliott of Lynchburg
                Bertrand, 1909
                Ray, 1913, Married Mandy Neipier of Lynchburg
                Viada Gordon, 1915, Married E. R. Shelton of Lynchburg
                Lillian Christian, 1912, Married Thomas R. Linn of
                                                        Lynchburg
                Benjamin Colvin, 1914
                Lucile Sterne, 1923

HORSLEY, CRAWFORD R., died 1909, Married Florence Dyson, 1861-1945
   Children: Marion

HORSLEY, DR., WILLIAM N., 1832-1892, Married Fannie Megginson, 1845-1924
   Children: William Hunt, 1866-1887
                John Rolfe, 1868-1944, Married Annie Davidson

HOWERTON, A. HUNTER, 1860, Married Anna C. Hunter, 1865-1934
   Father: Samuel Decatur Howerton   Mother: Elizabeth Agnes Moore
   Children: Vara Agnes, 1887-1942, Married Jesse Dickerson
                Ernest Hunter, 1891, Married Laura Dickerson
                John B., 1895, Married Bertha Blankenship of Danville
                Luther Marshall, 1898, Married Iva Petty
                Eula Virginia, 1900, Married J. H. Fleshman
                Sarah Elizabeth, 1903, Married Hubert H. Caldwell
                Edward J., 1907, Married Lucile Marshall, 1909
                Abner C., 1910, Married Elsie Campbell of Bedford

HOWERTON, ODELL, 1891, Married Rosa Wilson of Campbell
Children: Frances Odell, 1918, Married Lawrence Callahan
Rachel M., 1921, Married Greydon Eddlen
Second wife: Lura Cheatham

HOWERTON, SAMUEL DECATUR, 1829-1902, Married Elizabeth Agnes
Moore, 1836-1926
Children: Luther, 1858-1931, Married Miss Moore of South Carolina
Hunter, 1860, Married Anna C. Hunter
Samuel, 1862-1900, Married Lula Cheatham, 1872
Mary Elizabeth, 1865-1934, Married Sam Davidson
Margarette J., 1868-1906, Married Elmo Chick
Thomas, 1870, Married Miss Lottie Caldwell of Craig
Jean, 1873
Layton, 1876, Married a Lady of South Carolina

HUBBARD, JOEL, 1869-1917, Married Mattie Faris of Pittsylvania
Children: Rebecca, 1898-1902
Joel IV, 1904, Married Miss Hand of Georgia
Mattie J., 1907-1907
Grace H., 1910, Married Mr. Summersgill of Texas
Robert C., 1912, Married Evelyn E. Shaver of Florida
William C., 1914
Alice, 1916-1922

HUBBARD, JOHN THOMAS, Married Lucy Hargrave Hardy, 1859

HUBBARD, WILLIAM B., 1857-1939, Married Callie Childress, 1868-
Children: Janie, 1892, Married Ira Southall

HUDGINS, JOHN CALVIN, Married Margaret Stewart of Claremont
No Children

HUDGINS, REUBEN BOATWRIGHT, Married Bessie Lee Patteson
Children: Lester P., 1922, Married Eleanor Phillips
Ruby Lee, 1923
R. B., Jr., 1924
Second wife: Olive Ellett Hinton

HUGHES, JOHN R., 1817- Married Mrs. J. S. Copeland, 1821-1912

HUGHES, ROBERT DOUGLAS, 1871, Married Haleyon Patteson, 1878
Father: John Hughes   Mother: Miss Nowlin
Children: Kathleen, 1900-1904
John P., 1898, Married Ettie Jones of Lynchburg
Robert, 1901, Married Mancon Walters of North Carolina

HUNTER, CHAPMAN KENDALL, 1896, Married Emma Young, 1900
Father: Charles W. Hunter   Mother: Lula F. Jones
Children: Chapman Kendall, Jr., 1934

HUNTER, CHARLES JONES, Married Alice Lee Smith
    Children: Howlette Essel

HUNTER, CHARLES W., 1854-1900, Married Lula F. Jones, 1864-1920
    Children: Charles Evant, 1887, Married Nina Simmons of Roanoke
                Carrie Oliva, 1899, Married Marion G. Willis of
                                          Fredericksburg
                Chapman Kendall, 1896, Married Emma Young, 1900, of
                                      South Carolina
                Duval W., 1900, Married Carmel Rothrock of North Carolina

HUNTER, MARSHALL, 1905, Married Edythe Josephine Martin, 1908

HUNTER, MOSLEY W., 1869-1930, Married Myra Hopkins Martin, 1877
    Children: Mary Mosley, 1899-1907
                Robert Garland, 1900
                Thomas Allen, 1901, Married Estelle Thomas.
                Rachel Lucile, 1903, Married Thomas Edgar Moore
                Marshall Augustus, 1905, Married Edyth J. Martin
                James Milton, 1906, Married Evelyn Virginia Moore
                Anna Virginia, 1908, Married William Erick Taylor
                Nettie Bell, 1909, Married Bernard L. Moore
                William Hampton, 1911, Married Dorothy Phelps
                Sherman Benjamin, 1912
                Ryland Hopkins, 1916, Married Nancy Robertson

HUNTER, RYLAND HOPKINS, 1916, Married Nancy Robertson
    Father: Mosley W. Hunter   Mother: Myra Hopkins Martin
    Children: Ann Hopkins, 1946

HUNTER, THOMAS ALLEN, 1901, Married Estelle Thomas
    Father: Mosley W. Hunter   Mother: Myra Hopkins Martin
    Children: Madeline
                Katherine
                Ealine
                Rebecca

HURT, BARNETT, Married Frances Gregory
    Children: Samuel Barnett, 1833-1911, Married Anna Lee Hughes,
                                        1856-1942

HURT, SAMUEL BARNETT, 1833-1911, Married Anna Lee Hughes, 1856-1942
    Father: Barnett Hurt   Mother: Frances Gregory
    Children: Nannie D., 1875, Married J. Paul Walker
                Preston Conway, 1878, Married Annie V. Calhoun of Roanoke
                John Rudolph, 1880
                Samuel N., 1881, Married Mrs. Longfield of Indiana
                Julia Lee, 1883, Married Dr. J. S. Archibald of Illinois
                Sallie Davis, 1887, Married O. V. Henson of Illinois
                Robert Barnett, 1890, Married A. M. Chockley of California
                Jesse Hughes, 1892, Married Mrs. Fannie E. Gills
                Clarice Royal, 1895, Married Dr. F. W. Keopf of Ohio
                Ellen Stasy, 1899, Married Frank Southall of Amelia

INGE, DABNEY, 1878-1938, Married Mildred Paulette
    Father: William Paschal Inge   Mother: Martha Ferguson
    Children: Nellie, Married Robert Roach
                Zela, Married Palmer Ranson
                Laura, Married Bernard Richardson
                Richard, Married Rosa Martin
                Toby E., Married Helen Garrett
                Claiborne

INGE, FRED T., 1874, Married Berta Doss, 1879
    Father: Turner Inge   Mother: Bettie Bagby
    Children: Julian W., Married a lady from Chicago
                Lillian, Married Preston Coleman
                Mary, Married Spurgeon Coleman
                Aubrey, Married Miss Phelps
                Rachel, Married Harrell Rogers
                Mabel, Married Pete Christian of Europe
                Elsie, Married Mr. Burnett of Lynchburg
                Lilie, Married Preston Sandidge of Lynchburg

INGE, HOLMSEY, 1881, Married Mary Hamilton
    Father: William Paschal Inge   Mother: Martha Ferguson
    Children: Rachel, 1916, Married Harry Ranson
                Holmsey, Jr., 1919, Married Alice Smith, 1922

INGE, HOLMSEY, JR., 1919, Married Alice Smith, 1922
    Father: Holmsey Inge   Mother: Mary Hamilton .
    Children: Joice Lorine, 1944

INGE, JAMES T., 1906, Married Lonelle Hamilton, 1906
    Father: Taylor R. Inge   Mother: Mamie Gordon
    Children: Ralph H., 1940

INGE, JOEL HENRY, 1866- Married Lillie B. Ranson, 1867-1930
    Children: Ella, 1891, Married H. D. Harrup
                J. B., Married Wilmet Smedley of Pennsylvania
                Otey, 1903
                Louise, Married Lawrence Young
                Eva, Married Frank T. Cawthorn

INGE, TAYLOR R., 1872, Married Mamie Gordon of Forest
    Father: William Paschal Inge   Mother: Martha Ferguson
    Children: Lloyd, Married Neva Davis
                Wiley
                James, Married Lonel Hamilton
        Twins (Mamie
              (Malcolm, Married Jane Gray Paulett

INGE, THOMAS HENRY PEYTON, 1861-1944, Married Arrissa Mary Frances
                                            Wade   1866

INGE, THOMAS HENRY PEYTON, (continued)
Children: Allison T., 1885, Married Mary Moses 1897
             Nannie, Married Will Nash
             Henry Peyton, Married Miss Anderson of Dallas, Texas
             Mamie, Married George M. Dixon
             Della
             Willie D.
             Josiah
             Virgie, Married Grover Beasley
             George B.
             Howard C.
             Gladys D., Married Elkin Hamilton

INGE, TURNER, Married Bettie Bagby
Children: Dave, Married Nannie Rakes
             John, Married a lady from North Carolina
             Ashley Bernard
             Tom, Married Laura Cheatham
             Fred T., 1874, Married Berta Doss, 1879
             Susie, Married Frank Inge
             Mary, Married Nathan Scruggs
             Sallie, Married Daniel Cyrus
             Gertie, Married Leslie Torrence
             Pearle, Married Stephen Cyrus

INGE, WILLIAM E., 1919, Married Madelene Ferguson, 1914
Children: Frank, 1938
             Carrie Jane, 1940
             Samuel, 1944

INGE, W. P., 1863, Married Hattie Davis
Children: Carl, Married Macie Inge
             Beatrice, Married W. C. Garrett

INGE, WILLIAM PASCHAL, 1834-1913, Married Martha Ferguson, 1834-1913
Children: Claiborne, 1860-1916, Married Bettie Rush 1856-1916
             W. P., 1863, Married Hattie Davis
             Joel, 1866, Married Lillie Ranson
             Virginia L., 1869, Married John D. Hamilton
             Taylor R., 1872, Married Mamie Gordon
             Robert, 1875
             Dabney, 1878-1938, Married Mildred Paulette
             Holmsey, 1881, Married Mary Hamilton

INGE, WILLIS, 1812-1891, Married (second wife) Elizabeth Ann Wade,
                                                            1824-1905
Children: Victoria Alice, 1847-1909, Married Mr. Wright of
                                                   Buckingham
             Zachariah Taylor, 1848-1915, Married Scottie Morgan
             John Henry, 1849-1928
             James Thomas, 1850-
             Thomas S., 1852-1915, Married Willie Ann Coffee, died
                                                            1882

INGE, WILLIS (continued)
                    Nannie A., 1854-1909, Married J. C. Fuqua, died 1906
                    George William, 1856- Married Mollie Chambers
                    Samuel D., 1858-1914
                    Charles Wesley Statham, 1859-1911
                    Joel Walker, 1860-1908
                    Stonewall Jackson, 1862- Married Ora Fore

INGE, ZACHARIAH TAYLOR, 1848-1915, Married Scottie Morgan
        Father: Willis Inge   Mother: Elizabeth Ann Wade
        Children: Bessie, Married Harry James of Richmond
                   Thomas
                   Samuel
                   Waller

INGRAM, JOSHUA, 1820-1912, Married Elizabeth Woodson, 1840-1883, of
                                                            Nelson
        Children: Thomas J., 1868, Married Lizzie Hardy of Lynchburg
                    Joseph, 1870-1882
                    Rosa Lee, 1872-1938, Married Thomas W. Tuggle
                                          Second husband: W. J. Wilkerson,
                                                            1875-1946
                    Kemper, 1876-1889
                    Mollie, 1881, Married Mr. Peters of Richmond

IRBY, GEORGE
        Children: Robert, 1863-1931
                    Lizzie Gray, 1872

IRBY, ROBERT, 1863-1931, Married Mary Ann Coleman, 1863-1944
        Father: George Irby
        Children: Lula Gray, 1885
                    Mary, 1889, Married John Edward Sears

IRBY, TERRY C., 1848-1928, Married Rosa E. Woodson, 1875
        Children: T. E., 1900, Married Vivian Mays
                    D. G., 1902, Married Gracie Elder
                    J. T., 1904, Married Dottie Crowder, 1900

IRVING, EDWARD A., 1859-1917, Married Rosa Virginia Gilliam, 1862-1896
        Children: Frank M., 1891, Married Lacie Jamerson, 1897
                    Second wife of Edward A., Lily Norman
                                                    Gilliam

IRVING, FRANK M., 1891, Married Lacie Jamerson, 1897
        Father: Edward A. Irving   Mother: Rosa Virginia Gilliam
        Children: Edward Jamerson, 1919-1945

193

ISBELL, DAVID D., 1839-1912, Married Laura Alice Stratton, 1856-1932
    Father: Robert Isbell   Mother: Martha T. Boaz
    Children: V. Myrtle, 1877-1904
                Harry G., 1880, Married Rosamond Johnson of Nelson
                Donald D., 1882, Married Mary Leon Presgrave of Loudon
                Isabel, 1886, Married John W. Greenlay of Massachusetts
                Dorothy D., 1894, Married Roland M. Wilson of Massachusetts

ISBELL, LEWIS DANIEL, died 1889

ISBELL, ROBERT, 1807, Married Martha T. Boaz
    Children: Lucian, 1835-1849
                Robert B., 1836-1921
                William E., 1837-1924
                David D., 1839-1912, Married Laura Alice Stratton, 1856-
                                                                      1932
                Frederick M., 1843-1863
                Amasa A., 1845-1865
                Milton, 1847-1936
                Anna, 1833-1908
                Nannie P., 1840-1925
                Laura V., 1849-1924

JAMERSON, BRYANT THOMAS, 1868, Married Nannie E. Garrett, 1874-1946
    Children: Bessie Jane, 1893, Married A. L. Crews
                Ernest Thomas, 1896, Married Marissa Cole
                                    Second wife: Ruby Cobb
                Lacie McKenny, 1897, Married F. M. Irving
                Mary Ethel, 1899, Married R. E. Roach
                Charles Berkley, 1902-1910
                Kester Winifred, 1905, Married Cora Williams
                Grace Elizabeth, 1908, Married Russel R. Neely
                Bernard Earl, 1911
                Nona Crawley, 1913, Married B. C. Massey
                Frances Juanita, 1916 , Married Thomas C. Raine

JAMERSON, CARLTON, Married Mary Woody
    Father: Daniel W. Jamerson   Mother: Berta McCormick
    Children: Lola
                Carlton
                Dianne
                Brinda Gene

JAMERSON, CHARLES WILLIAM, 1867-1947, Married Amanda Virginia Worley
                                                              1869-1942
    Father: Robert Jamerson   Mother:
    Children: Janie, Married Emmett Miton of Craig
                Fannie, Married Clay Perdieu
                Warren, 1897-1945, Married Sallie Thornhill, 1901

194

JAMERSON, J. E., ("DUTCH"), 1902, Married Lula Smith
    Father: R. F. Jamerson   Mother: Ella Walton
    Children: James Robert, 1930
              William, 1934
              Mary Lou, 1945

JAMERSON, DANIEL W., 1877-1940, Married Berta McCormick
    Children: Raymond W., 1900, Married Nellie Godsey
              Melvin, 1902, Married Pansy Litchford
              Thelma, Married B. A. Thornhill
              Christine, Married Glenn Daniel
              Carlton, Married Mary Woody of Nelson
              Elsie, Married Robert Lucado
              Annie, Married Wiley Campbell of Amherst
              Margaret, Married Murray Payne of Richmond

JAMERSON, MELVIN, 1902, Married Pansy Litchford
    Father: Daniel W. Jamerson   Mother: Berta McCormick
    Children: Floyd Lee
              Melvin
              Watkins
              Cecil
              Donald Ray

JAMERSON, OSCAR T., 1888, Married Mary Ann Wooten, 1889
    Children: Rachel, 1909, Married Charlie McCormick
              Gladys, 1914, Married Mack Reynolds, 1903
              Thomas Jackson, 1917, Married Gertie Guill
              Frances Florine, 1919, Married Samuel Woodson
              Mary Elizabeth, 1923, Married Mott McCormick
              George Herbert, 1926, Married Mildred Mays

JAMERSON, R. WALTON, Married Frances Smith, 1902
    Father: R. F. Jamerson   Mother: Ella Walton
    Children: Elizabeth
              Walton

JAMERSON, RAYMOND W., 1900, Married Nellie Godsey
    Father: Daniel W. Jamerson   Mother: Berta McCormick
    Children: Edward

JAMERSON, ROLAND F., 1875-1943, Married Ella Walton, 1875
    Children: Louise, 1897, Married E. S. Meanly of Toana
              Paul, 1897-1913
              Walton, 1899, Married Frances Smith
              Eldridge, 1902, Married Lula Smith
              Russell, 1905, Married Rebecca Martin
              Josie, 1909, Married Tommy Ferguson
              Mary, 1912, Married T. M. Harris
              Carrie, 1915, Married Hugh Martin
              Raymond, 1918

JAMES, CHARLES F., 1888, Married Ada B. McCain of Alabama
 Children: Charles F., Jr., 1913, Married Elizabeth Scott of Florida

JAMES, EDWARD C., 1866, Married Fannie Thornhill, 1863
 Children: Carol
     Dorothy, Married Meador Farmer

JANATKA, RICHARD G., 1907, Married Margaret F. Coleman, 1909

JENKINS, C. S., 1892, Married Lilly Sullivan of Nottaway
 Children: C. S., Jr., 1921
     Josephine, 1918, Married Jack Dickerson of Lunenburg

JENKINS, HARRY, 1902, Married Mattie E. Beard, 1891, of Bedford
 Father: Robert S. Jenkins Mother: Addie Cawthorn
 Children: Roby O., 1923, Married George Monroe Webb
     Helen, 1926, Married Twyman Baldwin
     Robert Preston, 1928

JENKINS, JOEL W., 1855-1920, Married Eunice Cheadle
 Children: Joel W., Jr., 1897, Married Miss Hamilton

JENKINS, ROBERT S., 1858-1930, Married Colyer Abbitt
 Children: William Abbitt, 1889
         Second wife: Addie Cawthorn
 Children: Robert Julian, 1900, Married Beula Crews
     Harry Wellington, 1902, Married Mattie Beard, 1891
     Richard Temple, 1907
     Eunice Earl, 1904
     Mary Frances, 1910, Married Alfred B. Abbitt

JENNINGS, ALLEN, 1700, Married Miss Gilliam

JENNINGS, CLAUDE, 1907, Married Gertrude Wooten, 1911
 Father: Emory Jennings Mother: Lena Pulliam
 Children: Alice Lina, 1929
     Martha T., 1930
     Bettie Jane, 1932-1932
     Ester Claudine, 1937

JENNINGS, CURTIS CLYDE, 1907, Married Mayme Jo Cawthorn, 1911
 Children: Iris Lynette, 1935

JENNINGS, EDWARD LUTHER, died 1922, Married Martha S. Hardy, 1861-1934

JENNINGS, EMORY, 1862-1943, Married Lena Pulliam, 1877
 Children: Claude, 1907, Married Gertrude Wooten, 1911

JENNINGS, FRANK E., 1892, Married Alma Drinkard, 1890
    Father: Henry B. Jennings   Mother: Nannie G. Parks
    Children: . F. E., Jr., 1916, Married
                  Lloyd, 1924, Married Dorothy Bryant of Lynchburg
                  Louise, 1929

JENNINGS, GEORGE LeGRAND, 1907, Married Bradley Virginia Cawthorn,
                                                                1913
    Father: G. N. Jennings   Mother:
    Children: James Cawthorn, 1935

JENNINGS, GRANVILLE PARKS, 1886, Married Fannie Christian, 1889
    Father: Henry B. Jennings   Mother: Nannie G. Parks
    Children: Agnes Goode, 1920, Married Ashton Cocke of Fluvanna
                           Second husband: Charlie Spain of
                                         Petersburg
              George, 1922, Married Miss Thompson of Woodbridge
              Thomas, 1924
              Frances, 1927

JENNINGS, HENRY B., 1856-1922, Married Nannie G. Parks, 1856-1917
    Children: H. B., Jr., 1884
              Nannie L., 1885, Married Ernest Stratton
                         Second husband, Mr. Atkinson
              Granville Parks, 1886, Married Fannie Christian, 1889
              Lottie, 1888, Married Newton Gillispie of Tazewell
              Frank E., 1892, Married Alma Drinkard, 1890
              Ethel, 1893, Married Billie Kirkpatrick of Rockbridge
              H. S., 1896, Married Vera Drinkard 1892
                         Second wife of Henry B., Mary F. Brough

JENNINGS, HORACE STUBBS, 1895, Married Vera Virginia Drinkard, 1896

JENNINGS, JAMES, died 1868

JENNINGS, JOHN DANILE, 1907, Married Ruth Morris, 1913
    Father: Samuel Joel Jennings   Mother: Ella Walker Cawthorn
    Children: Jane Adair, 1943

JENNINGS, MARY ELIZABETH, 1826-1900

JENNINGS, ROBIN, Revolutionary Soldier

JENNINGS, SAMUEL JOEL, 1881-1947, Married Ella Walker Cawthorn, 1881
    Children: John Daniel, 1907, Married Ruth Morris

JOHNS, THOMAS WINSTON, 1818-1904, Married Mary Elizabeth Dudley,
                                                    1820-1898
    Children: Mary Elizabeth, Married William Henry, Trent
              Alice
              Nannie
              Thomas Winston, Jr.
              Bettie
              William Dudley
              Anna Deane

JOHNS, THOMAS WINSTON, (continued)
                Fannie, Married Edmund Winston Mosely of Bedford

JOHNSON, CHARLIE, 1912, Married Nellie V. Lucado, 1911
    Children: Margaret L., 1936
                Carolyn A., 1937

JOHNSON, CHARLES L., 1882, Married Ruth Smith
    Father: W. R. Johnson   Mother: Alice Dickerson
    Children: Elon, 1903, Married Nellie Sarver
                Alice Celine, 1905, Married Moorman Tuck of Lynchburg
                Taylor F., 1907, Married Catherine Mowyer of Lynchburg
                Mabel Twyman, 1908, Married Willie Tanner
                Charlie Darlane, 1912, Married Nettie Lucado
                Milton Carl, 1915, Married Helen Sheiner
                Cawthorn Elbert, 1917
                Willard Cadell, 1919, Married Lucile Godsey

JOHNSON, E. H., 1914, Married Emma Price of Charlotte
    Children: Bettie, 1939
                Elsie, 1941
                Lawrence, 1943

JOHNSON, HARRY G., 1897, Married Gladys Patterson, 1902
    Father: William T. Johnson   Mother: Virginia Inge
    Children: Dorothy Lee, 1924
                Rebecca E., 1926
                Barbara A., 1933

JOHNSON, HERMAN, 1907, Married Gracie Cumby, 1909
    Children: Arwild, 1931
                Clarke, 1933
                Larry, 1943

JOHNSON, JOSEPH PITZER, 1887, Married Eula May Smith, 1893
    Children: Ralph Walker, 1920
                Alice May, 1921-1923
                J. P., Jr., 1924
                Shirley Lee, 1929
                Harold Daniel, 1932
                Garland Fox, 1938

JOHNSON, RICHARD WASHINGTON, 1866, Married Rose Anna Armistead, 1881
    Children: Claude D., 1900-1944
                Ernest E., 1902

JOHNSON, WILLIAM R., Married Alice Dickerson
    Children: William T., Married Jennie Inge
                Jimmie
                Dannie, Married Cora Durrum
                Charlie L., Married Ruth Smith
                Pitzer, Married Eula May Smith

JOHNSON, WILLIAM T., 1873-1920, Married Virginia Inge, 1877
    Children: Estelle, 1894, Married Joe Blackburn of Lynchburg
                            Second husband: Luyellen Marsureau of
                                                                Baltimore
                    Nora M., 1896-1918, Married Edward Evans
                    Harry G., 1897, Married Gladys Patterson, 1902
                    Myrtle, 1899, Married Samuel J. Evans

JOHNSTON, DUDLEY M., 1891, Married Mary James, 1894, of Staunton
    Children: Charles F., 1921
                    Emma I., 1924

JOHNSTON, LEONARD SHEARER, 1858-1919

JOHNSTON, LITITIA, E. M., 1817-1903

JOHNSTON, MINOR HARTWELL, 1893-1911

JOHNSTON, WILLIAM FRIEND, 1849-1912

JONES, DR. DAVID CRAWFORD, 1802-1859, Married Eliza Walton, 1810-1893
    Children: Dr. William Rowland, 1839- Married Drucilla Allen of Ky.
                    Frank Boggs, 1843-1915, Married Nannie Elliott, 1845-1929
                    Ida W., 1846-1942
                    Cornelia Chapman, 1848-1925
                    Bell, 1854-1943, Married Samuel Payne
                    Ann Elizabeth, 1827- Married George Fuqua
                    Sallie Paul, 1834-1901, Married James A. Walker, 1835-1914
                    Alice, Married John Bass

JONES, FRANK B., 1843-1915, Married Nannie Elliott, 1847-1929
    Father: Dr. David Crawford Jones   Mother: Eliza Walton
    Children: Elliott R.
                    Frank Orman, Married Macca Bates
                    William S., Married lady from Chicago
                    Marvin S., Married Sallie Dickerson
                    Annie E., Married William D. Robertson
                    Herbert S., Married Eunice Furbush

JONES, HERBERT STROTHER, 1888, Married Eunice Ellen Furbush, 1895
    Father: Frank B. Jones 1843-1915 Mother: Nannie Elliott, 1847-1929
    Children: Nannie Ellen, 1920, Married A. W. Covington
                    Jane Onel, 1919, Married C. E. Moseley of Lynchburg
                    Herbert S., Jr., 1923, Married Mildred Ehoff of Baltimore
                    Charlie M., 1925

JONES, J. CHAPMAN, Married Miss Hunter
    Children: Dr. Herman, Married Miss Yeats of Roanoke
                    Lula, Married C. W. Hunter
                    Nina
                    Dr. Chapman

JONES, JAMES FRANKLIN, 1875, of Amherst

JONES, ROBERT ALEXANDER, 1874, Married Fannie Hudson, of Amherst

JONES, SAM "JUMP", 1878, Married Edna Earl Hudson, 1892
    Children: Malcomb Rucker, 1915, Married Inez Harris
                Edna Evelena, 1920, Married Mr. Williams of West Va.

JONES, VICTORIA L., 1838-1852)
                       Daughters of W. A. Jones
JONES, C. A., 1842- 1853)

JONES, WALTER MASSEY, 1880, of Amherst

JORDAN, J. E., 1898, Married Maggie G. Cardwell, 1894
    Children: Eula Mae, 1911, Married C. D. Connor of Lynchburg
                Sadie Virginia, 1913, Married N. C. Covington of Prospect
                James B., 1915-1919
                Margaret Gertrude, 1917, Married J. D. Guill
                Thurman L., 1919, Married M. Leonard of Sutherland
                James Edward, Jr., 1921
                Ronald Romer, 1926

KELLY, LAWSON, Married Sarah Harker LeGrand

KELLY, LEONARD N., Married Susan Harris LeGrand, 1839-1867

KERN, JOHN THOMAS, 1919, Married Frances Moore, 1921

KIDD, F. FLOYD, Married Martha Taylor Kidd

KINDRED, ELISHA THOMAS, 1837-1904, Married Mary Trent Tinsley,
                                            1844-1936
    Children: Tinsley, 1866-1927
                Weekley, 1868-1889
                Sidney, 1869-1871
                Della, 1872, Married Grayton Boylston of South Carolina
                Minnie May, 1876
                Mary Carlotta, 1877
                Alexander Goode, 1885

KINNEY, H. W., 1861-1937, Married Ella Stevens of West Virginia
    Children: J. S., Married Miss Moss of Danville
                Pollard
                Harry
                Jefferson

KINNEY, JUDSON S., 1892, Married Willie Moss of Danville, 1892
    Children: Judson, Jr., 1919, Married M. Kilby
                 Robert, 1922, Married Margeret Bailey
                 Laura
                 Kennon W., 1923, Married Gertrude Tilden
                 Ellen E., 1928

KINNEY, W. N., 1880, Married Rena Carlton

KOFELD, McKIE RAYE, 1937

KYLE, M. FREELAND, 1861-1919, Married Nancy Robertson, 1867-1925
    Father: R. R. Kyle   Mother: Amanda Bethel, 1829-1923
    Children: Lillie, 1890, Married Leslie Coleman
                 Mace, 1888, 1897
                 Adlie, 1893, Married Susie Kyle of Nelson
                 Virginia, 1897, Married A. Wooldridge

KYLE, R. R., 1824-1893, Married Amanda Bethel, 1829-1893
    Children: Wilton, Married Burnie Dunn
                 Dibrel, Married Annie Davidson
                 M. Freeland, 1861-1919, Married Nancy Robertson
                 Ida
                 Willie, 1869-1939, Married Florence Watts of Amherst
                 Lelia
                 Jack
                 Aubrey, Married Virginia Watts of Amherst

LANGHORNE, WILLIAM A., Married Mary Buckner
    Children: Maurice Buckner
                 Fannie Berely, 1848, Married Hugh Frye of Richmond
                 William Archer, 1850-1876
                 Devreux Alexander
                 Elizabeth Allen
                 Robert C.
                 Mattie, 1856-1946, Married A. F. Anderson
                 Beverly R.
                 Mary Potter, Married T. B. Bond of Petersburg
                 Sallie Cary
                 D. Allen, 1856-1917, Married Miss Brabham
                 Kent, Married D. C. Talbert of Kentucky
                 Lucy M.
                 Maude, Married William J. Nelson of Staunton
                 Harry Holmes

LANGRAN, GEORGE F., Married Earle Marks, 1890
    Children: George F., Jr., 1912
                 James Carter, 1914, Married Anna C. Carter of Nelson

LANGRAN, JAMES CARTER, 1914, Married Anna C. Carter
    Father: George F. Langran   Mother: Earle Marks
    Children: Catherine Earle
              James C., Jr.
              Virginia Ballard
              Mary Vance

LAUGHAN, JOHN HOUSTON, 1882, Married Georgie Alma Hartness, 1879
    Children: Theodore Hadges, 1906, Married Miss Pryor of Lynchburg
              John Divine, 1907, Married Miss Robinson of Richmond
              Kermit Oliver, 1909, Married Miss Griggs of North Carolina
              Landis Leneve, 1911, Married Raymond Kofelgt of Penn.
              McKie Parke, 1913, Married Mr. Farley

LAUGHAN, KERMIT OLIVER, 1909, Married Miss Griggs
    Father: John Houston Laughan   Mother: Georgie Alma Hartness
    Children: Kermit Oliver, Jr., 1939

LAWSON, JOHN RAYMOND, 1894, Married Rachel Ferguson, 1905
    Children: John Raymond, Jr., 1925
              Samuel Robert, 1928
              Frederick Hopkins, 1930
              Harry Gordon, 1931

LAWSON, SAMUEL ANDREW, Married Mollie Hobson
    Children: John Raymond, Married Rachel Adelia Ferguson
              Flora, Married Watt H. Stanley
              Harry Hobson, Married Anna Bell Honaker
              B. Maxwell, Married Gertrude Gregory
              Richard K., Married Helen Dickerson
              Roland W., Married Helen Cowan
              Samuel Alfred, Married Faye Babcock
              Mildred, Married Anderson Scruggs

LAWSON, S. ALFRED, 1911, Married Helen Fay Babcock, 1911

LAYNE, EDDIE L., Married M. C. Durrum, 1878
    Father: William H. Layne   Mother: Nannie McCary
    Children: Taylor, 1901, Married Nannie Cumby, 1903
              Manie Lewis, died 1920
              Lula Iola, 1907, Married Eddie T. Guill
              Ossie May, 1910, Married Howard Blanks of Halifax

LAYNE, JIMMIE, Married Betsy Drinkard

LAYNE, WILLIAM H., Married Nannie McCary
    Children: Robert Daniel, Married Lula Brown of Bedford
              Willie
              Charlie
              Berta, Married Charles Williams
              Eddie L., 1875, Married M. C. Durrum, 1878
              Aubrey, 1877-1943

LEE, SAMUEL J., 1851-1931, Married Matilda Wooldridge
   Children: J. T.
                W.
                R. T.
                Lula Kathern
                Anna Lois
                A. H.
                Herman L., 1901-1918
                S. J.

LEE, S. TILDEN, 1903, Married Margaret E. Wheeler of Campbell
   Father: Tilden Lee   Mother: Anna Bondurant
   Children: Roland Wayne, 1937
               Winifred Ann, 1940
               Barbara Jean, 1943

LEE, TILDEN, 1873-1903, Married Anna Bondurant
   Father: S. J. Lee   Mother: Matilda Wooldridge
   Children: Lucile, 1901, Married Rufus Burnett
               Samuel Tilden, 1903, Married Margaret E. Wheeler

LEE, WALTER C., 1888, Married Bessie J. Martin, 1902

LeGRAND, ARCHER ALEXANDER, 1803-1879, Married Caroline Matilda
                                          Hunter, 1809-1957
   Children: Elizabeth Anderson, 1828-1886 Married Richard C. Harvey
               William Archer, 1830-1901, Married Elizzbeth M. Shearer
                         Second wife: Mrs. Mollie
                                    Shearer Price
               Mary Adeline Walker, 1831-1869 Married Josiah L. Sears
               Caroline Matilda, 1832-1905, Married Peter A. LeGrand
                         Second husband: Robert Taylor
                         Third husband: Richard Bright
               Arrissa Candice, 1834-1845
               Josiah Benjamin, 1836-1860, Married Perlina Cock
               Thomas Edward, 1841-1903, Married S. Anne Smith
               Samuel A., 1850-1865
               John Luther, 1856-1873
               Credilla, died in infancy
                         Second wife of A.A., Cordylle Pugh
                         Third wife of A. A., Mrs. John Hancock

LeGRANDE ETHELBERT, 1799-1868, Married Lucy D. Stratton, 1812-1901
   Children: Elizabeth Woodson, 1832-1911, Married Peter L. Stratton
               William A., 1833-1846
               Frances Walker, 1835-1836
               Judith Ann, 1837-1851
               James Daniel, 1839-1920, Married Mary E. Harding
               Henry Douglas, 1840-1918, Married Susan Christian Walker,
                                            1844-1923
               Charles Walker, 1842-1862
               Sarah Frances, 1844-1887, Married Jesse S. Thornhill
               John A., 1846-1850
               Thomas Stratton, 1848-1891

LeGRANDE, ETHELBERT, (continued)
                    Mary E., 1851-1877
                    Sarah Virginia, 1853-1891, Married Robert F. Reveley

LeGRANDE, HENRY D., 1840-1918, Married Susan C. Walker, 1844-1923
    Father: Ethelbert LeGrande   Mother: Lucy D. Stratton
    Children: Anna D., 1869-1943
                 Bessie, 1871, Married J. Albert Stratton
                 Samuel W., 1873, Married Mary Kindston of Washington
                 Willie, 1875-1876
                 Charlie C., 1876-1900
                 John W., 1878, Married Jane Jones, Of Ohio, died 1946
         Twins   (Iza, 1880
                 (Fannie, 1880
                 Lellie E., 1883- died in infancy
                 Sallie, 1885

LeGRAND, THOMAS A., 1791-1846

LeGRAND, THOMAS EDWARD, 1841-1903, Married S. Anne Smith
    Father: Archer Alexander LeGrand   Mother: Caroline Matilda Hunter
    Children: Thomas E., Jr., 1871, Married Mattie Auguire
                 Mary Sue, 1873, Married W. A. Kelly
                 Luther Benjamin, 1875, Married Ruth S. Mayo of Lynchburg
                 Nannie A., 1878, Married W. D. Mason of Rice
                 William Josiah, 1882, Married Lula Drinkard, 1886

LeGRAND, WILLIAM JOSIAH, 1882, Married Lula Drinkard, 1886
    Father: Thomas Edward LeGrand   Mother: S. Anne Smith
    Children: Mary Ann, 1909
                 Lucy Matilda, 1911
                 Thomas Edward, 1912
                 Willie Josephine, 1915, Married R. L. Carter of Roanoke
                 Charles McElroy, 1917-1918
                 Elizabeth Lobelia, 1919
                 Alfred Archer, 1921
                 William Hunter, 1926

LEWIS, ABNER I., 1798-1877, Married Susan Alvis, 1801-1876
    Children: Ella Sue, 1831-1887, Married Joseph S. Watson
                 Eliza Emma, 1824-1900, Married Lane
                                        Second husband: Morgan Watson
                 Mary Ann, 1833
                 Abner H., 1834-1879, Married Jane Davidson
                 Shedrach Alvis, 1828-1887, Married Virginia A. Pankey,
                                                    1830-1870
                                        Second wife: Mildred Davis
                                                    1835-1936

LEWIS, AMANDA, 1859-1898, Married Carey Childress

LEWIS, CAROLINE, 1825-1839

LEWIS, CHARLES DAVIS, 1906, Married Ruby Caldwell
    Father: Charles Edward Lewis   Mother: Viola Moss
    Children: Clark
                 Dan
                 Virginia

LEWIS, CHARLES EDWARD, 1875, Married Viola Moss, 1877
    Father: S. A. Lewis   Mother: Mildred Davis
    Children: Moss, 1904, Married Frances Bramer of Roanoke
                 Charles Davis, 1906, Married Ruby Caldwell

LEWIS, DANIEL, Married Martha Paris
    Children: Ellen, 1838-1897
                 Angie, 1840-1890, Married Samuel Farrar
                 Joe, 1846-1863
                 Victoria, 1847- Married George L. Ferguson
                 Emiline, 1848-1936, Married Robert H. Browning

LEWIS, GEORGE, 1854, Married Miss Childress

LEWIS, JOANNA, 1850-1937, Married Richard Carter

LEWIS, JOHN LLOYD, 1874, Married Myrtle Dove Jennings, 1879-1946
    Father: William H. Lewis   Mother: Amanda W. Lee
    Children: Walker Olive, 1909, Married C. C. Pearce of Farmville
                 Lloyd Nollie, 1912, Married Teressa Raden of Florida
                 Martha Louise, 1916, Married Edward Carter Martin

LEWIS, JOHN, Married Susan Webb

LEWIS, JOHN R., 1827-1864

LEWIS, JOHN ROBERT, 1862, Married Ella Bruce Mitchell
    Children: John Robert, Jr.
                 William
                 Ella, Married Maurice E. Gordon
                 Lukin

LEWIS, JOHN WILLIAM, 1855-1942, Married Annie O. Purdum, 1857-1920
    Children: Alvis Watson, 1886, Married Roxie Campbell of Prince Edward
                                  Second wife: of Wisconsin
              William Edward, 1888, Married Jean Harris of Prince Edward
              James V., 1890, Married Ruby Hubbard of Prince Edward
              John Fillmore, 1893, Married Lillian Clayton of North
                                                            Carolina
              Walter Tweedy, 1895-1905

LEWIS, MARTHA, 1836-1905, Married Charles H. Coleman

LEWIS, MARY ANN, 1832-1906, Married John Garrett

LEWIS, SUSAN E., 1831-1896

LEWIS, THOMAS, 1848-1921, Married Delie Dawson
    Children: Herman, 1876
                  Fay, 1879, Married Mr. Noble of Florida
                  Lola, 1882
                  Paul, 1885

LEWIS, WILLIAM A., 1852-1942, Married Nannie Webb

LEWIS, WILLIAM D., 1830-

LEWIS, WILLIAM H., 1848-1916, Married Amanda W. Lee, 1848-1907
    Father: William I. Lewis   Mother: Amy G. Portwood
    Children: Augustus William, 1870-1885
                  John Lloyd, 1874- Married Myrtle Dove Jennings, 1879-1946
                  Annie Alma, 1888, Married Courtney Woodson

LEWIS, WILLIAM I., 1799-1857, Married Amy G. Portwood, 1803-1890
    Children: William H., 1848-1916, Married Amanda W. Lee, 1848-1907

LIGON, LESLIE N., 1875, Married Annie Guthrie
    Father: William H. Ligon   Mother: Nannie Cunningham
    Children: Leslie N., Jr., Married Mrs. Virginia Hook of North Carolina
                  Margaret C.
                  Willis H. II, Married Virginia Rose of Covington
                  James G., Married Bettie Graney of New York

LIGON, THOMAS CECIL, 1904, Married Isabel Allen, 1904
    Father: T. J. Ligon   Mother: Kate Sears
    Children: Thomas Cecil, Jr., 1937
                  Katherine Ann, 1940

LIGON, T. J., 1880, Married Kate Sears, 1880-1911
    Father: W. H. Ligon   Mother: Nannie Cunningham
    Children: Samuel Willis, 1904-1928
                  Thomas Cecil, 1904, Married Isabel Allen, 1904
                  Willard Dupuy, 1907, Married Mary Brightwell, 1911
                  Hilda Lucile, 1909, Married J. R. Gardner
                              Second wife of T. J.: Janie Logan Gilliam
    Children: Lawrence R., 1917
                  William Hollis, 1919, Married Gladys Dickerson
                  John Jeter, 1923

LIGON, WILLIS H., Married Nanie Cunningham of Prince Edward
    Children: Leslie N., Ligon, Married Annie Guthrie
                  Thomas Jeter, Married Kate Sears, Second wife, Logan Gilliam
                  Elva, Married

LUCADO, ELISHA, 1846-1903, Married Catherine Conner
    Children: William H., Married Beulah Hamilton
                Florence, Married John H. Bingham
                Joseph, Married Maude Morris
                Robert, Married Nannie Marsh
                        Second wife: Mrs. Lizzie Wilcox
                Littleton T., Married Ethel Childers
                Mollie, Married John Torrence
                Edward, Married Kate Lucado
                Ira, Married Alene Barlow
                Della, Married Robert Doss

LUCADO, HARRY, 1912, Married Vennice Hamilton, 1913
    Children: Clinton Wayne, 1936
                Frances Geraldine, 1938

LUCADO, JAMES HENRY, 1892, Married Mattie Gladys Nowlin, 1898
    Father: William H. Lucado, Mother: Beulah Hamilton
    Children: Doris, 1920, Married W. W. Cunningham of Wisconsin
                Edith Nowlin, 1918

LUCADO, JOSEPH, Married Maude Morris, 1882-1935
    Father: Elisha Lucado   Mother: Catherine Conner
    Children: Lottie, Married LeRoy Marks
                Catherine, Married George Perdue

LUCADO, LITTLETON T., 1885, Married Ethel Childers, 1890
    Father: Elisha Lucado   Mother: Catherine Conner
    Children: Basil J., 1913, Married Lorene E. Bass, 1920, of Halifax
                Laurence Elisha, 1916, Married Pearl Harris, 1916
                Eva Lynelle, 1927
                Nellie, Married Charlie Johnson
                Irene, Married_____ Trent
                R. E., Married Irene Trent, 1920
                Anis L., 1928

LUCADO, R. HARRY, 1882, Married Nannie Lou Marsh
    Father: Elisha Lucado,   Mother: Catherine Conner
    Children: Clinton
                Harry
                Robert
    2nd. Wife of R. H. Lucado, Lizzie Wilcox

LUKIN, DR. F. H., 1874, Married Allie T. Thornton, 1882
    Children: F. H., Jr., 1909-1944

LUSADI, VINCENT, Married Caroline Moses
    Children: Jean Caroline

MANN, CLIF, Married Miss Simms
    Children: Ryland M., 1906, Married Hazel Reynolds, 1909

MANN, HERMAN H., Married Rosa Crews
    Children: Frances, 1932
                 Lois, 1934
                 Herman Ray, 1939
                 Tony, 1945

MANN, JOHN ANDREW, 1866-1942, Married Anna C. Wright, 1878
    Children: Lelia, 1900
                 Ernest, 1903, Married Thelma Ghun
                 John Andrew, Jr., 1906, Married Irene Ferguson, 1910

MANN, JR., JOHN ANDREW, 1906, Married Irene Ferguson, 1910
    Father: J. A. Mann   Mother: Anna C. Wright
    Children: Mildred, 1931
                 Kenneth, 1939

MANN, RICHARD MORTON, 1870, Married Carrie Pollard, died 1899
                             Second wife: Eunice Gregory, 1881-1904

MARKS, M. HASKINS, Married Rosa Lee
    Father: W. D. Marks   Mother: Allie Turner
    Children: Elsie, Married Don Perdiew
                 LeRoy, Married Lottie Lucado
                 Florence, Married Ed Ranson
                 Louise, Married Strode Burks
                 Gladys, Married Mike Thornhill
                 William, Married _____
                 Hughes, Married_____

MARKS, RICHARD D., 1910, Married Virginia Smith, 1908, of Cumberland
    Children: Richard D., Jr., 1932

MARKS, THOMAS HOLMES, 1880, Married Fannie Megginson, 1884
    Father: W. D. Marks   Mother: Allie Turner
    Children: Allie, 1907

MARKS, W. D., 1848-1924, Married Allie Turner, 1850-1901
    Children: Ida B., 1874-1922
                 M. H., 1877, Married Rosa Lee
                 T. H., 1880, Married Fannie Megginson
                 S. E., 1882-1920, Married Lucy Christian of Nelson
                 J. R., 1886, Married Florence Dixon of Buckingham
                 Earl, 1890, Married George Langran of Texas

MARSH, EDWARD J., 1877, Married Cara Winona Hamilton, 1882

MARSH, G. T., 1871, Married Virgie T. Davis, 1877
    Children: Herman Thomas, 1903, Married Frances Flinn of Campbell
                Harry Walker, 1903, Married Lillian Hillsman
                Rachel, 1910, Married A. Victor Jones of Campbell
                Jessalyn, 1914, Married E. R. Davis of Lynchburg
                Aspin L., 1917, Married Miss Kirby of Lynchburg
                Randolph P., 1920, Married Miss Dobbs of Norfolk
                Theresa, 1901, Married Dean A. Pugh

MARSH, THOMAS, 1840-1934, Married Elvira Gordon, died 1934

MARSHALL, SR., D. H., Married Elizabeth Hunter
    Children: Thomas, Married Miss Dickey of Nelson
                John
                Hunter
                Robert, Married Miss Harvey
                Willie, Married Susie Coleman
                D. H., Jr., Married Mary Coleman

MARSHALL, JR., DOUGLAS HANCOCK, 1857-1914, Married Mary Walker of
                                                        Coleman, 1870
    Father: D. H. Marshall   Mother: Elizabeth Hunter
    Children: Mary Elizabeth, 1890
                William Douglas, 1892, Married Ruth Caldwell
                Abbitt Hancock, 1893, Married Margaret Virginia Carter,
                                                        1900-1933
                Schuyler Benjamin, 1895, Married Pearl Virginia Caldwell,
                                                        1895
                Byron Walker, 1898, Married Janie Drucilla Nichols
                David Glover, 1900, Married Irene Martin
                Susin Betty, 1902, Married Lester Walker Jenkins
                Sarah Grace, 1905, Married Willie Cadmus Rudd, 1903
                Douglas Perreeza, 1907
                Ruby Isabelle, 1911

MARSHALL, ELLIOTT HUNTER ("DOCK"), 1877, Married Emma C. Cheatham,
                                                        1877
    Children: Elliott Wilkins, 1898, Married Susie Hunter Caldwell, 1896
                Josephine Christian, 1902, Married Thomas W. Harvey, 1890
                William Franklin, 1905, Married Nannie Cochran Caldwell, 1905
                Mary Lucille, 1909, Married Joseph Howerton

MARSHALL, ELLIOTT WILKINS, 1898, Married Susie Hunter Caldwell, 1896
    Father: Elliott Hunter Marshall   Mother: Emma C. Cheatham
    Children: Margaret Hunter, 1921
                Eliotte Wilkins, 1923
                Jane Marie, 1925
                Robert Thomas, 1926
                Beatrice, 1928

MARSHALL, GLOVER BENJAMIN, 1891, Married Addie Harvey
    Father: William Benjamin Marshall   Mother: Susie Ellis Coleman
    Children: Wilson Benjamin, 1919
                 Mary Thelma, 1921

MARSHALL, HENRY MORTON, 1867-1943, Married Blanch Gilliam
    Second wife, Alice Gilliam
              Child: Henry Morton Marshall, 1826-1947

MARSHALL, HENRY WILKINS, 1825-1895, Married Sarah Hancock, 1828-1907
    Children: Paulina, 1849-1917
                 William Atkins, 1850-1918, Married Ellie Hamlet, 1847-1939
                 Mary C., 1852, died in childhood
                 Margaret A., 1853-1939, Married Willis Williamson
                 John W., 1855-1915, Married Lottie Smith, -1918
                 Nathan T., 1857, died in childhood
                 Lacy Thornton, 1858-1943, Married Ida Coffman
                 Nathan D., 1860-1937
                 James H., 1862-1897, Married Jennie Reynolds, 1864
        Twins   (Edwin C., 1864-1943, Married Sallie Smith, 1861-1945
                 (Edgar T., 1864
                 Charles P., 1866-1947, Married Elizabeth Price, 1875
                 Rosa F., 1868
                 David M., 1870-1930

MARSHALL, JAMES BEARD, 1779- Married Jesse Bell Jones, 1775.

MARSHALL, JOHN BAXTER, Married Mary Pearl Sears, 1874
    Children: Bessie Evelyn
                 Mary E.
                 Flossie Sears
                 John Kenneth, Married Louise Scruggs, died 1945
                 Sally Dupuy
                 Kate
                 Annie Laurie, Married Mr. Moseley; 2nd. Husband Eugene
                                                                    Sears

MARSHALL, JOHN HENRY, 1824-1902, Married Susan Catherine Thornton,
                                                          1832-1895
    Children: John H., Jr., 1854-1928, Married Mattie Gilliam, 1859-1904
                            Second wife: Fannie Gilliam
                 Maryetta V., 1855-1869
                 Janie Morton, 1857-1941
                 William Thornton, 1858-1938
                 Frank Thomas, 1860-1941
                 Richard D., 1861-1862
                 Mattie Rudd, 1863-1938, Married Joseph U. Harwood
                 Sallie Brooks, Married Joel Watkins
                 Henry Morton, 1867-1943, Married Blanche Gilliam
                            Second wife: Alice Gilliam
                 Anne Belle, 1870-1934, Married N. R. Featherston
                 James E. Marshall, Married Margaret Nichols
                 Lucy Daniel, Married Eugene W. Gilliam

MARSHALL, JR., JOHN H., 1854-1928, Married Mattie Gilliam, 1859-1904
    Children: J. R., Married Belle Gilliam of Farmville
                 Second wife of John H., Fannie Gilliam

MARSHALL, JOHN KENNETH, Married Louise Scruggs, died 1945
    Father: John Baxter Marshall   Mother: Mary Pearl Sears
    Children: John Kenneth, Jr., 1941

MARSHALL, JOHN PATTERSON, 1886, Married Reva May Cheatham, 1885
    Father: William Benjamin Marshall   Mother: Susie Ellis Coleman
    Children: Herman Patterson, 1910
                Reva Mildred, 1912, Married Richard Montague Taylor
                Frances Lucile, 1915
                Helen Holmes, 1917
                Sallye Isabel, 1919, Married Walter Twyman Coleman
                Marjorie Magdalene, 1921
                Jack, 1923
                Joseph Wingfield, 1925
                Sarah Grace, 1927

MARSHALL, JOSEPH HENRY, 1899, Married Emma Frances Rush, 1898
    Children: Thornton Henry, 1922

MARSHALL, J. R., Married Belle Gilliam
    Father: John H. Marshall, Jr.   Mother: Mattie Gilliam
    Children: Mattie Elizabeth, Married Charlie B. Carson

MARSHALL, NATHAN D., 1868-1941, Married Myrtle Lee White, 1869
    Children: Elna S., 1890, Married W. W. Overton
                Mary D., 1897, Married S. M. Golliday of Nelson
                Atwell D., 1898, Married Margaret Caldwell
                Pauline White, 1901, Married G. C. Cocke of Charlotte
                John E., 1903, Married Josephine Dobenthien of California
                George Hunter, 1909

MARSHALL, ROBERT ELLIOTT, 1845-1915, Married Mary Nathan Harvey,
                                        1847-1925
    Children: Nathan Douglas, 1868-1941, Married Myrtle Lee White, 1869
                Wilkin Jones, 1870
                Evie May, 1872-1938, Married Thomas H. Ford
                Bernice, 1875, Married Norman Pugh
                Elliott Hunter ("Dock"), 1877, Married Emma C. Cheatham,
                                          1877
                James Board, 1879, Married Jessie Jones
                Howard Blanton, 1881- Married Mary Willie Caldwell, 1886
                Travis Taylor, 1883, Married Sarah Catherine Cheatham
                Robert Collier, 1887, Married Modessia Mulliken
                Nannie Elizabeth, 1889, Married Ira Spoonhour
                Gladys Wade, 1891, Married Sylvester Pugh, 1884

MARSHALL, ROBERT LEE, 1865, Married Ada Scott Fleshman, 1866-1923
    Children: Bertie Synthia, 1886-1903, Married Rosser Wooldridge
                Elizabeth, 1888, Married W. T. Sublett of Campbell

MARSHALL, WILLIAM BENJAMIN, 1857-1932, Married Susie Ellis Coleman,
                                                  1862-1898
    Father: D. H. Marshall, Sr.   Mother: Elizabeth Hunter
    Children: Mary Olive, 1882, Married Oscar F. Cheatham, 1876
                William Douglas
                John Patterson, 1886, Married Reva May Cheatham, 1889
                Annie Walker, 1885, Married Aldridge Cheatham, 1885
                Lula Bell, 1890-1925, Married Melton W. Martin, 1885
                Grover Benjamin, 1891, Married Addie Harvey
                Martha Alice, 1894, Married John David Plunkett, 1892
                Susie Abbitt, 1896, Married Moses Nash, died 1914
                        Second husband: Josh Harvey

MARSHALL, WILLIAM FRANKLIN, 1905, Married Nannie Cochran Caldwell,
                                              1905
    Father: Elliott Hunter Marshall   Mother: Emma C. Cheatham
    Children: Mary Lucy, 1931
                Juanita Sears, 1936

MARTIN ASHERIAH, Married Lucy Dunchcomb Durham
    Children: Elizabeth
                Carolin

MARTIN, B. H. W., 1852-1932, Married Mary Alice Moore, 1855-1884
    Father: Howlett Martin
    Children: J. Edgar, 1876, Married Alice Harvey
                        Second wife: Thelma Webb
                Thomas Howlett ("Tip"), 1878, Married Estelle McLaughlin
                Mollie, 1882, Married Forest Moore
                Emmett B., 1880, Married Maude Moore
                      Second wife of B.H.W., Esmonia C. Grow,
                                        1870
    Children: Hiram O., 1890, Married Mattie Grow
                Myrtle, 1892-1936, Married Charlie Goodman
                Spurgeon, 1894-1901
                Ashby C., 1896, Married Irma Drinkard, 1892
                M. Gibbs, 1898, Married Lillian Drinkard
                Annie Walker, 1900, Married Bennett Harding
                Eural, 1902, Married Ercie Martin, 1905
                Suhling, 1904, Married Dorothy Martin, 1908
                Leonard, 1907, Married Louise Drinkard, 1911
                Emza, 1909-1911
                Estelle, 1911, Married Edwin Moore

MARTIN, CARL E., 1921, Married Sallie Reynolds, 1923

MARTIN, CHARLES, 1923, Married Elsie Marion Drinkard, 1924
    Children: Samuel R., 1945

MARTIN, EMMETT BLACKWELL, 1880, Married Maude Moore, 1881
    Father: B. H. W. Martin   Mother: Mary Alice Moore
    Children: Marjorie, 1903, Married Louis Moore
                 Emmett B., Jr., 1905-1932
                 Edythe Josephine, 1908, Married Marshall Hunter
                 Gladys, 1911, Married G. W. Taylor
                 Alise, 1914, Married Melvin W. Drinkard
                 Lloyd, 1917, Married Burnett Smith
                 Ruby, 1921, Married C. T. Moses, Jr.
                 Helen, 1924

MARTIN, ETHELBERT PAYNE, 1854, Married Agnes Johnson
    Children: Elizabeth, Married Dan Jacobs of Lynchburg
                 Edward
                 Berkley, Married Edna Landrum
                 Alma
                 Plunkett
                 Allen, Married Elizabeth Harvey

MARTIN, E. KINKLE, 1885, Married Mary Adams of Cumberland
    Father: J. W. C. Martin   Mother: Martha Virginia Moore
    Children: Marjorie, 1910, Married Dave Anderson of Charlotte
                 E. Carter, 1913, Married Louise Lewis
                 Robert K., 1914, Married Virginia Parks
                 Sallie, 1915, Married Tommy Martin
                 John Adams, 1918
                 Beverley, 1920, Married Ella Martin
                 G. C., 1923

MARTIN, FITZHUGH LEE, 1869-1947, Married Mary Eliza Garrett, 1882
    Father: William Francis Martin   Mother: Martha Smith
    Children: William Lewis, 1902, Married Estelle Beard
                 Beulah Lee, 1904, Married Lewis Ferguson
                 F. L., Jr., Married Lorine Reynolds
                           Second wife: Carrie Jamerson
                 Rebecca Elizabeth, 1907, Married Russell Jamerson
                 Lavinia, 1908-1917
                 Mary Louise, 1921, Married Joseph Hawkins of New York

MARTIN, FREEMAN C., 1822- Married Martha C. Harvey, 1831
    Children: Samuel Hunter, 1859-1910, Married Elvira B. Harvey,
                                                           1860-1893
                                        Second wife: Anna C. Pugh
                                                           1867-1913

MARTIN, JR., FRED HUNTER, 1918, Married Shirley Harvey, 1922
    Father: Hunter F. Martin   Mother: Lockie Maxwell
    Children: Fred Hunter, III, 1943

MARTIN, HARRY C., 1907, Married Bessie Roark, 1906, of Halifax
    Children: Horace Lee, 1929
                 Joel David, 1935
                 Nellie Jane, 1940
                 Clinton Douglas, 1942

MARTIN, HERBERT OTWAY, 1923, Married Irene Walter Trent, 1922

MARTIN, HESTER E., Married Joseph Crews

MARTIN, HUNTER FREEMAN, 1889, Married Lockie Belle Maxwell
    Father: Samuel Hunter Martin   Mother: Elvira B. Harvey
    Children: Fred Hunter, 1918, Married Shirley Harvey
                 Glenn Samuel, 1920, Married Ophelia Self, 1920, of Buckingham

MARTIN, JAMES ALLEN, Married Miss Harris
    Father: L. E. Martin   Mother: Leva Ann Brooks
    Children: J. A., Jr., 1938
                 Helen E., 1941
                 Robert H., 1942
                 Eunice Ann, 1945

MARTIN, JAMES D., 1842, Married Susan C. Woodson, 1836-1916
    Children: Dodridge, 1868-1918, Married Alice Kirby of Floyd
                 Reese Franklin, 1870-1945, Married Gay Kirby of Floyd
                 Walter Ryland, 1872, Married Lang Garland of Roanoke
                 Olivia, 1874, Married Sterling Scruggs
                 Emory Hughs, 1878- , Married Annie Laury Taylor, 1874

MARTIN, J. E., Married Irene Childress
    Children: Valentine, 1809- Married Elizabeth J. Plunkett, 1814
                 Thomas Benton, 1834
                 William Plunkett, 1836
                 Mary Adeline, 1838
                 Richard Seldon, 1839
                 James D., 1842, Married Susan Woodson
                 Silas Hill, 1845
                 John Wilkins, 1848
                 Steven Ambrose, 1851
                 Ethelbert Payne, 1854

MARTIN, JOEL HOLMES, 1875, Married Mollie S. Wright, 1879-1945
    Father: William Alexander Martin   Mother: Mariah Catherine Harvey
    Children: J. W., 1900, Married Maude Sidney Ferguson, 1907
                 Tressie B., 1899, Married Wade Ferguson
                 Carrie C., 1902, Married Roland Smith
                 Blanche C., 1911, Married Emmet Day
                 Wesley A., 1915, Married Susie Moon
                 Albert Fletcher, 1920, Married Margaret Almond, 1919
                 Eva Louise, 1923, Married Willie Mayberry

MARTIN, JOHN EDGAR, 1876, Married Alice Harvey
    Father: B. H. W. Martin   Mother: Mary Alice Moore
                 Second wife: Thelma Webb, 1906
    Children: Carrie Jane, 1943

MARTIN, JOHN W. C., 1858-1934, Married Martha Virginia Moore, 1865-1913
Father: Howlett Martin
Children: Wilmer, 1883-1897
E. Kinkle, 1885, Married Mary Adams of Cumberland
Etta F., 1890, Married Lytton Harvey
R. Marshall, 1893, Married Ethel Tatum of Cumberland
Howlett B., 1896, Married Estelle Dickerson
Leslie N., 1899, Married Estelle Coleman
Second wife: Dorothy Woodson
John Graydon, 1901, Married Nellie Moore
Alonza W., 1905, Married Ethel Chenault
W. D., 1907-1937, Married Mattie McCain of Alabama

MARTIN, JOHN GRAYDON, 1901- Married Nellie C. Moore, 1902
Father: John W. C. Martin   Mother: Martha Virginia Moore
Children: Warren, 1927
Graydon, 1928
Verta, 1932
Calvin, 1944

MARTIN, JOHN LACY, Married Ola Thacker
Father: Lacy Blassengame Martin   Mother: Anna Bernice Cawthorn
Children: John Lee
Bonita Rose
Wanda Gayle

MARTIN, LACY BLASSENGAME, 1886-1944, Married Anna Bernice Cawthorn
Father: Samuel Hunter Martin   Mother: Elvira B. Harvey
Children: Elvira Bernice
John Lacy, Married Ola Thacker
Rosa Elizabeth, Married Richard D. Inge

MARTIN, LEONARD E., 1907, Married Lucile Drinkard, 1911
Father: B. H. W. Martin   Mother: Esmonia C. Grow
Children: Everett W., 1931
Virginia Gertrude, 1934
Rachel A., 1940

MARTIN, LUTHER ELBERT, 1858-1932, Married Leva Ann Brooks, 1864-1941
Children: Charles Edward, 1888-1930, Married Drucy Lee Layne, died
1946
Mattie Elizabeth, 1890, Married W. A. Moon
John David, 1893, Married Ollie Baber
James Allen, 1896, Married Rebecca Elizabeth Harris, 1905
William E., 1898, Married Irene Cyrus
Mary Brucie, 1900, Married Arthur C. Almond
Vara Frances, 1903, Married David Cyrus
Lucy E., 1907-1911

MARTIN MAURY GIBBS, 1898, Married Lillian Fuller Drinkard, 1901
Father: B. H. W. Martin   Mother: Esmonia C. Grow
Children: Evelyn Drinkard, 1923, Married Herbert H. Moore, Jr.
Maury Gibbs, Jr., 1925
Alice Walker, 1932

MARTIN MAURY GIBBS, (continued)
          Alfred Carroll, 1936
          Barbara Kathleen, 1941
          Geraldine Kay, 1944

MARTIN, OTHO W., 1885, Married Lula Goodman
    Father: T. H. Martin   Mother: Mattie Emza Moore
    Children: Clark, 1907-1938
             Carrie Emza, 1909, Married Henry C. Moore
             Christine Odell, 1911, Married Hubbard Moore
             Isabel, 1914, Married Bob Moore
             Otho W., Jr., 1918, Married Hazel Lee Coleman
             Annice, 1921, Married Maurice Williams
             Ellen Rebecca, 1924, Married Beverly Martin
             David Lee, 1927, Married Lillian Martin Bethel

MARTIN, PRYOR D., 1849-1896, Married Judie A. Martin, 1853-
    Children: Lillie, 1870, Married Samuel R. Martin
             Alice, 1875-1930, Married John Martin
             Pervis, 1876, Married Ella Williams
             Elnora, 1879-1926, Married Tom Cumby
             Lucy, 1881-1933, Married George Williams
             Travis, 1883, Married Mattie Driskill
             Florence, 1885, Married Humphrey Wooldridge
             Mary, 1887, Married Buck Blackwell
             Isabelle, 1892, Married Richard Grady
             Willie, 1893, Married William Strong
       Twins {Julia, 1895, Married Lewelyn Giles
             {Julian, 1895-1933, Married Bell

MARTIN, R. B., 1912, Married Isabel Martin, 1914
    Father: T. M. Martin   Mother: Miss Grow
    Children: Allen Randolph, 1935
             Bentley Wray, 1943

MARTIN, ROBERT K., Married Virginia Parks
    Father: E. Kinkle Martin   Mother: Mary Adams
    Children: E. Kinkle, 1940
             Colyer Ann, 1942
             Lu Ella, 1943

MARTIN, ROBERT MARSHALL, 1892, Married Ethel Lee Tatum, 1893
    Father: John W. C. Martin   Mother: Mattie Virginia Moore
    Children: James Marshall, 1917, Married Margaret Drinkard, 1915
             Edythe Christian, 1918, Married Riley T. Megginson, 1915
             Mabel Etta, 1920, Married Oscar T. Whitten, 1920
             Ethel Lee, 1925, Married David T. Robertson, 1921
             John Gordon, 1927
             Garland Keith, 1930
             June Juanita, 1935

MARTIN, ROBERT W., 1853-1932, Married Mary W. Nash, 1860-1938
    Children: Donie, 1876
                  Myra H., 1877, Married Mosely W. Hunter
                  Rosa, 1880
                  David A., 1881
                  James A., 1883-1947, Married Bertha V. Wooldridge
                  Milton, 1885
                  Daisy L., 1887
                  Ryland, 1889
                  Mary L., 1891
                  Rexford, 1893
                  Annie, 1895
                  Douglas, 1897
                  Curtis E., 1899
                  Bessie J., 1902
                  Rupert N., 1904

MARTIN, RUSSELL, 1915, Married Kate Reynolds, 1919
    Children: Nerlyn, 1946

MARTIN, SAMUEL HUBERT, 1900, Married Mary Willis Ranson
    Father: Samuel Hunter Martin   Mother: Anna C. Pugh
    Children: Annie Christian
                             Second wife of S.H.: Jessie Harvey
    Children: Donna Lee

MARTIN, SAMUEL HUNTER, 1859-1910, Married Elvira B. Harvey, 1860-1893
    Father: Freeman C. Martin   Mother: Martha C. Harvey
    Children: Hunter Freeman, 1889, Married Lockie Belle Maxwell
                  Elizabeth C., 1891, Married S. C. Ranson
                  Lacy Blassengame, 1886-1944, Married Anna Bernice Cawthorn
                             Second wife of S.H.: Anna C. Pugh
                                         1867-1913
    Children: Mary Christian, 1895, Married Samuel Henry Dickerson
                  Samuel Hubert, 1900, Married Mary Willis Ranson
                         Second wife: Jessie Harvey

MARTIN, SAMUEL R., 1867-1932
    Children: Ada B., 1889, Married Willis Mann
                  Duff, 1893, Married Lelia Worley of Lynchburg
                  Hollie May, 1898, Married Willis Mann
                  Floyd Winston, 1901, Married Hester Davidson, 1904
                  Samuel Walker, 1905, Married Mary E. Layne

MARTIN, SIDNEY M., 1882-1947, Married Etta Bingham, 1878-1942
    Father: Thomas Howlett Martin   Mother: Enza Moore
    Children: Charlie, 1904, Married Winfred Harvey
                  Lois, 1905, Married Taylor Coleman
                  Mary Jane, 1914, Married W. L. Burcher
                  Joyce, 1918, Married Floyd Coleman
                  Bessie, 1916, Married Jack Cobbs
                  Lyncoln, 1920, Married Beula Hudson

MARTIN, S. R., 1851-1936, Married Rebecca Elizabeth Moore, 1852-1918
Father: Howlett Martin
Children: Emmitt G., 1875-1878
            Alexander B., 1877-1878
            R. C., 1879-1902
            W. E., 1881-1905
            A. H., 1889-1909
            Ella, 1892-1903
            T. M., 1886, Married Lillian Pearl Grow, 1890

MARTIN, THOMAS HOWLETT, 1855-1945, Married Emza Moore, 1862-1908
Children: Travis W., 1881-1947, Married Miss Stewart of Lynchburg
            Sidney M., 1884, Married Etta Bingham of Radford
            Otha W., 1886, Married Lula Goodman
            Mattie Sue, 1888, Married Clarence Drinkard
            Mary, 1890, Married Royal Coleman
            Alice R., 1892, Married Herman R. Moore
            T. Raymond, 1894, Married Ruth Drinkard, 1895
            Colena, 1896-1940, Married Marvin Drinkard
            Flemming, 1899, Married Mary Harris
            Anna Bell, 1902-1924

MARTIN, JR., THOMAS RAYMOND, 1919, Married Nannie Morris, 1919
Children: Alice Faye, 1943
            Gaynell, 1944

MARTIN, WILLIAM A:, 1840-1926, Married Mariah Catherine Harvey, 1843-1911
Children: William W., 1867
            Lizzie P., 1870, Married J. J. Cumby
            Joel H., 1875, Married Mollie S. Wright
            Nora, 1878, Married James L. Davidson
            Leonard C., 1885, Married Vassie Bagby of Pittsylvania
            Mary A., 1887, Married Charlie Seay
            John T., 1872-1872
            James N., 1874-1874
            Taylor, 1881-1936, Married Cora Studenrock of Pulaski

MARTIN, WILLIAM FRANCIS, died 1904, Married Martha Smith
Children: Fitzhugh Lee, 1869-1947, Married Mary Eliza Garrette, 1882
            Emma, Married Will Davidson
            Mamie, Married LaFayette Smith
            Ila Virginia, Married James Blackwell
            Willie, Married M. Foster of Lynchburg
            Fields, Married Nannie Foster of Lynchburg

MARTIN, WILLIAM LEWIS, 1902, Married Estelle Beard
Father: Fitzhugh Lee Martin   Mother: Mary Eliza Garrette
Children: Mary Lottie, 1927
            Dorothy Beatrice, 1931

MATTHEWS, WILLIAM, Married Frances Daniel
                  Second wife: Harriet Spencer
                  Third wife: Margaret Porter
                  Fourth wife: Margaret Gilliam

MAYBERRY, WILLIAM T., 1873, Married Mary Peo, 1879
   Children: Allen, 1897, Married Virginia Goin, 1900
               William W., 1898, Married Lena Goin, 1904
               Leonard H., 1900, Married Gracie Doss, 1899
               Leslie, 1902, Married Ruby Goodman, 1902
               Thomas A., 1904, Married Gracie Cheatham
               Riley M., 1905
               Lillie C., 1907, Married Leonard Doss
               Hallie E., 1908-1944, Married Lellie Wicker of Amherst

MAYS, WILLIAM ARTHUR, 1883, Married Margaret Thompson, 1893, of Smythe
   Children: Walter Lee, 1913, Married Louise Whitehead
               Clarence, 1916, Married Clarine Kesner
               Marie, 1918, Married Buster Bolton
               Lena, 1920, Married Ernest Pollard.
               Gilbert, 1922, Married Irene Page

MAYS, JOHN, Married Mollie_____
   Children,   Cassie, Married J. E. Handy.
               William Arthur, 1883, Married Margaret Thompson, 1893

MAXEY, LOIS MAY, 1926-1929

MAXEY, REVA MAY, 1901-1929

MAXWELL, BENJAMIN HARRISON, 1881- Married Rosa Lee Nichols of
                                    North Carolina
   Father: W. B. Maxwell
   Children: Earline, 1915, Married Mr. Smith of Baltimore
               Mellon, 1918, Married Miss Wimnah of Utah
               Margaret, 1922, Married John Goin
               Ella, 1924, Married Leonard Harvey
               James E., 1921, Married Miss Hay of Texas
               Arlis, Married Alice Burge, 1923
               Clemmy, 1928
               Lillie, 1933
               Raymond, 1927

MEADOWS, J. S., 1874, Married Berta Davis, died, 1944
   Children: Carrie, 1908, Married Howard Williams

MEGGINSON, JOSEPH C., 1829-1917, Married Eliza Alvis of Buckingham
   Father: Samuel Megginson   Mother: Mary Johnson
   Children: William Stevens, 1856- Married Susie Hill of Buckingham
               James B., 1857-1889, Married Bettie Lewis, 1858
               Mariah E., 1859, Married James Patteson
               Lucy, 1864-1864
               Ida. B., 1861-1881, Married Edward Coleman, 1861
                             Second wife of J. C.: Sarah Elizabeth
                                         Spencer
   Children: Joseph Alexander, 1865-1901, Married Rosa Hardy, 1870-
                                      1931
               Mary Elizabeth, 1868-1892, Married John Carnefix

MEGGINSON, JOSEPH C., (continued)
Twins   (Thomas J., 1870-1936
     (Robert E., 1870-1933
     Roberta B., 1873-1916, Married T. P. Robertson
     Edna F., 1876
     Alice V., 1879, Married Charlie Grow, 1872-1920
     John K., 1881-1941, Married Elsie Morgan, 1897

MEGGINSON, JOHN K., 1881-1941, Married Elsie Morgan, 1897, of Buckingham
     Father: Joseph C. Megginson,   Mother: Elizabeth Spencer
     Children: Elizabeth, 1922, Married Richard Leigh Burke, Jr.
       Joseph R., 1923, Married Ethelyne Torrence, 1924, of
                                    Lynchburg
       Jacqueline, 1927
       Dorothy, 1933

MEGGINSON, SAMUEL, 1803- Married Mary Johnson, died 1893
     Children: Sallie, 1840, Married James Davidson of Buckingham
       Samuel T. ("Buster") 1850-1933, Married Lugenia Everett
                              Patteson, 1855-1910
       Joseph C., 1829-1917, Married Eliza Alvis of Buckingham
                   Second wife: Elizabeth Spencer

MEGGINSON, SAMUEL THOMAS ("Buster"), 1850-1933, Married Lugenia
                              Everett Patteson, 1855-1910
     Father: Samuel Megginson   Mother: Mary Johnson
     Children: Benjamin Everett, 1880
       Ida Florine, 1891, Married John Beale of Buckingham
       John William, 1887, Married Mamie Curie of Nelson
       Samuel Thomas, Jr., 1891, Married Virgie Spradlin, 1896
       James Napoleon, 1896, Married Miss Hall of Norfolk
       Lula, Married Willie Beale
       Mollie, Married Willie Beale

MEGGINSON, SAMUEL T., JR., 1891, Married Virgie Spradlin, 1896
     Father: Samuel T., (Buster)   Mother: Lugenia Everett Patteson
     Children: Riley Thomas, 1915, Married M. Christian Martin, 1918
       Lucy, Married Mr. Gilliam
       Edith, Married George Williams
       Nancy, Married Paul Hughes
       John
       Wallace Ragland
       Mollie
       Jeane
       Mary Anna

MEGGINSON, WILLIAM, Married Amanda Bocock, 1805
     Children: Joseph
       John
       William, Married Martha McCraw of Buckingham
       Thomas
       Henry
       Mary, Married Capt. Jeter Davidson of Buckingham
       Judith T.

MEGGINSON, WILLIAM, (continued)

Twins
(Martha, Married Mathew Farrar
(Jane, Married Peleg Bosworth of Lynchburg
Mariah, Married James Farrar

MITCHELL, D. H., 1869-1942, Married Rosa Wooldridge, 1879
Children: O. B., 1900, Married Christine Nucomb of Petersburg
Collie, 1902, Married Myrtle Rice of Richmond
Hollie, 1903, Married Paul Cawthorn
Berkley, 1905-1940, Married Miss Smith of Lynchburg
Vara, 1909, Married Holcomb Wood
C. W., Married Margaret Fulp

MITCHELL, EUEN TALMADGE, 1895, Married Emily Frances Gunter, 1894.
Father: Charlie Wesley Mitchell   Mother: Nealy Sweeny
Children: Sarah Catherine, 1926, Married Harry B. Giles
Raymond Wyse, 1928
Charles Vernell, 1917, Married Pearle H. Burnett, 1918
William Garland, 1920, Married Rachel Lee Phelps, 1923
Hilda Carolyn, 1922, Married W. G. Buckey of Missouri

MITCHELL, FLOYD L., 1903, Married Clara Viola Guill, 1905
Father: Charlie Wesley Mitchell   Mother: Nealy Sweeney
Children: Helen Louise, 1926, Married W. W. Ford, Jr.

MITCHELL, L. M., 1866-1946, Married Willie Wooldridge
Children: Bessie, 1900, Married H. A. Torrence
Susie Estelle, 1902, Married C. A. Harvey of Lynchburg
Katie, 1904, Married Ernest Burford of Roanoke
Allen, 1907, Married Ann Mays
John D., 1909, Married Katie Cyrus

MITCHELL, ROBERT MILLER, 1888, Married Cora Ann Gordon, 1890
Father: Charlie Mitchell   Mother: Nealy Sweeny

MITCHELL, CHARLIE WESLEY, 1863-1930, Married Nealy Sweeney, 1867-
1914
Second wife Emma J. Sweeney
Children: Robert M., 1888, Married Lola Gordon, 1890
Willie W., 1889, Married Della Wooldridge, 1895
Julian B., 1891, Married Mela Coleman
Mildred E., 1893-1894
Ewen T., 1895, Married Emily Gunter
Lemuel C., 1897
Floyd L., 1903, Married Clara Guill
Mattie L., 1900, Married Irvin Wooldridge
Curtis Lewis, 1909,

MITCHELL, WILLIAM M., 1839-1912, Married Sarah Coffee, 1833-1919
    Children: Ella B., 1877, Married John R. Lewis
                Susie, 1871, Married G. E. Perdue
                Charles Wesley, Married Nealy Sweeney
                    Second wife: Emma J. Sweeney
                D. H., Married Rosa Wooldridge
                L. M., Married Willie Wooldridge

MOOMAW, JR., BENJAMIN F., Married Evelyn Makine Robertson
    Children: Benjamin F., III, 1940

MOON, D. P., 1890, Married Mary F. Dean, 1896
    Father: Archer Moon
    Children: Susie, 1912, Married W. A. Martin
                J. D., 1913, Married Lucile Carrico
                Hazel, 1915
                Rachel, 1919, Married Noton Webb
                Lucile, 1921, Married Willie Jacobs of Bedford

MOON, W. A., 1888, Married Mattie Martin
    Father: Archer Moon
    Children: William
                Margaret
                Roy

MOORE, ALONZA, 1859-1927, Married Ella Harding, died 1933
    Father: Thomas B. Moore   Mother: Martha V. Boaz
    Children: Mundy
                H. H.

MOORE, CLARENCE FLETCHER, 1895, Married Grace Coleman, 1896
    Father: T. Burge Moore   Mother: Nannie Rebecca Burge
    Children: Clarence Chandler, 1919-1946
                Irene Rebecca, 1921
                Coleman Burge, 1923, Married Mildred Louise Smith, 1924
                Ruby M., 1925-1925
                Doris Clayton, 1927
                Helena, 1838-1938

MOORE, CORNELIAS A., 1875-1944, Married Frances Burge, 1876
    Father: Robert Washington Moore   Mother: Hester A. Burge
    Children: Ruth, 1895, Married Robert Wheeler of Campbell
                Robert, 1899, Married Mary Grow, 1898
                Ina, 1902, Married Hardin Harvey of Campbell
                F. E., 1905, Married Hartwell Burge
                H. C., 1908, Married Carrie Martin, 1909
                V. D., 1911, Married Raymond Hamilton
                E. B., 1914, Married E. Phelps
                C. B., 1917,-1921
                Bernice Rice, 1919, Married Rebecca Whitten

MOORE, EDDIE, Married Mollie Watts of Lynchburg
    Father: Robert Washington Moore
    Children: Eddie, Married a lady from West Virginia

MOORE, EDGAR T., 1904, Married Rachel Hunter, 1903
    Father: Edward W. Moore   Mother: May Ocie Burge
    Children: Jean Caroline, 1935
                 Sandra Hopkins, 1939

MOORE, EDWARD W., 1868-1940, Married May Ocie Burge, 1874
    Father: Thomas B. Moore   Mother: Martha V. Boaz
    Children: Hince, 1902, Married Stella Chenault, 1902
                 Edgar T., 1904, Married Rachel Hunter, 1903
                 Virginia E., 1911, Married Milton Hunter, 1906
                 Royal, 1914, Married Verna Kern, 1915

MOORE, EDWIN MURPHY, 1910, Married Estelle Martin. 1911
    Father: H. Milton Moore   Mother: Alice Irene Moore
    Children: Minnie Evalena, 1930
                 Thomas Benjamin, 1932

MOORE, FLETCHER B., 1838-1931, Married Martha R. Moore, 1845-1914
    Children: Neola E., Married Thomas Howerton
                 James W., Married Elizabeth Baldwin
                 Baker B., Married Eliza Conner
                 William W., Married Maggie M. Shaner
                 Rebecca, Married John H. Crews

MOORE, HENRY CORENLIUS, 1908, Married Carrie Emza Martin, 1909
    Father: Cornelias A. Moore   Mother: Frances Burge
    Children: Richard Earl, 1935-1943
                 Fred Wallace, 1939
                 Edward Huston, 1942
                 Mildred Christine, 1943
                 Henry Cornelius, Jr., 1946

MOORE, JR., HERBERT H., Married Evelyn D. Martin
    Children: Harold Wayne, 1940
                 Freddie Lee, 1942

MOORE, HUNTER MILTON, 1890, Married Alice Irene Moore, 1888
    Father: Alonza Moore   Mother: Ella Harding
    Children: Edwin M., 1910, Married Estelle Martin, 1911
                 Jesse Clyde, 1912, Married Katherine Martin, 1912
                 Aubrey I., Married Vera Kern, 1912

MOORE, JESSE CLYDE, 1912, Married Katherine Martin, 1911
    Father: H. Milton Moore   Mother: Alice Irene Moore
    Children: Alice Jean, 1932
                 Elsie Carolyn, 1938
                 Myrtle Mae, 1942

MOORE, JOHN C., 1826-1920, Married Susan Burge
    Children: Thomas B., Married Susan Martin
                 Alice, Married Walker Martin
                 Emza, Married Thomas Martin
                 Rebecca, Married Samuel Martin

MOORE, JOHN C:, 1877-1945, Married Ellen Hubbard, 1876
    Father: Thomas Burge Moore   Mother: Frances Susan Martin
    Children: Thomas Kenneth, 1899, Married Katherine Alvis of Huntington
                 Walker Clark, 1900, Married Mary Coleman, 1904
                 Nellie Clifton, 1902, Married Graydon Martin, 1901
                 Louis, 1904, Married Margie Martin, 1903
                 Hubbard Cardwell, 1907, Married Christine Martin, 1912

MOORE, LOUIS, 1904, Married Margie Martin, 1903
    Father: John C. Moore   Mother: Ellen Hubbard
    Children: Jessalyn, 1926
                 Nellie Margarete, 1929
                 Thomas Carlton, 1931-1942
                 Susan Jennette, 1934
                 Rebecca Ann, 1936
                 Jeraldine, 1939
                 Louis Walker, 1941
                 Eva Celesce, 1942

MOORE, MARVIN, 1890, Married Ida Grow, 1896
    Children: Lyle Clifton, 1919-1945
                 Virginia Irene, 1921, Married Edgar Tuck of Halifax
                 John Patterson, 1924
                 Marvin, Jr., 1926
                 Doris Aileen, 1928
                 Virgle Alton, 1932

MOORE, ROBERT WASHINGTON, 1828-1909, Married Hester A. Burge,
                                            1832-1904
    Children: Wesley Emory, 1850-1930, Married Miss Grow
                              2nd. Wife, Mary Overton
                 Washington, Robert, 1853-1930
                 T. Burge, 1856-1940, Married Nannie Rebecca Burge, died 1933
                 John Tompkins, 1859-1892
                 William Fletcher, 1861-1947; Married Sarah Jane Taylor
                            2nd. wife, Maey Ellen Hudson
                 Rosa Blanche, 1864-1940, Married Homer C. Babcock
                 Edward Hall, 1867-1897,
                 Francis Boggs, 1870
                 Cornelias A., 1875-1944, Married Frances Burge, 1876

MOORE, R. C., 1888, Married Maude Gregory, 1881-1946
    Father: William Fletcher Moore   Mother: Sarah Jane Taylor
    Children: Hilda, 1914
                 Lawrence, 1916, Married Melva Kofink of New York, 1909
                 Calhoun, 1918, Married Roma Saul of Pennsylvania, 1920
                 William, 1923

MOORE, SAMUEL AND JAMES, Killed in Civil War.

MOORE, THOMAS B., 1831-1908, Married Martha V. Boaz, 1839-1873
    Children: Hunter M., 1857-1937, Married Bertha Paris, died 1938
                 Alonza, 1859-1927, Married Ella Harding, died 1933
                 Willis B., 1862-1926, Married Lelia Bethel, died 1936
                 Martha V., 1864-1913, Married John C. Martin, died 1934
                 Laura, 1866-1872
                 Edward W., 1868-1940, Married May Ocie Burge, 1874
                 Robert B., 1870-1908, Married Mary Scruggs of Amherst

MOORE, T. BURGE, 1856-1942, Married Nannie Rebecca Burge, died 1933
    Father: Robert Washington Moore   Mother: Hester A. Burge
    Children: Fannie Burge, 1878, Married J. D. Hamilton
               Lula, 1884, Married Mr. Harris
               Robert E., 1882
               Cabelle, 1884-1940, Married Alma Hamilton
               Hester A., 1886
               Edmonia, 1888-1930, Married Howard Phelps
               Florine, 1890, Married Tommy T. Phelps
               Wiley Floyd, 1892
               Clarence Fletcher, 1895, Married Grace Coleman

MOORE, THOMAS BURGE, 1854-1926, Married Frances Susan Martin,
                                                        1846-1943
    Father: John C. Moore   Mother: Susan Burge
    Children: Minnie Eva, 1874-1900, Married Thomas Gardner
               John C., 1877-1945, Married Ellen Hubbard, 1876
               Alice Irene, 1888, Married H. Milton Moore, 1894

MOORE, THOMAS KENNETH, 1899, Married Katherine Alvis
    Father: John C. Moore   Mother: Ellen Hubbard
    Children: Charles Kenneth, 1940

MOORE, WESLEY EMORY, 1850-1930, Married Susie Josephine Grow,
                                                        1849-1888
    Father: Robert Washington Moore   Mother: Hester A. Burge
    Children: Rev. Lloyd, 1874, Married Miss Ivey
               Forest, 1879, Married Mollie Martin, 1882
               James I., 1884-1947, Married Ruth Overton Burge, 1889
               Herman Robert, 1886, Married Alice Martin
               Genevia, Married Dr. Rucker
               Maude, Married E. B. Martin
               Susie, Married G. Wirt Taylor
                   Second wife of W. E.: Mary Overton, died 1920

MOORE, WALKER CLARK, 1900, Married Mary Coleman, 1904
    Father: John C. Moore   Mother: Ellen Hubbard
    Children: Mary Ellen, 1934

MOORE, REV. WASHINGTON, Married Elizabeth Cardwell of Campbell

MOORE, WILEY F., 1894, Married Claudie Cash, 1906, of Amherst
    Father: T. Burge Moore   Mother: Nannie Rebecca Burge
    Children: Alton, 1929
               Claude Allen, 1937

MOORE, WILLIAM FLETCHER, 1861-1947, Married Sarah Jane Taylor of
Amherst
Father: Robert Washington Moore Mother: Hester A. Burge
Children: R. C., Married Maude Gregory
Annie Laurie, 1890
Rev. Raymond, Married Gladys Witt

MORGAN, MILDRED, 1931, Daughter of Leslie Morgan of Clarksville

MORGAN, WILLIAM H., 1861-1934, Married Lula B. Carson

MORTON, DR. CHARLES, Married Mary Lavalett Gilliam, 1850
Children: Charles Francis, 1872-1898
Marshall, 1874
Mary Evelyn, 1877, Married Lucius Dillon of Botetourt
Evangeline, 1879, Married Mr. Martin of Georgia
Henry Wilson, 1881
John Taylor, 1884, Married Florence Massie of Nelson
William Gilliam, 1886-1941
Elsie V., 1889-
Robert Finley, 1891

MORRIS, CHARLES H., 1858-1920, Married Addie Ferguson, 1868-1946
Children: Lawrence, 1884, Married Tarry Hatch of Disputana
Joel, 1887, Married Chessie Wright, 1886
Bessie, 1890, Married Thornton R. Carter
John D., 1893-1932
Dillie, 1896, Married Leonard W. Carter
Odelle, 1898-1929, Married Mott McFadden
Abednigo, 1900, Married Nannie Carter, 1902
Nannie, 1903, Married Julian McFadden
Janie, 1906, Married Walter Frazier of Lynchburg
Jennings, 1908, Married Mamie Camper of Buchanan
Neva, 1910, Married Willie Hamilton

MORRIS, JAMES DILLARD, 1886-, Married Helen Gregory
Father: R. N. Morris Mother: Mary E. Ferguson
Children: James N., Married Lucile Woodall
Thelma, Married T. Hunter Dickerson

MORRIS, JAMES N., Married Lucile Woodall
Father: J. D. Morris Mother: Helen Gregory
Children: Shirley

MORRIS, JOSEPH HENRY, 1848-1925, Married Mary F. Cheatham, 1844-1904
Children: Leslie Thomas, 1873-1941, Married Bessie Chilton, 1872-1948
Ava, 1875-1937, Married R. F. Ramsey
Earn, 1877, Married R. C. Fleshman
Lena, 1879
Nannie, 1881, Married W. E. Dickerson
Eltha, 1883

MORRIS, JUDSON JOEL, 1913, Married Frances Lorene Martin, 1916
    Father: J. T. Morris
    Children: Shirley Mae, 1937
               Richard Glenn, 1941

MORRIS, LUTHER EMMETT, 1882, Married Rosa Healon Wright, 1885

MORRIS, LUTHER J., 1880, Married Alice Jane Proffitt, 1892
    Father: R. N. Morris   Mother: Mary E. Ferguson
    Children: Garland Jackson, 1922

MORRIS, NICHOLAS, 1849-1913, Married Mary Davidson Garrette, 1835-1896
    Children: Emily, 1871, Married B. C. Chernault
               William Thomas, 1873, Married Maggie Spiggle
                            Second wife of Nicholas: Laura
                                       O'Brien Lindsay
                            Third wife: Lucy Harper Wooldridge
    Children: Lucy, 1910, Married Mr. Crowell of South Boston

MORRIS, ROBERT HAROLD, 1919, Married Margie Webb
    Father: Robert Walter Morris   Mother: Hallie Torrence
    Children: Robert Harold, Jr., 1944

MORRIS, ROBERT NAT., 1858-1915, Married Mary E. Ferguson, 1852-1900
    Children: Mary F., 1871-1944, Married Henry Bingham
               Rhoda A., 1872-1941, Married S. A. Gilbert
               Robert W., 1874, Married Hallie Torrence
               William H., 1876-1891
               Lillie B., 1878, Married H. Winston Ferguson
               Luther J., 1880, Married Alice Jane Proffitt, 1892
               Maude O., 1882-1935, Married Joseph Lucado
               Ossie S., 1884, Married J. Shelton Ferguson
               James Dillard, 1886- Married Helen Gregory
               Mamie P., 1888-1944, Married James Beasley
               Charles Lelon, 1891, Married Ida Hawley
               Wiley M., 1893, Married Gertrude McKenzie Harris
               Jesse M., 1897, Married J. L. Gordon

MORRIS, ROBERT WALTER, 1870, Married Hallie Torrence, 1877
    Father: R. N. Morris   Mother: Mary E. Ferguson
    Children: Betty, 1901, Married Richard Meade Webb
               Verna, 1906, Married Richard Hamilton, 1904
               Vara, 1908, Married Herman E. Robertson
               William David, 1910, Married Lola Moore, 1909
        Twins   (Rachel, 1913, Married Leonard Fred Day
               (Ruth, 1913, Married John Daniel Jennings
               James Earl, 1917, Married Frances Whitten of Chase City
               Robert Harold, 1919, Married Margie Webb

MOSES, C. T., 1844-1896, Married Mary Woodson, 1845
    Children: W. A., 1868, Married Carrie Smith, 1874
               Thomas W., Married Matilda Clara Mann
               James Drury, 1871, Married Carrie Walton, 1877
               R. L., Married Miss Bryant

MOSES, C. T., (continued)
        Charlie
        Leonard

MOSES, CHARLES THOMAS, 1897, Married Virginia Godwin of Nansemond
    Father: Thomas W. Moses   Mother: Matilda Clara Mann, 1876
    Children: Caroline, Married Vincent Lusadi
                Virginia, Married H. Webster Babcock
                Charles, Thomas, Jr., Married Ruby Martin
                Clara Whitney, Married Mr. Herndon of Chatham

MOSES, THOMAS W., 1873, Married Matilda Clara Mann 1876
    Children: Charles Thomas, 1897, Married Virginia Godwin
                Nettie, Married F. C. Dresser of Canada

MOSES, W. A., 1868, Married Carrie Smith, 1874
    Father: C. T. Moses   Mother: Mary Woodson
    Children: Don, 1896-1942, Married Willie Smith
                Mary, 1897, Married A. T. Inge
                Hunter, 1903, Married Ella Blanks of Lynchburg

MOSS, RICHARD TOLER, 1844-1924, Married Virginia Scruggs, 1847-1904
    Children: Mattie Sue
                Daisye M., 1889, Married Hugh Sanders of Richmond
                Viola, Married C. E. Lewis
                Mary Fannie, Married J. C. Abbitt
                Anna Belle, Married W. C. Harvey
                Janie, Married D. E. Walton
                John

MOSS, WILLIAM OSCAR, 1894, Married Mattie Sears, 1897
    Children: Nancye Griffin, 1924

MURPHY, F. L., 1886, Married Mary Hester Babcock, 1890
    No Children

McCAIN, ADFIELD S., 1909, Married Maude Mullen, 1909, of Alabama
    Children: Grace M., 1934
                Susan B., 1939
                Maude M., 1942
                Henrietta, 1945

McCORMICK, CHARLES PERROW, 1908, Married Susie Pauline McCormick, 1910
    Father: Saul McCormick   Mother: Tiny Phelps
    Children: Clyde Eugene, 1932
                Carl Marnard, 1934
                Charles Harold, 1937
                Permelia Louise, 1939

McCORMICK, E. W., Married "Sis" Childress
    Children: Berta, Married Daniel Jamerson
                Mary E., Married Floyd Woody
                Eugene, Married Rosa Stevens

McCORMICK, E. W., (continued)
                Cora, Married B. W. Robertson
                Nannie, Married Leonard Nordwell
                John Thomas, Married Jessie Ledbetter
                            Second wife: Amilia McCormick
                Charlie, Married Ethel Ledbetter
                Tiny, Married J. D. Phelps
                Walker, Married Effie Childress
                Carrington
                John T., Married Annie L. Stevens, 1900

McCORMICK, JOHN T., Married Annie L. Stevens, 1900
    Father: E. W. McCormick
    Children: Hubert, 1918, Married Helen Coffee of Nelson
                    Robert, 1920, Married Marjorie Coffee of Nelson

McCORMICK, LEIGHTON, 1899, Married Myrtle Childress, 1903
    Father: William Benjamin McCormick   Mother: Emma Franklin
                                                            Claybrook
    Children: Lucille, 1925
                  James, 1927
                  Leighton, Jr., 1929
                  Adelle, 1932
                  Eloise, 1934
                  Dorothy, 1939

McCORMICK, LEWIS S., 1888, Married Queeney Almond, 1890
    Children: Charlie, Married Rachel Jamerson
                  Lewis, Married Eva Williamson
                  Bennie, Married Florence Tyree
                  Bolden, Married Miss Newan
                  Calvin, Married Margaret Gallier
                  Wiley
                  Mirlene, Married Jamie Ferguson
                  Miner
                  Makey

McCORMICK, OSCAR D., 1915, Married Lucy Woody, 1918
    Father: Oscar Leonard McCormick   Mother: Nora Stevens
    Children: James Coleman, 1944
                  Shirley Ann, 1935

McCORMICK, OSCAR LEONARD, 1892, Married Nora Stevens
    Father: Saul McCormick   Mother: Amelia Burks
    Children: Oscar D., 1915, Married Lucy Woody
                  Elizabeth, 1918, Married W. C. Woody
                  James Otis, 1920, Married Lillian B. Woody
                  Ivanhoe, 1922, Married Helen Proffitt

McCORMICK, SAUL, Married Amelia Burks
        Children: Edna, 1887, Married Truman Woody
                        Berta, 1889, Married William Hargrove
                        Frank, 1889, Married Pearl McCormick
                                    Second wife: Tiny Phelps
                        Oscar Leonard, 1892, Married Nora Stevens
                        Johnny, 1894, Married Annie Stevens
                        Morton, 1896
                        Clyde, 1898
                        Earl, 1900, Married Mabel Robertson
                        Perrow, 1902, Married Susie McCormick

McCORMICK, WILLIAM BENJAMIN, 1848-1907, Married Emma Franklin
                                          Claybrook, 1846-1932
        Children: Leighton, 1899, Married Myrtle Childress, 1903

McCORMICK, WILLIAM B., 1878, Married Nettie Ferguson, 1896
        Children: Louise, 1916, Married John Darding of Lynchburg
                        William Mott, 1918, Married Mary Jamerson
                        Bessie L., 1920, Married James Roberts of Concord
                        Mattie Pearl, 1922, Married Pete Martin of Lynchburg
                        Helen R., 1924
                        C. V., 1926
                        Elwood, 1928
                        Charles, 1930

McCORMICK, WILLIAM F., died 1926, Married Tiny Hughes of Buckingham
        Children: Eva, Married George Stanley of Amherst
                        William, Married Mrs. Clark of Pennsylvania
                        Jessie, Married John Thomas McCormick
                        Mattie Lou, Married George Stevens
                                      Second wife of W.F.: Martha Hughes of
                        Rosa,   Buckingham
        Children: Married Harry Gibson
                        Second Husband, H. L. Hays
                        Third Husband, Mr. Newel
                        Herbert, Married Eva Charles
                        Carrington

McDEARMON, CLARENCE LEWIS, Married Willie Guthrie Anderson
        Father: Clarence Stickley McDearmon   Mother: Mamie E. Tucker
        Children: C. Lewis, Jr., 1938
                        Mary Anna, 1941

McDEARMON, CLARENCE STICKLEY, 1871, Married Mamie E. Tucker
        Father: William James McDearmon   Mother: Mary Frances Stickley
        Children: James Wilber, Married Olive Raiford of Southampton
                        Mary Frances, Married Elliot Cheatham of Florida
                        Mildred Tucker
                        Clarence Lewis, Married Willie Guthrie Anderson
                        Richard
                        Elizabeth, Married Samuel B. Witt of Richmond

McDEARMON, JAMES DANIEL, Married Pearl Farrar
    Father: William James McDearmon   Mother: Mary Frances Stickley
    Children: Elaine, Married H. Y. Spencer
              Mary, Married R. D. Sears

McDEARMON, COL. SAMUEL D., 1814-1871, Married Mary Walton
    Children: William James, 1844-1925, Married Miss Stickley
              Samuel D., Jr.
              Mary, Married David Plunkett
                      Second husband: Cornelius Hill
              Victoria
              Hampton, Married Miss Wright

Mc DEARMON, WILLIAM JAMES, 1844-1925, Married Mary Frances Stickley,
                                                1851-1890
    Father: Col. Samuel D. McDearmon   Mother: Mary Walton
    Children: Clarence S., 1871, Married Mamie Tucker of Amherst
              Morton Lacy, 1870, Married Mamie Dyson
              Mary M., 1873, Married S. M. Thornton
              James Daniel, 1877, Married Pearl Farrar
              John R., 1879-1886
              Nulty C., 1882, Married Edmund H. Cawthorn
              William A., 1885-1924, Married Mary L. Farrar
              Alma G., Married Norman Farrar

McFADDEN, ELIJAH, Married Edith Virginia Ferguson

McGILL, WALTER, Married Sallie Burke, 1875-
    Children: Betty, Married Dr. John McKee

McKINNEY, DANIEL, 1830-1896, Married Virginia Walton, died 1903
    Children: Joel, 1867-1887
              Annie, 1869-1923
              Charles, 1877, Married Mary Cheatham, 1879

McKINNEY, FRANK W., 1855-1916, Married Mary McKinney
    Father: John H. McKinney   Mother: Maggie Walton
    Children: Frankie

McKINNEY, JOHN H., 1819-1886, Married Miss Statham
                       Second wife: Maggie Walton
    Children: J. Walton, 1852-1937, Married Eva Peers
          · Charlie, 1853, Married Miss Beatty of Glade Springs
              Lou
              Cornelia, Married R. B. Poore
              Frank W., 1855-1916, Married Lelia Peers
                      Second wife: Mary McKinney of Amherst
              Luther: 1858-1928
              Lizzie, Married Mr. Watts of Lynchburg
              Kate, Married Mr. Wright of Richmond
              William C., 1868-1919
              Mattie, Married H. C. Elliott of Roanoke
              Fannie
              H. Winston

McKINNEY, J. WALTON, 1852-1937, Married Eva Peers, 1856-1904
    Father: John H. McKinney Mother: Maggie Walton
    Children: (Margaret, 1880, Married H. C. Elliott of Roanoke
      Twins   (Virginia, 1880,-1908, Married Mallory Dunnington of
                            Lynchburg
           Helen, 1884-1934, Married Tell Adams of Lynchburg
           Mary, 1886-1925, Married Mr. Hoskins of Tennessee
           Walton Holmes, 1893
           John Peers, 1900-1907

McKINNEY, SAMUEL HENRY, Married Mary Lizzie Averett of Baltimore
    Children: Janie
           Mary, Married Frank W. McKinney

McPHILLIPS, EDWARD, 1897, Married Otis Virginia Coleman, 1897
    Children: Hilda D., 1931
           E. W., 1933

McPHILLIPS, PATRICK H., 1895, Married Lizzie May Phillips, 1907
    Children: Patrick H., Jr., 1931
           Margaret Ann, 1938

NASH, HUNTER S., 1907, Married Willie S. Burks, 1909
    Children: David Sylvester, 1929
           Buford Hunter, 1933
           Binford Burks, 1933
           Paul Thomas, 1936

NASH, MOSES MARTIN, died 1914, Married Susie Abbitt Marshall, 1894
    Children: Moses Martin, Jr., 1914, Married Alice Franklin

NASH, WILLIAM THOMAS, 1881, Married Ariana E. Godsey, 1883-1916
    Children: Bertha M., 1900
           Maggie L., 1902
           Mattie M., 1905
           Charlie T., 1908
           Annie S., 1910
           Nellie Davis, 1915
                 2nd. Wife, Mary Lenie Inge, 1888
    Children: Henry Elliott, 1920
           Mildred Lynett, 1921
           Richard T., 1924

NESTER, EUNICE, 1910, Married Miss Grishaw, 1910
    Children: Albert, 1930
           Virgle Curtis, 1933
           Joyce Minie, 1942

NOWLIN, ABRAM, Married Mildred Watkins
    Children: Elizabeth, 1789
           William W., 1791
           Sarah, 1791
           Thomas W., 1895
           Martha C., 1797
           Peter, 1799

NOWLIN, ABRAM, (continued)
           Bryant, 1802
           Samul, 1806
           Abrum P., 1809

NOWLIN, ALLIE BENJAMIN, 1856-1921, Married Emma Catherine Wooldridge,
                                                         1856
   Father: Perkins Nowlin   Mother:
   Children: Mary Patteson, Married W. W. O'Brien
                Mittie Odelle, Married W. L. Coleman
                Maude, 1889, Married J. N. Phelps
                Bertha, 1891, Married E. W. Austin of Illinois
                Lucy
                Floyd, 1895-1924
                Mattie Gladys, 1898, Married James H. Lucado
                Alethia C., Married C. H. Manning of Pennsylvania

NOWLIN, JAMES BENJAMIN, 1849-1932, Married Annie E. Wingfield, 1871
   Father: Thomas Watkins Nowlin   Mother: Ann Tombs Carnefix
   Children: James Tucker, 1892-1942, Married Lena Campbell
                Annie Lee, 1898, Married William B. Dove, 1898

NOWLIN, JOHN H., 1839-1901, Married Sallie Woodson, 1856-1925
   Children: Julia, Married Bernard S. Thorpe
                Albert Sidney, 1878-1944, Married Annie Mosley Thornhill,
                                              1891
                Mary, Married John Moon of Albemarle
                Laura, Married Walker LeGrande
                William Henry, 1884-1947, Married Fannie Wood, of Campbell
                Bessie, Married Frank L. Cisna of Pennsylvania

NOWLIN, SAMUEL WALKER, 1843-1915, Married Emma Chapman of Giles
   Father: Bryant Nowlin   Mother: Miss Perkins

NOWLIN, THOMAS WATKINS, 1795-1872, Married Ann Tombs Carnefix, 1814
   Children: Elizabeth Mildred, 1833-1834
                Martha Jane, 1834-1869
                George Washington Perkins, 1836-1909
                Samuel Mosbey, 1840-1911, Married Fannie Cook of Wytheville
                Mary Susan, 1841
                John William, 1844
                Sarah Frances, 1842-1929, Married Dave Rogers
                Thomas Edwin, 1838-1908
                Bryant Hunter, 1846, Married Molly Patterson of Wytheville
                James Benjamin, 1849-1932, Married Annie E. Wingfield, 1871
                (Annie Branch Gibbs, 1851-1921, Married H. E. Burton
     Triplets   (Daniel Adams Christian, 1851-1894
                (Henry Patteson, 1851-1852
                David Hunter, 1855-1856
                Robert C., 1857-1857

NOWLIN, WILLIAM C., Married Jeannie Walker
   Children: Robert Watkins, 1881-1942, Married Annie Robertson

NOWLIN, W. C., died 1924, Married Nannie Wooldridge
    Father: Perkins Nowlin   Mother:
    Children: Burton
                Charlie
                Alton

O'BRIEN, BENJAMIN WALKER, 1850-1947, Married Virgie Ferguson, 1870
    Children: Francis P., 1906, Married Mary Goin
                Rachel, 1909, Married Charlie McFadden
                Hildren Walker, 1903

O'BRIEN, FRANK ALLEN, 1874, Married Marie Ida Torrence
    Father: Robert Alexander O'Brien   Mother: Mildred Kyle Conner
    Children: Mildred Eva, 1896, Married Elwood Alvis
                Robert Alfred, 1898-1947, Married Ocie Jones of Williamsburg
                Kate Elizabeth, 1900
                Charles Abbitt, 1902-1902
                Mary Lucile, 1903, Married Louis Dahl of Farmville

O'BRIEN, JAMES HOWARD, 1880, Married Nettie Conner, 1887
    Children: Clyde Garvis, 1910, Married Ellen Sweizer of Wheeling
                Ouida, 1908, Married Owen Persinger of Alleghaney
                Claudine
                James Howard, Jr.
                Nelwyn
                Maurine
                    Second wife: Margaret Smith, 1908
    Children: Thomas Ellis
                Richard Smith

O'BRIEN, JENNINGS L., Married Mary Sears Tweedy, died 1913
    Father: Robert Alexander O'Brien   Mother: Mildred Kyle Conner
    Children: Joseph
                Edith
                Ann, Married Jack Davis

O'BRIEN, ROBERT ALEXANDER, 1847-1928, Married Mildred Kyle Conner,
                                        1854-1893
    Children: Frank Allen, 1874, Married Marie Ida Torrence, 1875
                Judith Albertha, 1876, Married W. P. Gills
                Robert Edward, 1877, Married Helen C. Weaver of West Va.
                William Walker, 1880, Married Mary P. Nowlin, 1883
                Thomas Henry, 1882, Married Catharine Peppleman of
                                  Philadelphia
                Jennings L., 1884, Married Mary Sears Tweedy, died 1913
                Mary Elizabeth, 1886, Married S. G. Johndroe of Vermont
                Ada Elaine, 1889
                Ira Conner, 1891-1892
                Lucy J., 1892

O'BRIEN, WILLIAM WALKER, 1878, Married Mary Patteson Nowlin, 1883
    Father: Robert Alexander O'Brien   Mother: Mildred Kyle Conner
    Children: Evelyn Christine
                Garland Patteson
                Maynard Gordon
                Hiram L.
                Phoebe Catherine
                Isabel, Married Mr. Haug of Switzeland
                Dorothy, Married Mr. Perkins of Richmond
                William David, Married Bessie Gunter
                Robert Allen, Married Miss Brownlee

O'CONNOR, DENNIS of Ireland, 1824-1883, Married Susan Smith of
                                Chesterfield, 1833-1900
    Children: William E., 1856-1925, Married Miss Harvey of Prince Edward
                J. F., 1858
                J. J., 1861
                M. E., 1859, Married P. R. Wooldridge
                Kate S., 1863
                M. J., 1865
                Bettie S., 1867, Married J. H. Stanley

ODEN, BENJAMIN F., died 1930, Married Bettie Burke
    Children: Vernie, Married Mr. Covington

ODONELL, PHOEBE SWADER

ODONELL, WILLIAM

ODOR, HENRY ALLEN, 1898, Married Annie Katherine Martin, 1896
    Father: Thomas W. Odor   Mother: Lizzie Coleman
                        Second wife: Beatrice Louise Dodd
    Children: Thomas William II, 1918

ODOR, JOSEPH A., 1823-1899, Married Arana Cheatham, 1830-1885
    Children: Walter W., 1860-1931, Married Miss Wingo of Giles
                Robert Smith, 1862-1928
                Thomas W., 1863, Married Lizzie Coleman, 1874
                Josiah Ellis, 1866-1916, Married Madaline Coleman
                Conrad, 1868-1931, Married Myrtia Coleman of Campbell
                Floyd P., 1870-1903, Married Mollie Kirk of West Va.
                R. Clark, 1872-1872

ODOR, THOMAS W., 1863, Married Lizzie Coleman, 1874
    Father: Joseph A. Odor   Mother: Arana Cheatham
    Children: W. Pierce, 1893, Married Caroline Vogel, 1894-1944
                Annie R., 1896, Married Russell Harper of Nottoway
                Henry Allen, 1898, Married Annie Martin
                             Second wife: Miss Dodd of Lynchburg
                Ella C., 1902, Married Mr. Rexrode of Highland
                Sarah Catherine, 1905-1913

OSBORNE, WILLIAM E., 1825-1894, Married Miss Epps

OULD, W. CARROLL, 1896, Married Addie Childers, 1904
    Father: Dr. W. L. Ould   Mother: Florence Baulow
    Children: Lyle Davis, 1928
                James Carroll, 1930

OULD, DR. W. L., 1873, Married Florence Baulow, 1871 of Halifax
    Children: W. Carroll, 1896, Married Addie Childers, 1904
                Herman, 1898, Married Ethel Shields, 1906, of Campbell
                Ruth, 1903, Married Robert Manton of New Hampshire

OVERTON, JAMES EDWARD, 1836-1920, Married Katherine Adelaid Braford
                                                            Abbitt

(OVERTON, SAMUEL H., 1833-1900)

(OVERTON, MARIE E., 1837-1909   )

(OVERTON, ANNA W., 1863-1890   )   Brothers and sisters

(OVERTON, KATE C., 1872-1889   )

(OVERTON, WILLIAM H., 1865-1891)

OWEN, JAMES ALBERT, 1868-1926, Married Willie Hughes
    Father: Nicholas Owen, Jr.   Mother: Lucinda Carson
    Children: William Albert, 1893, Married Nellie Abbott
                Thomas, 1895-1918
                James Palmer, 1900, Married Helen English of Franklin
                John Daniel, 1906, Married Lucy Coffey of Lynchburg

OWEN, NICHOLAS, JR., 1833, Married Lucinda Carson
    Children: Thomas Edward, 1864-1943, Married Willie Coleman
                Nona L., 1866-1910
                Sallie E., 1868, Married E. H. Carson
                James Albert, 1868-1926, Married Willie Hughes

OWEN, WILLIAM ALBERT, Married Nellie Abbott
    Father: James Albert Owen   Mother: Willie Hughes
    Children: Roman, 1926

PACK, DR. H. B., died 1935, Married Ollie Mae Jennings
    Children: H. B. Jr., 1912, Married Lucy Smith Caldwell
                Lucile, 1921, Married Leon R. Anderson of Alabama

PACK, JR., H. B., 1912, Married Lucy Smith Caldwell
    Father: H. B. Pack, Sr.   Mother: Ollie Mae Jennings
    Children: H. B., III, 1942

PAGE, CHARLES B., 1884, Married Grace B. Coleman, 1890
    Father: Washington Meredith Page   Mother: Mary Susan Doss
    Children: Susie J., 1909, Married Robert Carter of Franklin
                Mary V., 1911, Married T. R. Deaner
                Vera V., 1914, Married Willie Pugh
                Gladys, 1915, Married Uriel Carson
                Elmo C., 1917, Married Louise Bowman of Gladys
                Agnes, 1919, Married Earl Wilkerson
                Vernel, 1921, Married Kent Guthrie of Naruna
                Irene, 1923, Married Gilbert Mays
                Charles W., 1924
                Lewis L., 1926
                Spurgeon Ray, 1933

PAGE, THOMAS L., 1875, Married Sallie Roberta Doss, 1883
    Father: Washington Meredith Page   Mother: Mary Susan Doss
    Children: Percy H., 1905, Married Ottie Austin of Amherst
                Elsie Mae, 1907, Married Robert Wells of Farmville
                George W., 1910, Married Virginia Lucado
                Nora R., 1914, Married Lawson Lucado
                Samuel, 1915, Married Lena Stanley
                Virginia Bell, 1919, Married Eugene Dunkley of Farmville
                Albert H., 1922
                Ruth O., 1925, Married John Spiggle

PAGE, WASHINGTON MEREDITH, Married Mary Susan Doss
    Children: Willie W., 1874, Married Lizzie Austin
                Thomas L., 1875, Married Sallie R. Doss
                Samuel C., 1877, Married Annie Phelps
                Jannie H., Married Edward Phelps
                Virginia, 1881, Married Robert Phelps
                James H., 1883, Married Eva Bryant
                Charles B., Married Grace Coleman
                Rosa, Married John Harvey
                Edgar, Married Mary Smith
                Robert

PANKEY, JOHN R., 1853-1919, Married Sallie Allen, died 1892
    Father: William Tyler Pankey   Mother: Sarah Frances Gary
    Children: William Allen, 1877, Married Jessie K. Kahle of Bluefield
                Drusa Jones, 1879, Married Walter P. Wright
                Mary Randolph, 1886-1919, Married Jesse LeGrand of
                                                            Lynchburg

PANKEY, R. P., 1869, Married Elizabeth Carter, 1878
    Children: Witt, 1896-1914
                Minnie, 1897, Married Edward Pentecost
                Elsie, 1900, Married Wade May
                Mabel, 1904, Married Roy Harvey
                J. L., 1905, Married Bernice Ford
                R. L., 1908, Married Bernice Wood
                Martha, 1910, Married Fred Jennings
                T. C., 1915, Married Estelle Jennings
                Dan, 1919-1928

PANKEY, WILLIAM TYLER, 1821-1880, Married Sarah Frances Gary, 1831-
                                          1909, of Buckingham
        Children: John R., 1853-1918, Married Sallie Allen of Kentucky
                                                    died, 1892
                     Laura, 1856, Married A. H. Abbitt
                     Mattie E., 1859
                     William Tyler, Jr., 1861
                     Christopher Lee, 1863-1896, Married Ethel Wallace, died
                                             1896, of Charlottesville
                     George T., 1866
                     Charles Ernest, 1868-1888
                     Samuel L., 1871

PARIS, LEWIS D., 1907, Married Mattie Leet, 1901
        Father: Walker Daniel Paris   Mother:
        Children: Mollie, 1931

PARIS, THOMAS HENRY, 1840-1911, Married Lucinda Mahone, 1840-1911
        Children: Willie Albert, 1868-1938, Married Bertha Chenault, 1867-1933
                     Annie Rebecca, 1872-1945, Married Robert Garrett of Amherst
                     James Manson, 1877, Married Gertie Thomas of Lynchburg
                     Walker Daniel, 1879-1940, Married Susie Sublet
                                        Second wife: Mildred Farmer
                     Jesse Day, 1881, Married Janie Bondurant of Lynchburg

PARKS, GURNEA, Married Colyer Swan, 1891
        Children: Virginia, Married Robert K. Martin

PARRISH, HENRY TUCKER, 1829-1913, Married Virginia Catherine Ragland,
                                                    1855-1940
        Children: Travis Tucker, 1881-1882
                     Nathaniel Ragland, 1884, Married Mary Slusher
                     Francis V., 1890, Married Helen Burk

PATTESON, JOHN HUNT, 1845-1921, Married Bettie Patteson Nowlin, 1846-1929
        Children: Bessie, Married R. A. Hamilton
                     Henry Christian, 1871
                     Charlie Perkins, 1873, Married Miss Smith of Tennessee
                     William Duiguid, 1881, Married Mrs. Edna Beale, 1901,
                                                    of Buckingham
                     Elsie, Married Robert Hughes
                     John Robert, 1889, Married Lillian Couch of Lynchburg
                     Lucy, Married Mr. Drinkard

PATTESON, JOEL WALKER, 1860-1916, Married Maggie F. Bryant, 1867-1886
                                    Second wife: Mary Leola Torrence,
                                                    1876-1947
        Children: Lougenia, Married Lewis Doss
                     Gladys, Married H. G. Johnson
                     Earle, Married C. H. Robinson

238

PATTESON, WILLIAM DUIGUID, 1881, Married Mrs. Edna Beale, 1901
    Father: John Hunt Patteson   Mother: Bettie Pateson Nowlin
    Children: Robert Booth, 1921, Married Catherine Doss
                William Duiguid, Jr., 1924
                Charles Christian, 1927
                Thomas Carroll, 1931
                Edmond Lee, 1936
                Viola, 1926
                Barby Beale, 1929
                Lucy, 1934

PAULETTE, A. WALTER, 1861, Married Ada Jennings, 1866
    Children: Samuel Russell, 1892, Married Jeanette Garrette, 1880
                John, 1894
                Jesse Tipton, 1900

PAULETTE, BRUCE HARMON, 1914, Married Frances Harvey, 1922
    Father: Robert Jefferson Paulette   Mother: Annie C. Wheeler
    Children: Bruce Harmon, Jr., 1946

PAULETTE, C. J., 1882, Married Ethel Ferguson, 1894

PAULETTE, E. L., 1881, Married Janie Jones of Fauquier
    Children: Lucie C.
                Jane Gray, Married J. M. Inge

PAULETTE, HARVEY H., 1815-1901, Married Fannie J. Moseley, 1832-1905
    Children: Samuel Tilden, 1876, Married Lottie F. Fore, 1890

PAULETTE, JOSEPH PRESLEY, 1889, Married Alice Warriner, 1892
    Father: Richard Paulette   Mother: Maggie Farrar
    Children: William Ronald, 1918
                Helen, 1923
                Nellie, 1925, Married Ashby Paulette

PAULETT, OSCAR CLEVELAND, 1884, Married Ethel Judith Calhoun, 1890
    Children: Kermit Calhoun, 1915
                Joseph Edwarn, 1918, Married Lorean Williams of Lynchburg
                Mary Alice, 1923, Married Ryland Staples

PAULETTE, RICHARD, 1862-1931, Married Maggie Farrar, died 1891
    Children: Annie, Married Benjamin Gallier

PAULETTE, ROBERT JEFFERSON, 1880, Married Annie Christian Wheeler, 1889
    Children: Virginia Dare, 1908
                Robert Jefferson, Jr., 1910
                Bruce Harmon, 1914, Married Frances Harvey, 1922
                Dwight Minefee, 1919, Married Miss Jefferson
                Phillip Ashby, 1921, Married Nellie Paulette
                Woodruff Burke, 1923
                Gwendolyn Fay, 1926
                James Pretlow, 1928
                Temple Layne, 1931
                Kathleen Augusta, 1911, Married Curry Lawler of Lynchburg
                Christine Wheeler, 1916, Married Jack Moseley of Lynchburg

PAULETTE, SAMUEL RUSSELL, 1894, Married Jeanette Garrette
    Father: A. Walter Paulette   Mother: Ada Jennings
    Children: Andrew Calvin, 1923, Married Shirley Moran of Texas
                 S. Russell, 1928
                 Leon, 1933

PAULETTE, SAMUEL TILDEN, 1876, Married Lottie F. Fore, 1890
    Father: Harvey H. Paulette   Mother: Fannie J. Moseley
    Children: Ella, 1906, Married Oscar F. Fleshman
                 Howard T., 1909
                 Willard T., 1912, Married Addie Lena Ferguson, 1921

PAULETTE, TOBY E., 1852-1917, Married Mary E. Baker, 1858-1899

PAYNE, SAMUEL, Married Belle Jones, 1854-1943
    Children: Dr. Mosby H., 1891

PAYNE, SR., WALTER J., 1886, Married Irma Coleman
    Children: Walter J., Jr., 1907
                 Hallie C., 1910, Married Mr. Amene of New Jersey
                 Margaret A., 1913, Married Mr. Kobryznski of New Jersey
                 Doris, 1915
                 Nell, 1920, Married W. R. VanHoose

PEERS, GEORGE T., 1830-1908, Married Jenny Sackett, 1838-1896
    Father: Thomas R. Peers
    Children: Evelyn, 1856-1904, Married J. Walton McKinney
                 Lelia, 1858-1893, Married F. W. McKinney
                 Charlie, 1864-1924, Married Alice Budd of Richmond
                 Loulie, 1870, Married Emmett Taylor, 1868-1947

PEERS, THOMAS R., Married Mary Petty

PENICK, ROBERT, 1826-1902, Married Caroline M. Harvey, 1827-1904
    Children: Elizabeth Frances, 1850
                 Martha J., 1852-1933, Married Charlie Mann
                 Celestia Glover, 1854-1869
                 Charles Millard, 1857-1859
                 Robert Ida, 1861
                 Sarah Blassenggame, 1863-1925
                 Sue Jessie, 1866
                 Lillie Belle, 1869- Married James Moses

PENN, WILLIAM, died, 1806, Married Martha Stovall, 1766-1833
    Children: William, Married Elizabeth Childers, 1821-1903
                 George S., died 1867

PERDIEU, HENRY ARCHER, 1874, Married Leaette Doss, 1878-1936
    Children: Mott, 1897, Married Eunice Ferguson
                 Charlie, 1899, Married Macie Bryant of Lynchburg
                 Mary, 1901, Married Richard Smith
                 Virginia, 1904, Married Walter Bergman
                 Thurman, 1907, Married Nettie Page
                 Walter, 1910, Married Hazel Lavinder of Richmond

PERDIEU, H. C., 1886, Married Frances E. Jamerson, 1892
 Children: Alpha L., Married Kathleen Roberts
              Davovan, Married Elsie Clay Marks
              Clarence A., Married Eula Jane Arrowood
              Charles E.
              Nellie Virginia

PERDIEU, WALTER D., 1913, Married Elsie Marks, 1905
 Children: Phyllis Ann, 1933
              Donna Ray, 1935
              Dorothy, 1936
              Barbara Odelle, 1939
              Walter D., Jr., 1944

PERDUE, DOTRIDGE E., 1879, Married Susie M. Mitchell, 1871
 Children: George W., 1907, Married Catherine Lucado, 1914

PERDUE, GEORGE W., 1907, Married Catherine Lucado, 1914
 Father: Dotridge E. Perdue   Mother: Susie M. Mitchell
 Children: William Raymond, 1933
              Charles L., 1935
              Lucye Mozelle, 1937
              Ronald Wayne, 1939

PHELPS, EVERETT, Married Audrey Morris Williamson, 1923
 Children: Everett Wayne, 1946

PHELPS, J. N., 1878, Married Maude Nowlin, 1889
 Father: Richard T. Phelps   Mother: Bettie Agnes Wooldridge
 Children: Binford Taylor, 1912, Married Ercell Christian of Nelson
              Elizabeth Nowlin, Married S. Smith
              J. N., Jr., 1916, Married Pauline Banton of Nelson
              William, 1920
              Allen, 1924
              Calvin, 1927

PHELPS, RICHARD T., died 1923, Married Bettie A. Wooldridge, died 1927
 Children: Mary Agnes, 1872, Married Tom Coleman
              Roberta W., 1875-1944, Married J. W. Harvey
              James Nelson, 1878, Married Maude Nowlin
              Thomas R., 1880, Married Clara Lee Phelps
              Luther C., 1883, Married Annie Kidd of Nelson
              Early Jane, 1886, Married W. A. Wells
              Maggie V., 1889, Married Tom M. Gardner
              Eugene N., 1892
              Walter P., 1895, Married Mary S. Chenault

PHELPS, S. B., 1874, Married Mary Alice Gardner, 1877
 Father: Thomas Jefferson Phelps   Mother: Elizabeth F. Harris
 Children: Weta, 1904, Married Rufus Morris
              Margaret Elizabeth, 1906, Married Aubrey Inge
 Twins   (Minnie Eva, 1909, Married Howard Marsh
              (Carlton B., 1909-1909
              Mary Lillian, 1910, Married Robert Armentrout

PHELPS, S. B., (continued)
        Louise, 1912, Married Roy Wells
        Winfred Odell, 1915-1924
        Samuel Clyde, 1917, Married Dorothy Davis

PHELPS, THOMAS JEFFERSON, 1844-1889, Married Elizabeth F. Harris,
                                              1845-1928
    Children: Ellie A., 1872, Married Harvey Lee Rogers
                S. B., 1874, Married Mary Alice Gardner
                Maude H., 1876, Married George Burks
                Minnie, 1878, Married John Burks
                Howard W., 1881, Married Edmonia Moore
                Clara L., 1883, Married Thomas R. Phelps
                Thomas T., 1887, Married Florine Moore

PHELPS, THOMAS R., 1880, Married Clara Lee Phelps, 1883
    Father: Richard T. Phelps   Mother: Bettie A. Wooldridge
    Children: Norton J., 1904
                Clayton, 1906, Married Jenett Cling of Glouster
                Flossie, 1908, Married Walter Moore
                Carlisle, 1909, Married Della Robertson
                Christine, 1911, Married David Harvey
                Dorothy, 1915, Married Hampton Hunter
                Vivian, 1917, Married Elmore Crews
                Rachel, 1921, Married William Mitchell

PHELPS, WALTER, Married Mary S. Chenault
    Father: Richard T. Phelps   Mother: Bettie Agnes Wooldridge
    Children: Burleigh, Married Alice Guill
                Ethel Lee
                Elaine
                Helen, Married Leonard Anderson

PITTMAN, THOMAS H., Married Martha A. Wingo
    Children: Henry R., 1833-1912, Married Elizabeth F. Paris, 1823-1907
                William Albert, 1849
                Nancy Fitzhugh, 1846
                Robert Hipkins, 1851
                John Wilson, 1854-1855
                Clement Judson, 1856-1906
                Martha, 1824-1864

PLUNKETT, CHARLES TALIAFERRO, Married Viola Clark

PLUNKETT, DAVID ADOLPHUS, Married Miss McDearmon
    Children: Willis Archer (Cudge), 1848-1889, Married Harriett Baker,
                                              1848-1883

PLUNKETT, HUBBARD THOMAS, 1903, Married Letha May Rice
    Father: John Samuel Plunkett   Mother: Anna C. Coleman
    Children: Howard Thomas
                Glenna Gay
                Jean
                Jack

PLUNKETT, JOHN, Married Cynthia Ann Maria Staples
    Second wife: Emily Ann Staples
    Children: Sarah Frances, Married Dr. William Henry Abbitt
                 Mache, Married Benjamin Hunter
                 Emma, Married Mr. Hunter
                 Second husband: Mr. Hunt

PLUNKETT, JOHN DAVID, Married Mary McDearmon

PLUNKETT, JOHN DAVID, 1892, Married Alice Marshall, 1894
    Father: John Samuel Plunkett   Mother: Anna C. Coleman
    Children: John Garland, 1914, Married Reva Robertson
                 Susie, 1919, Married John Cook

PLUNKETT, JOHN SAMUEL, 1859-1937, Married Anna C. Coleman, 1870
    Children: Mary Sue, 1888, Married William T. Coleman
                 Velma Clarrice, 1891-1891
                 John David, 1892, Married Alice Marshall
                 Paul Patteson, 1895
                 Anna Louise, 1897, Married Warwick G. Marshall
                 Alma Catherine, 1899, Married Theodore Zastrow
                 Harry Gordon, 1901, Married Caral West
                 Hubbard Thomas, 1903, Married Letha May Rice
                 Richard Burke, 1905, Married O. J. Haskins
                 George Clifford, 1908, Married Louise Morris

PLUNKETT, RICHARD BURKE, Married O. J. Haskins
    Father: John Samuel Plunkett   Mother: Anna C. Coleman
    Children: Martha Ann
                 Richard Burke, Jr.
                 Audry Jo

PLUNKETT, WILLIS ARCHER (CUDGE), Married Harriet Baker, 1848-1883
    Father: David Adolphus   Mother: Miss McDearmon
    Children: Annie Lou, 1869-1924, Married John H. Robertson
                 Ida F., 1871-1891
                 Mary Frances, 1873, Married Allen Rucker
                 Hattie Willis, 1877, Married Thomas A. Deane
                 John B., 1880, Married Maude Hawkins of Roanoke
                 Charles C., 1882-1882

POE, C. C., 1907, Married Blanche Babcock
    Father: John Robert Poe   Mother: Lillie Mae Pugh
    Children: Helen Mae, 1934
                 C. C., Jr., 1940

POE, JOHN ROBERT, Married Lillie Mae Pugh
    Children: C. C., 1907, Married Blanche Babcock
                 Eras, Married E. J. Paulette

POWELL, ATWILL, Married Clara Marsh, 1908

PRICE, ALFRED, 1913, Married Evelyn Doyne, 1916
    Children: Evelyn Farmer

PRICE, WILLIAM H., 1824-1870

PUCKETT, LENWOOD D., Married Bettie Lula Torrence, 1885
    Children: Virginia, Married Mr. Payne of Darlington Heights

PUGH, DEAN A., Married Theresa Marsh, 1901

PUGH, JOHN G., 1831-1868, Married Henrietta M. Pugh, 1838-1929
    Children: Ella, 1861-1939, Married Samuel M. Wooldridge

PUGH, L. N.

PUGH, MRS. MOLLIE F., 1843-1923

PULLIAM, HERBERT CARRINGTON, 1895, Married Bessie Gertrude Dowdy,
                                                 1908
    Father: William Vaughter Pulliam   Mother: Sallie Elizabeth Alvis
    Children: Herbert Carrington, Jr.

PULLIAM, J. K., Married Miss Godsey
    Children: Harvey, Married Blanche Davidson
                    Second wife of J.K.: Ellie Gertrude Ferguson

PULLIAM, JOHN, 1832-1917, Married Martha Steele

PULLIAM, WILLIAM VAUGHTER, 1852-1923, Married Sallie Elizabeth Alvis,
                                                1856
    Children: Thomas Anderson, Married Miss Cheatham
                    Herbert Carrington, 1895, Married Bessie Gertrude Dowdy,
                                                 1908
                    J. K., Married Miss Godsey
                          Second wife: Ellie Gertrude Ferguson
                    Clyde

PURYEAR, JOHN D., Married Sallie Abbitt, died 1918
    Children: Benjamin, 1878-1918, Married lady from Lynchburg

RAGLAND, NATHANIEL HARDEN, 1818-1888, Married Martha Walker Trent,
                                                1827-1907
    Children: Mary Elizabeth, 1849-1928, Married Capt. John H. White of
                                            Accomac
                    Thomas Trent, 1850-1893
                    Sallie Massie, 1852-1932, Married J. H. Featherston
                    Virginia Catherine, 1855-1940, Married Judge H.T. Parrish
                    Charles Massie, 1858-1935, Married Mary Sands of Richmond
                                    Second wife: Bonnie Daniel of
                                                 Texas

RAGLAND, NATHANIEL HARDEN, (continued)
          William Henry, 1861-1943, Married Madge Urquhart of Ark.
          Nathaniel Harden, Jr., 1864-1937, Married Jeane Broad of
                                         Texas
          Martha, Married Mathew Troy of Alabama and Texas
          Ella Barrett, 1871, Married Rev. J. D. Leslie of Texas

RAMSEY, EDWARD, 1913, Married Kathryn Lester, 1913
    Father: R. F. Ramsey   Mother: Ava T. Morris
    Children: Mary Ellen, 1933
                 Frances, 1939

RAMSEY, ROBERT FLOYD, 1875, Married Ava Thornton Morris, 1874-1937
    Children: Edward, 1913, Married Kathryn Lester, 1913

RANSON, CHARLES S., Married Mary Eisemon
    Father: William Frank   Mother: Claudie Dickerson
    Children: William Carroll
                 Ann
                 Eleanor Faye

RANSON, HARRY, W., Married Rachel Inge
    Father: William Frank Ranson   Mother: Claudie Dickerson
    Children: Louise
                 Mary Edith
                 Ruth
                 Harry Eugene

RANSON, JAMES F.,Married Pearle Foster
    Father: William Frank Ranson   Mother: Claudie Dickerson
    Children: Mary Willie
                 Pearle Katherine

RANSON, JAMES H., 1880-1946, Married Miss Richardson

RANSON, JOHN, 1793-1860, Married Phoebie Gunter
    Children: William, 1821
                 Robert, 1823-1910
                 Ann Eliza, 1825-1890
                 James, 1827-1870
                 John P., 1830-1864
                 Henry, 1832-1924
                 Thomas G., 1840-1916
                 Phoebe, died 1840
                            Second wife: Mary Ann Flood
    Children: Samuel, 1844-1936, Married Pocahontas Paulette
                 Peter C., 1846-1912
                 Frank N., 1848-1868

RANSON, OTIS R., Married Gladys Almond
    Father: William Frank Ranson   Mother: Claudie Dickerson
    Children: Charlene

RANSON, S. C., 1885, Married Bettie Martin, 1891
    Father: Samuel M. Ranson   Mother: Pocahontas Paulette
    Children: Samuel Edward, 1912, Married Florence Marks
                William Blass, 1914, Married Emma L. Ranson
                Odell Pocahontas, 1921
                Boyd Calvin, 1923, Married Odell Mann of Charlotte
                Isabelle, Married Roy Gowen of Buckingham
                Etta C., 1930

RANSON, SAMUEL M., 1844-1936, Married Pocahontas Paulette, 1851-1936
    Children: Susan Gertrude, 1878
                William Frank, 1880-1932, Married Claudie Dickerson
                John Paulette, 1882, Married Hattie Garrette, 1880
                Courtney Johnson, 1888-1895
                Sallie Ann, 1890-1892
                Mattie Kate, 1893, Married Daniel Walker Dinkins, 1886-1944
                Samuel Calvin, 1885, Married Bettie Martin, 1891

RANSON, WILLIAM FRANK, 1880-1932, Married Claudie Dickerson
    Father: Samuel M. Ranson   Mother: Pocahontas Paulette
    Children: Sallie K., Married Clarence M. Evans
                Mary W., Married Hubert S. Martin
                Otis R., Married Gladys Almond
                Charles S., Married Mary Eisemon
                James F., Married Pearl Foster
                Harry W., Married Rachel Inge

RAY, HOLCOMB POWHATAN, 1899, Married Laura Lavirt Abbitt
    No Children

REDDING, JAMES RICHARD, 1922, Married Harriet Smith, 1924
    Father: Rev. R. E. Redding   Mother: Mae Dick
    Children: James Richard, Jr., 1946

REDDING, REV. R. E., 1861, Married Mae Dick, 1889, of North Carolina
    Children: Dick, 1920-1926
                James Richard, 1922, Married Harriet Smith, 1924
                C. W., 1924

REYNOLDS, ALBERT C., Married Dorothy Tweedy, 1914

REYNOLDS, HOMER D., 1898, Married Emma Robertson, 1900
    Children: Shirley, 1922, Married Hazel Jones
                Clyde, 1924, Married Hulda Wilkerson
                Doris, 1926
                Harold, 1928, Married Ruby Lucado
                Alfred, 1930
                Marle, 1936
                Ralph, 1938
                Cecil, 1941

REYNOLDS, JESSE HERBERT, 1883, Married Alice Hagood, 1894, of Danville
    Children: Corean, 1924, Married Lyle Davidson of Campbell
                Marvin, 1916, Married Frances Phelps, 1921

REYNOLDS, JESSE HERBERT, (continued)
        Lonnie, 1921, Married Belle Martin, 1927
        Garland, 1929
        Katie, Married Russell Martin
        Sallie, Married Carl E. Martin
        Cleo, Married Martin Coleman

REYNOLDS, LONNIE, 1921, Married Belle Martin, 1927
        Father: Jesse Herbert Reynolds   Mother: Alice Hagood
        Children: Lonnie, Jr., 1947

REYNOLDS, MILTON R., 1871-1937, Married Carnelia Turner, 1876-1937
        Children: Homer D., 1899, Married Emma E. Robertson, 1900
                     Percy J., 1900, Married Elizabeth Coleman
                     Lorine, 1903, Married Hugh Martin

REYNOLDS, W. R., died 1940, Married Lizzie Myrtle Peake of Pittsylvania
        Children: Virginia, 1907, Married H. N. Hunt of Amherst
                     Hazel, 1908, Married Ryland M. Mann, 1906
                     Sadie, 1910
                     Iris, 1913

REYNOLDS ---, Married Sallie Bocock
        Children: Charles
                     Ann

RICHARDSON, CLARENCE, 1909, Married Carrie Gowin, 1908
        Children: Lloyd E., 1931
                     Hermon H., 1933
                     Otis, 1935
                     Ruby J., 1941

RICHARDSON, JAMES LEE, Married Sarah Lorene Torrence
        Father: Wiley Richardson   Mother: Lizzie Fore
        Children: Dorothy Lee
                     Eleanor

RICHARDSON, PRESLEY, Married Miss Baker
        Children: Thomas P., Married Rebecca McCune
                                 Second wife: Vick Crosby of Amelia
                                 Third wife: Rebecca Noble
                     Thalie, 1874, Married R. E. Paulette
                     T. R., 1878, Married Alice Dickerson
                     Inez, 1881
                     T. E., 1883, Married Hallie Mosby of Lynchburg

RICHARDSON, THOMAS MARSHALL, 1915, Married Mildred Carter, 1920
        Father: Thomas R. Richardson   Mother: Alice Witt Dickerson
        Children: Catherine Gray, 1944

RICHARDSON, THOMAS R., 1878, Married Alice Witt Dickerson, 1889
    Children: Jessie, 1910, Married Eddie Carwile of Campbell
                 Bernard Carson, 1912, Married Laura Inge, 1914
                 Curtis Eugene, 1913, Married Merle Dinkins, 1914
                 Thomas M., 1915, Married Mildred Carter, 1921
                 Samuel Wiley, 1918, Married Fay Etta Harvey, 1918
                 Rebecca, 1921, Married Edwin Carter

RICHARDSON, WILEY, Married Lizzie Fore
    Children: James, Married Lorene Torrence
                 Bernard
                 Herbert, Married Kathlene Coleman
                 Grace, Married J. M. Cobb

RILEY, GEORGE WASHINGTON, 1885, Married Hettie Viar, 1879
    Children: J. D., 1913
                 L. R., 1914
                 B. S., 1918

ROBERTSON, BAXTER W., Married Cora McCormick
    Children: Mabel, 1907, Married E. C. McCormick
                 Della, Married Carlisle Phelps
                 Curtis W., 1913, Married Louise Doss, 1914
                 Oscar L.
                 Pearl, Married Roy Burks
                 Lester

ROBERTSON, CASWELL F., 1830-1917, Married Ella Shearer, 1856-1917
    Children: John S., 1881-1902
                 W. H., 1884, Married Rosa Bondurant, 1884
                 James O., 1888, Married Mabel Carson

ROBERTSON, CLARE LAMAR, 1898-1926

ROBERTSON, DR. D. MOTT, 1858-1919, Married Alberta Carter, 1864-1907
    Father: Dr. David P. Robertson   Mother: Mary A. D. Glover
    Children: Mary, 1888
                 Ethel, 1889, Married P. W. Murray of Newport News
                 Susie, 1891
                 Alberta, 1893
                 David P., 1894-1913
                 Ruby, 1896
                 Clare, 1898-1926
                 Ella, 1901
                          Second wife: Nena Chilton
    Children: D. Mott, Jr., 1915
                 Dorothy, 1918, Married Carlton Sundin of Massachusetts

ROBERTSON, D. N., 1898, Married Ruth Coleman, 1898
    Father: Therious P. Robertson   Mother: Berta Megginson
    Children: Annie Virginia, 1919, Married John Clifton Harvey
                 Roberta, 1924, Married Tyler Coleman
                 Elizabeth, 1928
                 Ulelia, 1931

ROBERTSON, DR., DAVID P., 1819-1892, Married Mary A. D. Glover,
1831-1899
Children: Ann Elizabeth, 1851-1853
            William Horace, 1853-1858
            James Samuel, died 1856
            John H., 1856-1934, Married Fannie C. Moore, died 1886, of
                                            Buckingham
                        Second wife: Annie Lou Plunkett
            Dr. David Mott, 1858-1919, Married Mary A. Carter
                        Second wife: Nena Chilton
            Mary Bridget, 1860, Married Jesse Wood of Campbell
            Robert G., 1862-, Married Miss Carter of Amherst
                        Second wife: Fannie Perrow of Campbell
            Charles Joseph, 1854-1854
            Minnie Jackson, 1865, Married W. F. Wood of Campbell
            William I., 1867
            George, 1869-1869

ROBERTSON, DAVID THOMAS, 1920, Married Ethel Lee Martin, 1925
    Father: W. H. Robertson   Mother: Rosa Bondurant

ROBERTSON, ELDRIDGE COLE, 1834-1900, Married Mary A. E. Johnson,
1843-1919
Children: Therious P., 1870-1946, Married Berta Megginson,
                                            1873-1916
                        Second wife: Irvine Coleman, 1896
            George W., 1872, Married Cora Vest
            Thomas H., 1884, Married Natlia Coleman
            Nancy, Married Freeland Kyle
            Ulealy, Married Walker Carnefix

ROBERTSON, GEORGE W., 1872, Married Cora Vest, 1869-1938
    Father: Eldridge Cole Robertson   Mother: Mary A. E. Johnson
    Children: Eunice, 1898-1909
            Jim, 1900, Married Louise Anderson of Naruna
            Emma, 1901, Married Homer Reynolds
            May, 1903, Married Eldridge Wright of Bedford
                        Second husband: Henry Edwards of Lynchburg
            Lawrence, 1905-1915
            Dillard, 1907-1920
            Nellie, 1909, Married Courtney St. John of Charlotte
            Fred, 1911, Married Rachel Guill

ROBERTSON, HERMAN H., 1909, Married Vara E. Morris, 1911
    Father: Thomas H. Robertson   Mother: Natlia Coleman

ROBERTSON, JAMES O,, 1888, Married Mabel Carson, 1890
    Father: Caswell F. Robertson   Mother: Ella Shearer
    Children: (Jimmie C., Married Ruth Hudson of Lynchburg
    Twins   (Virgil, Married Margaret Davis of Lynchburg
            Alice, Married David Smith of Lynchburg

ROBERTSON, JOHN H., 1856-1934, Married Fannie C. Moore, died 1886
    Father: Dr. David P. Robertson   Mother: Mary A. D. Glover
    Children: Annie, Married Watkins Nowlin
               William D., Married Annie Jones
                   Second wife of John H.: Annie Lou Plunkett
    Children: Hattie, Married Henry Brinkley
               Minnie Lee, Married Arthur Williamson
               Lila, Married Raymond Schools
               Nell, Married Tyler Akers
               Charlie, Married Gertrude Born
               John, Married Edna Keeney
               Arthur, Married

ROBERTSON, JOHN SHEARER, 1881-1905

ROBERTSON, SHEARER B., 1923, Married Mary Catherine Torrence, 1924
    Father: W. H. Robertson   Mother: Rosa Bondurant
    Children: Sandra Fay, 1945

ROBERTSON, THOMAS H., 1884, Married Natlie Coleman
    Father: Eldridge Cole   Mother: Mary A. E. Johnson
    Children: Ernest, Married Pearl Wells
               Herman, Married Vera Morris
               Daisy, Married Lloyd Hamilton
               Elizabeth, Married Percy Thompson
               Walter, Married_____

ROBERTSON, T. P., 1869-1946, Married Roberta Megginson, 1873-1916
    Father: Eldridge Cole Robertson   Mother: Mary Johnson
    Children: David North, 1898, Married Ruth Coleman
               Christopher, 1903-1905
               Mary E., 1907, Married Thomas A. Garrette
                   2nd. wife of T. P. Robertson, Irvin Coleman
    Children: Emma, Married Leonard Garrette
               Irvin, Married Spencer Garrette, Jr.
               Florence

ROBERTSON, WILLIAM DAVID, 1884, Married Annie Jones, 1885-1933
    Father: John H. Robertson   Mother: Fannie C. Moore
    Children: Margaret Moore, 1908
               Frank Harker, 1910, Married Miss M. E. Taylor of N. C.
               Evelyn Makine, 1911, Married B. F. Moomaw of Roanoke
               Christine E., 1912
               Edith Pauline, 1915, Married Roland Kauffman of Baltimore
               Reva, Married J. Garland Plunkett
               William Roy, 1918, Married Beulah Dobbins, 1922, of West Va.
               Nancy, 1920, Married Ryland Hunter
               Annie Louise, 1923, Married H. W. Knight
               Harriet Lee, 1927

ROBERTSON, WILLIAM E., 1817-1898

ROBERTSON, W. H., Married Rosa Bondurant
    Father: Caswell F. Robertson   Mother: Ella Shearer
    Children: Elizabeth, 1913, Married Joel Asher of Brookneal
                Ruth C., 1914, Married Theodore Carson
                Howard, 1917, Married Anna B. Dickerson
                David T., 1920, Married Ethel Lee Martin
                Rosa L., 1922, Married Bert Broom of Philadelphia
                Shearer B., 1923, Married Catherine Torrence, 1924

ROBERTSON, WILEY HOWARD, 1917, Married Anna B. Dickerson, 1918
    Father: W. H. Robertson   Mother: Rosa Bondurant
    Children: Jeane Adair, 1939
                Anna Lee, 1941

ROBERTSON, WILLIAM ROY, 1918, Married Beulah Dobbins, 1921
    Father: William David Robertson   Mother: Annie Jones
    Children: Robbie Lou, 1942
                Brenda Leigh, 1947

ROBINSON, CALVIN H., 1906, Married Earle Patteson, 1906
    No Children

ROBINSON, RICHARD D., 1915, Married Elizabeth Davidson, 1914, of
                                         Buckingham
    Children: Elizabeth Dale, 1938
                Richard D., 1940

RODE, DAVID, 1924, Married Gracie Coleman, 1925

ROGERS, BERKLEY, Married Thelma Dinkins, 1912
    Children: James, 1936
                Wade, 1940
                Dan, 1943

ROGERS, DAVID, Married Bettie Phelps
    Children: Harvey Lee, Married Ellie Phelps
                Leslie, Married Cora M. Doss
                Welvey, Married Ethel Shepard of Lynchburg
                Effie, Married Mr. Shepard
                        Second husband: Henry Draper
                Mamie
                Homer, Married Margie Shepard of Lynchburg
                Abbitt, Married Miss Powell of Lynchburg
                Bettie' Lee, Married Mr. Powell of Lynchburg
                Buck, Married Mary B. North
                Fielding J., 1862-1914, Married Annie Doss, 1870
                Ira
                J. E., Married Daisy Doss
                Luana
                Rosa, Married Peter Nowlin
                Hop, Married Nettie North
                Ike
                Robert, Married Miss Brooks of Lynchburg
                Wallace
                Warren
                John

ROGERS, FEILDING J., 1862-1914, Married Annie S. Doss, 1870
    Children: James Ottie, 1892, Married Irene Coleman
                 Reva, 1893, Married Wirt H. Ayers

ROGERS, J. E., 1867-1934, Married Daisy Doss, 1877
    Children: Harold, 1901, Married Rachel Inge
      Twins   (J. Elbert, 1904
              (Robert L., 1904, Married Gracie McGann of Amherst
               Berkley, 1913, Married Thelma Dinkins

ROGERS, JOHN THADEUS, Married Laura Ackerman Topping
    Children: Percy, Married Martie Morgan
                 Lydia, Married Edwin Fore
                 Rupert, Married Grace Shade
                 Howard, Married Frances Adams
                 Ernest, Married Lou Covington
                 Bertha, Married Edwin McClintic

ROSSER, CHARLIE C., 1882-1936, Married Sallie Estelle Swan, 1888
    Children: Calvin Swan, 1907, Married Doris Swan of Buckingham
                 Annie, 1909, Married Robert Covington
                 Ouida, 1911-1914
                 Benjamin Alex, 1913
                 John William, 1916-1938
                 Eurlean, 1918, Married Carl Evans
                 James Howard, 1920, Married Louise Nash of Charlotte
                 Raymond Edward, 1922, Married Bettie Rector of Salem

ROSSER, JESSE MORTON, 1890,-1944, Married Virginia Adams, 1900
    Children: Jesse Morton, Jr., 1934

ROSSER, WILLIAM, 1834-1921, Married Susan Inge
    Children: Emma, 1858-1936, Married Alex Inge
                                Second husband: Charles Homberg
                             Second wife: Virginia E. Sweeney
    Children: Robert, 1869-1888
                 Lennie, Married E. E. Gills
                 Ada, Married R. A. T. Clement
                 Ella, Married C. A. Hancock
                 Bessie, Married Samuel A. Ferguson
                             Third wife: Mary P. Kelley

ROUTEN, GEORGE D., 1834-1903, Married Nannie C. Taylor, 1839-1897
    Children: Jesse Edward, 1875
                 Bettie Walker, 1877, Married Samuel E. Anderson, 1869-1943

ROUTEN, JOHN A., 1825-1896, Married Mary Gannaway, 1831-1896
    Children: Charlie, died at 30
                 Lizzie, died at 22
                 Addie, 1873, Married Homsie Tanner

ROUTEN, J. J., 1845-1910, Married Delia F. Woodson, 1856-1944
    Children: Robert Henry, 1873, Married Ella Drinkard, 1887
                 Mary Lucy, 1875, Married William Alvis, 1871-1944
                 Willie Melvin, 1877, Married Claude M. Drinkard, 1884
                 Rosa Susan, 1879, Married William Walker Scruggs, 1871

ROUTEN, ROBERT HENRY, 1873, Married Ella Drinkard, 1887
    Father: J. J. Routen   Mother: Delia F. Woodson
    Children: Wilton M., 1910, Married Lillian Lerner
                 Walter Henry, 1911
                 Shelton Ould, 1921
                 John Edward, 1925

RUCKER, DR. THOMAS R., 1872, Married Geneva Moore
    Children: Kathleen, Married Dr. C. C. Cochran of North Carolina
                 Ashby, Married Ada Bell Lovett of Georgia
                 Mary Peyton
                 Pauline, Married E. E. Sanne

RUSH, CHARLIE S., 1909, Married Lucile Reynolds, 1912, of Charlotte
    Children: Charlie, 1931
                 Rebecca, 1932
                 Goldie, 1935

SACKETT, CHARLES H., 1845-1928, Married Louisa Mosely, 1843-1891
    Father: Benjamin Sackett
    Children: Henry M., 1874-1928, Married Mina Otey of Lynchburg
                 Evy, 1876-1940, Married Dr. Sydnor
                 Anna Bell, 1877, Married W. D. Sale
                 Janie, 1879, Married A. W. Mosby of Lynchburg
                 Alice, 1880, Married Rev. A. E. Spencer of Georgia

SCHEFFLER, G. A., 1858-1946, of Germany, Married B. C. Binkley, 1858-1942
                                                                    of Ohio
    Children: E. L., Married Bertha Stonerock
                 Lottie, Married W. J. Fischer
                 C. N., Married Laura Taylor
                 G. A., Jr., Married Jennie Thompson
                 Albert L., 1892, Married Fannie Stephenson
                 Oscar L., 1895, Married Gay Smith

SCOTT, JOHN M., Married Ann Eleanor Abbitt
    Children: John
                 Eleanor

SCOTT, WALTER WINFIELD, 1888, Married Nannie Sue Hancock
    Children: Grace
                 Nancy

SCRUGGS, CURTIS, 1911, Married Miss Brown

SCRUGGS, ROY, 1930, brother of Curtis Scruggs

SCRUGGS, HENRY WILSON, 1914, Married Bessie Hamner Ferguson, 1915
    Father: John William Scruggs   Mother: Mary Garrette
    Children: Warren Dudley, 1937
               Phillip Wayne, 1941

SCRUGGS, JAMES LITTLETON, 1813-1887, Married Mary Woodson, 1817-1887
    Children: Ann, Married Richmond Green
               William M., Married Cordelias Gannaway
                           Second wife: Miss Anderson
                           Third wife: Miss Anderson
               Virginia, Married Richard T. Moss
               Fannie, Married C. Candler
               (John J., 1852-1933, Married Elizabeth Rosa Stone
    Triplets   (Thomas B., 1852-1929
               (Palmer, 1852- 1926

SCRUGGS, JOHN J., 1852-1933, Married Elizabeth Rosa Stone, 1855-1896
    Father: James Littleton Scruggs   Mother: Mary Woodson
    Children: James P., 1877-1940, Married Frances Dickerson
               Mary Virginia, 1880, Married W. A. Drinkard
               L. M., 1882-1932
               T. R., 1885, Married Fannie Drinkard
               Sallie, 1888, Married C. B. Blankenship
               Pocahontas, 1891, Married J. E. Wright of Charlotte

SCRUGGS, JOHN WILLIAM, 1880, Married Mary Garrette
    Father: Samuel A. Scruggs,   Mother: Adaline Hamersley
    Children: Louise, 1911-1945, Married J. K. Marshall
               Henry Wilson, 1914, Married Bessie Hamner Ferguson, 1915
               Charles Wiley, 1917, Married Ruth Smith of Alabama

SCRUGGS, SAMUEL A., 1824-1910, Married Adaline Hamersley, 1849-1926
    Children: James S., 1878, Married Rosa Wright of Buckingham
               John W., 1880, Married Mary Garrette
               Rawlings, 1883, Married Miss Hatcher of Bedford
               Lizzie, Married J. D. Childers
               Mattie, Married Dr. R. A. North
                     Second husband: Lee Davidson

SCRUGGS, STERLING, 1869-1935, Married Olivia Martin
    Father: William Scruggs   Mother: Cordelias Gannaway
    Children: Hubert Braxton, 1895, Married Myrtle Wright
               Howard Archebald, 1897, Married Preston Young
               Cordelia Christine, 1901-1947, Married Dr. Clarence Schuld
                                          of Indiana
               Annie Laurie, 1904, Married A. A. Babcock
               Helen Martin, 1905, Married W. R. Stratton
               Ivan Sterling 1913-1939, Married Zelma Witt of Lynchburg

SCRUGGS, WILLIAM, 1843-1924, Married Cordelias Ganaway, died 1878
                                             Second wife: Ella Anderson, died 1889
                                             Third wife : Lillie Anderson, died 1933
    Children: Sterling, Married Olivia Martin
                    Warren
                    Walker, 1870, Married Rose Routon, 1879

SCRUGGS, WILLIAM

SCRUGGS, WILLIAM WALKER, 1870, Married Rosa S. Routen, 1879
    Children: E. Carlisle, 1901, Married Colyer Abbitt
                    R. Clayton, 1907
                    Lacy C., 1903-1908

SEARS, EDWARD, 1808-1857, Married Jane Mathews, 1819-1857
    Children: Edward Algerman, 1857
                    John James, 1855-
                    William M., died 1857
                    Eleanora, died, 1857
                    Samuel D., 1847, Married Columbia Ann Gilliam, 1847-1915
                    Fannie Elizabeth, 1842-1923, Married W. D. Hix, 1836-1911

SEARS, EDWARD PERCY, 1872, Married Myrtle Gilliam, 1885
    Father: Samuel D. Sears   Mother: Columbia Ann Gilliam
    Children: Robert Daniel, 1909, Married Mary McDearmon, 1913
                    Eugene Mathews, 1911, Married Annie Laurie Marshall Moseley
                    John James, 1913, Married Nancy Jones, 1913
                    Henry Lester, 1915, Married Margaret Ramsey
                    Gertrude, 1922
                    Lavalette Ann, 1925, Married Mr. Guild
                    Edward Dupuy, 1907-1920
                    Samuel Gordon, 1917-1920
                    Myrtle, 1920-1926

SEARS, JEREMIAH, 1800-1857, Married Ann M. Tweedy, 1827-1890
    Children: Emma F., 1850
                    Lucy Alice, 1852-1928, Married R. F. Burke
                    John A., 1853-1923, Married Willie Ann Tweedy
                                    Third wife: Alice Urquhart
                    Jerre E., 1857-
                    Ann E., 1857-Married Benjamin Barnard

SEARS, JOHN, 1798, Married Susan LeGrand, 1806
    Children: Elizabeth, 1829, Married Thomas A. Caldwell

SEARS, JOHN EDWARD, 1889-1940, Married Mary Ann Irby
    Father: John A. Sears   Mother: Willie Ann Tweedy
    Children: Mary Gray, 1914, Married Ivey Holland
                    Dorothy Ann, 1918
                    Mattie Irby, 1919, Married Eames A. Powers
                    Robert Allen, 1923

SEARS, SAMUEL D., 1847-1895, Married Columbia Ann Gilliam, 1847-1915
    Father: Edward Sears   Mother: Jane Mathews
    Children: Edward Percy, 1872, Married Myrtle Gilliam
                Fannie, Married W. S. Taylor
                Bessie, Married A. R. Harwood
                Herman Dupuy, 1883, Married Ethel Pickett of North Carolina
                Lester Paul, 1885-1914
                Samuel ("Tad"), W., 1891-1938, Married Winnie Scott
                Mary Pearl, Married J. B. Marshall

SEAY, CHARLIE, 1876-1939, Married Mary A. Martin, 1887
    Children: Peyton, 1910, Married Frances Goin, 1925
                Hallie, 1912
                Frances, 1914, Married Hallie Ferguson
                Charlie, 1918
                Pauline, 1921, Married John Oxford
                Paul R., 1924
                Sadie C., 1927
                Bobbie, 1931
                James Randolph, 1934

SHANKS, ROBERT, Married Rebecca Lockett, 1898, of Botetourt
    Children: Ruby, 1916, Married Elbert Parsley of California
                Carrie, 1921, Married John Farrar

SHEARER, GEORGE W., 1851-1867

SHEARER, HENRY BROWN, 1830-1908, Married Judith LeGrand
                            Second wife: Anna Farmer
    Children: Georgiana
                William Henry, 1866, Married lady from West Virginia
                Crute
                Walter A., 1858, Married Alice Turner, 1857-
                          Second wife: Willie Hicks of Amherst
                Mariah, Married Robert A. Weakley
                Rose
                Fannie, Married James Nelson of New Jersey
                Oneida, 1868, Married Herman Nathan of New Jersey

SHEARER, HENRY CLAY, 1845-1925, Married Martha Jane Clark, 1842-1925
    Children: Elma Gessner, 1871, Married Raleigh H. Chilton
                Viola, 1874, Married Alexander Perryman
                Bessie, 1878, Married Raleigh H. Chilton

SHEARER, JAMES EDMUND, Married Mary Jane LeGrand
    Children: Mary Harriet, 1855-1914
                Elfieda, 1857-1891, Married Meem Diuguid of Lynchburg
                William Otway, 1859-1946
                James Wilber, 1861, Married Lucy Kyle of Campbell
                Peter Eugene, 1863
                Charles Edward, 1865, Married Minnie Kent of Amherst
                Rev. Louis Cable, 1868, Married Dasie Virginia Bell
                Esmond Gibbs, 1870
                Newton Henry, 1875
                Minnie Bell, 1877

SHEARER, REV. JOHN BUNYAN, 1832-1919, Married Lizzette Gissner of)
                                    Germany, 1832-1903)
) Brothers
SHEARER, JOHN AKERS, Married Ruth Webber   )   and
) Sisters
SHEARER, ANN LOUISE, 1850-1876   )

SHEARER, JOHN CABLE, 1864, Married Josephine Angle of Rocky Mount, 1867
    Father: William Newton Shearer   Mother:
    Children: Frances, 1898
                 William, III, 1900
                 Bertha, 1906
                 Josephine

SHEARER, WILLIAM NEWTON, Married Emily F. Turner
                         Second wife: Mary Etta Foreman
    Children: Mary Elizabeth, 1859, Married Nat Angle of Rocky Mount
                 Frances Alice, Married Rev. John W. Carroll
                 John Cable, 1864, Married Josephine Angle of Rocky Mount,
                                                                   1867

SHEPHERD, PETER JENNINGS, 1867, Married Allie Torrence, 1869-1940
    Children: Evie Lillian, 1894, Married B. H. Springer
                 Louise, 1896, Married Arthur Springer
                 Georgie, Married Carrington Burgess
                 Willie J., 1903, Married Ester Stimpston
                 Ruth, 1908, Married J. S. Crute

SHIREY, F. M., 1867, Married Mary Virginia Hawes, 1869
    Children: H. H., 1896
                 W. H., 1897, Married Elizabeth Meharg of Richmond
                 Virginia T., 1899
                 F. M., Jr., 1901, Married Viola Elton of Lynchburg
                 George A., 1903,
                 Louise B., 1906, Married Maurice Mendel of West Va.
                 Robert P., 1910, Married Edith Holland of Lynchburg
                 Horace W., 1913, Married Marye Stewart, 1919

SHOUSE, S. S., 1903, Married Helen M. Begoney, 1911
    Children: Virginia Lee, 1941
                 Samuel, 1942
                 Linda Ann, 1947

SHREVE, GEORGE, 1897, Married Ellie Hamlet, 1900, of Charlotte
    No Children

SIMMS, ELICE AUSTIN, 1840-1915, Married Mary Frances Furbush, 1846-1903
    Children: William Jefferson, 1874-1937
                 Macky B., 1875
                 Lillie May, 1877-1908, Married James M. Davidson
                 Mott Robertson, 1879-1901
                 Hunter W., 1881-1946, Married Mary Beulah Caldwell
                 Mary S., 1885, Married James Ammon Casey
                 Freddie, 1888-1888

SIMMS, HUNTER W., 1881-1946, Married Mary Beulah Caldwell
.Father: Elice Austin Simms   Mother: Mary Frances Furbush
Children: William Hunter, 1924
              Robert Elice, 1926
              Mott Twyman, 1928

SINGLETON, GEORGE HENRY, 1852-1943, Married Laura Elizabeth Gilliam
Children: Thomas Henry, 1898, Married Mary Vivian Clarke
              Richard Morton, 1904

SLAGEL, DAVID, 1836-1899, Married Callie Ellen Dunn
Children: Sallie, 1869-1927, Married John C. Harris

SLAYTON, C. W., 1903, Married M. Rigney, 1908, of Pittsylvania
Children: Bettie Mildred, 1930
              C. W., Jr., 1944

SMITH, CHARLES FREEMONT, 1863-1926, Married Lottie Bell Wilcott of
                                            Wisconsin, 1871-1912
Children: Charles R., 1899, Married Carrie Martin, 1901
              Hobert A., 1901
              Lola D., 1904, Married Rufus Watts of Amherst
              Dorothy, 1908, Married John Henry Moore

SMITH, CHARLIE HENRY, 1859-1938, Married Emma Walker Durrum, died 1923
Children: Frank James, Married Miss Spiggle
              Eula May, Married J. P. Johnson
              Annie Virginia, Married Mr. Evans
              Nettie Walker, Married Mr. Lawrence
              Pearl North, Married Mr. Beatries

SMITH, CHARLES R., 1899, Married Carrie Martin, 1901
Father: Charles Freement Smith   Mother: Lottie Bell Wilcott
Children: Charles Roland, Jr., 1926
              Mollie, 1924, Married Terrell Rogers
              Mildred, 1922, Married Coleman Moore
              Clifton B., 1929
              Ralph, 1931
              Watkins, 1935
              Daphine, 1941

SMITH, ELIJAH, 1844-1906, Married Margaret Ferguson, 1845-1909
Children: Ollie Thomas, 1870-1946, Married Mary O'Brien
                                      Second wife: Rena Wood
              Lucy, 1872, Married Sam Doss
              LaFeyette, 1871, Married Mamie Martin
                                      Second wife: Berta Wright
              Juttie, 1877-1946, Married John Wright
              Laura, 1879-1907
              Ruth, 1880, Married C. L. Johnson
              Elbert, 1882-1914, Married Addie Hamilton
                                      Second wife: Mattie Morris

SMITH, E. CARROLL, Married M. Avis Brown, 1906
Children: Randolph Carroll, 1944
              Vicki Camille, 1947

258

SMITH, E. HOLMES, 1883, Married Annie Guill, 1886
     Father: George N. Smith   Mother: Malatia Ferguson
     Children: Vara, 1907, Married L. L. Stanley
                 Lula, 1908, Married J. E. Jamerson
                 Grover, 1909, Married Neola Barlow
                 Burnett, 1911, Married Lloyd Martin
                 Beatrice, 1912
                 Mary
                 Helen

SMITH, E. LeROY, 1886, Married Addie Pace, 1885, of Halifax
     Father: M. C. Smith   Mother: Fannie M. Kitzmiller
     Children: Alice Lee, Married Charles Jones Hunter of Campbell
                 Frances M.
                 LeRoy Pace, Married Miss Loll of Pennsylvania
                 Harriet, Married J. R. Redding

SMITH, FIELDING, 1860-1923, Married Anna Catherine Durrum, 1870-1925
     Children: Jasper Jackson, 1890
                 John Thomas, 1892
                 Richard, 1894, Married Mary Perdieu
                 Mary Ann, 1896, Married Mr. Page
                 Ernest W., 1898, Married Virginia Almond, 1917
                 Callie, 1900, Married Mr. Flinchum of Lynchburg
                 Essie, 1902, Married Mr. Williams
                 Nona, 1904
                 Odelle, 1906

SMITH, GROVER E., 1909, Married Neola Inez Barlow, 1914
     Father: E. H. Smith   Mother: Annie Guill
     Children: Peggy Marye, 1934
                 Grover Alton, 1938
                 Judy Ester, 1947

SMITH, GEORGE N., 1859-1922, Married Malatia Ferguson, 1856-1931
     Children: Leola, 1891-1945, Married Marshall'Ferguson
                 E. Holmes, 1892, Married Annie Guill, 1886-1933
                              Second wife: Cora Durham, 1882
                 Edna N., 1884, Married Andrew Ferguson
                 George I., 1888, Married Octavia Guill, 1889-1946
                 Nannie V., 1895, Married Everet Blackwell

SMITH, H. BURNETT, 1911, Married Lloyd Walker Martin, 1917
     Father: E. H. Smith   Mother: Annie Guill
     Children: Gloria Ann, 1940
          Twins (Jerre Burnett, 1943
                 (Jane Annett, 1943
                 Phillis Kay, 1946

SMITH, LEONARD ELLIS, 1864-1947, Married Lena L. Jones, 1864-1901
Father: Thomas A. Smith   Mother: Nannie LeGrand
    Children: Gladys, 1892, Married A. B. White of Lynchburg
                 Nannie LeGrand, 1894-1899
                 Susie Ileen, 1897
                                Second wife: Willie C. Inge, 1881
    Children: Verta H., 1903, Married R. W. Stanley
                 Myrtle, 1905
                 Mary Elizabeth, 1906, Married W. W. Ford
                                Second husband: J. A. Bingham
                 Margaret Miller, 1908, Married J. H. O'Brien
                 Caroline M., 1911
                 Leonard Ellis, Jr., 1913, Married Alma Moon of Altavista
                 Thomas Archer, 1922

SMITH, M. C., 1862-1947, Married Fannie M. Kitzmiller, 1862-1943
    Children: E. LeRoy, 1886, Married Addie Pace
        Twins (C. W., 1888, Married Lucy Cabell Foster, 1890
              (S. Guy, 1888, Married Mary Purdum
                 W. I., 1892, Married Miss Gold of Tennessee
                 Gay, Married O. L. Sheffler
                 Ernest G., 1893, Married Miss Miller of Page County
                 Elmer, 1904, Married Genoa Dameron
                 Frances, Married R. W. Jamerson
                 Virginia, 1907-1945

SMITH, NAPOLEON, Married Susie Powell
    Children: Willie, Married Miss McCullough
                 Rosa
                 John, Married Lelia McCormick
                 Major
                 Howard
                 Harvey
                 Emmett
                 Alice
                 Walter, Married Lelia O'Brien

SMITH, RICHARD, 1894, Married Mary Perdieu
    Father: Fielding Smith   Mother: Anna Catherine Durrum
    Children: Eleanor, 1926
                 Eloise, 1928
                 Richard, Jr., 1934

SMITH, RICHARD EDWARD, 1900, Married Grace Mae Blanks, 1906
    Father: William Edward Smith   Mother: Annie Baker
    Children: Richard Edward, Jr., 1930
                 William Thomas, 1936
                 Barbara Mae, 1928

SMITH, RICHARD W., 1867, Married Eva Virginia Jones, 1870-1899
    Father: Thomas A. Smith   Mother: Nannie LeGrand
    Children: Second wife: Cornelia Davis, 1870-1926
                 Davis LeGrand, 1906, Married Edith Davidson
                 Frances, 1908
                 Richard, 1911, Married Dorothy Everetez of Amherst

SMITH, THOMAS A., 1836-1914, Married Nannie LeGrand, 1838-1884
    Children: Leonard Ellis, 1864-1947, Married Lena L. Jones, 1864-
                                                 1901
                                Second wife: Miss Paris
                Hunter G., 1870, Married Mrs. Grady of North Carolina
                Maggie, 1872-1911, Married James Caldwell
                Carrie, 1874, Married W. A. Moses
                Lucy
                Emma
                William Edward, 1866, Married Annie Baker
                Richard W., 1867, Married Eva Virginia Jones, 1870-1899
                        Second wife: Cornelia Davis, 1870-1926

SMITH, WILEY J., 1897, Married Winnie Myers of Washington County
    Children: Mary, 1917, Married W. A. McDearmon, Jr.
                Charlie, 1918, Married Sallie Sutton of Buckingham
                Edith, 1920, Married Francis B. Fitzgerald, Jr.
                Dora, 1922, Married Ernest Ranson
                Fred C., 1924
                Jimmie, 1927
                Garnet, 1929
                June, 1931

SMITH, WILLIAM EDWARD, 1866, Married Annie Baker, 1874-
    Father: Thomas A. Smith   Mother: Nannie LeGrand
    Children: Willie Anne, 1894, Married Don Moses
                Richard Edward, 1900, Married Grace Mae Blanks, 1906

SOUTHALL, ALGER R., 1903, Married Carrie Watson of Chatham
    Father: Luther M. Southall   Mother: Mary Paulette
    Children: Alger R., Jr., 1924
                Billy Watson, 1926
                Horton Miller, 1928
                Shirley Collene, 1929

SOUTHALL, IRA, 1887, Married Janie Hubbard, 1892
    Children: Albert, 1912
                Hazel, 1913
                Milton, 1914
                Mae, 1918
                Delores, 1920, Married Woodrow Southall
                Junior, 1922
    Twins   (Carroll, 1924
               (Caroline, 1924, Married Wilber Layne

SOUTHALL, LUTHER M., 1870-1940, Married Mary Paulette, 1879
    Children: Curtis A., 1901, Married Frances Dowdy of Lynchburg
                        Second wife: Ida Wayne Pick
                Alger R., 1903, Married Carrie Watson
                Gladys C., 1905, Married John A. Neal
                      Second husband: R. C. Hinman of Farmville
                Eleanor E., 1910

SPENCER, HAROLD Y., 1900, Married Elaine McDearmon, 1903
    Father: John Y. Spencer   Mother: Lizzie B. Pankey
    Children: Mary Yancy, 1946

SPENCER, JOHN Y., 1864-1916 , Married Lizzie B. Pankey, 1868-1946
    Children: H. Y., 1900, Married Elaine McDearmon, 1903

SPENCER, THOMAS HENRY, 1848-, Married Elizabeth May Hannah, 1856
    Children: Addie Plunkett, 1878
               Annie Elliott, 1878-1943, Married Mr. Howerton
               Alice Leola, 1879
               William Hannah, 1881
               Thomas Bernard, 1883
               Oscar Hunter, 1886
               Champie Kate, 1888
              . Robert Suppleton, 1892

SPIGGLE, G. W., 1913, Married Estelle Low of Prince Edward, 1916
    Father: John W. Spiggle   Mother: Harriet Lena Thornhill
    Children: G. W., Jr., 1937
               Lester Martin, 1939
               Melvin W., 1941

SPIGGLE, JAMES A., 1868-1918, Married Alma Durrum, 1876
    Children: Sallie Ann, 1893, Married Frank Smith
               Bernice L., 1895-1896
               Virginia, 1897, Married Cleveland Hall
               John C., 1900, Married Mazie Doss

SPIGGLE, JOHN C., 1900, Married Mazie Doss
    Father: James A. Spiggle   Mother: Alma Durrum
    Children: James, 1921, Married Ruth Page
               Mary Alma, 1929
               David Wilson, 1935

SPIGGLE, JOHN W., Married Harriet Lena Thornhill, 1881-1916
    Children: Annie Olivia
               Furman
               Martin
               John Henry, Married Edna Brown
               William Alfred
               Raymond North
               Winston Melvin, Married Gracie Wells of Lynchburg
               Alma Estelle, Married Lewis Harris
               Robert Leslie, Married Alice Woody
               Effie D.
               Ernest Bolton, 1910, Married Julia Watson
               ·Reed
               George Wilson, Married Miss Lowe
               Lillian Grace

STANLEY, J. H., 1853-1920, Married Bettie S. O'Connor
    Children: R. W., 1904, Married Verta Hamner Smith, 1903
                R. F., 1890-1939, Married Miss Griffith of Maryland
                Willie Ann, 1892, Married H. M. Burge
                J. H., Jr., 1894, Married Miss Pruden of Suffolk
                Mary E., 1897-1904
                W. H., 1899, Married Flora Lawson
                Josie H., 1901-1903
                John Carroll, 1906, Married Miss Silling of Staunton
                Edward H., 1911-1913

STANLEY, R. W., 1904, Married Verta Hamner Smith, 1903
    Father: J. H. Stanley   Mother: Bettie S. O'Connor
    Children: Jane Hamner, 1945

STANLEY, WATT HUGH, 1899, Married Flora E. Lawson, 1898
    Father: J. H. Stanley   Mother: Bettie S. O'Connor
    Children: Mary Watt, 1937

STANLEY, WILLIAM B., 1852-1914, Married Ann Elizabeth Viar, 1852-1945

STANLEY, WILLIAM HARRINGTON, 1879, Married Emma Vernon Ferguson,
                                              1882
    Children: L.L., 1903, Married Vara Rachel Smith
                Samuel Lawrence, 1905
                Willie B., 1907, Married Avis Cumby
                            Second wife: Lula Bryant
                Verna Victoria, 1910, Married George P. Doss
                M. A., 1912, Married Mabel Hall
                Erma May, 1914, Married Curtis Page
                Clarence H., 1916, Married Lillian Doss
                Lena, 1918, Married Samuel Lee Page
                Edwin T., 1920, Married Clara Williamson
                Zada A., 1922, Married Kelly Knight of Lynchburg
                Harry Byrd, 1924, Married Geane Cheatham

STAPLES, J. L., 1882, Married Florence Hopkins
    Children: B. L.

STAPLES, MARTHA, 1758-1831

STAPLES, WILLIAM, 1759-1831

STEELE, WILLIAM T., 1877-1938, Married Alice Burke, 1885
    Children: R. F. B., 1904, Married Louise Adams of Halifax
                William T., Jr., 1908, Married Mary Cover of Staunton

STEVENS, ANDREW J., 1873-1946, Married Lilly W. Franklin
    Father: Robert A. Stevens   Mother: Cordelia E. McCormick
    Children: Ernest J., Married Alice Bryant
                Herbert C., Married Lula Bryant

STEVENS, ERNEST J., Married Alice Bryant
    Father: Andrew J. Stevens   Mother: Lilly W. Franklin
    Children: Claude E.
                Eugene
                Robert
                Tommy
                Buck
                T.

STEVENS, HERBERT C., Married Lula Bryant
    Father: Andrew J. Stevens   Mother: Lilly W. Franklin
    Children: Minnie L.

STEVENS, IVERSON W., 1845-1927, Married Ida Jane Viar, 1859
    Children: Rosa, 1893-1945, Married Eugene McCormick
                Leonorah, 1896, Married Oscar Leonard McCormick
                Annie, 1900, Married John T. McCormick

STEVENS, ROBERT A., 1827-1917, Married Cordelia E. McCormick, 1854-1910
    Children: Robert H., 1869
                Andrew J., 1873-1946, Married Lilly W. Franklin
                James C., 1875, Married Beula Dickins, 1884
                William A., 1877-1943, Married Nannie McCormick
                Laura P., 1881, Married H. O. Carroll
                Archer H., 1884-1930, Married Virgie J. Gregory
                Grover C., 1886, Married Lucy Morris
                Maggie L., 1890, Married Cleveland Burks
                George P., 1879-1945, Married Mattie McCormick

STEWART, LAWRENCE LEE, 1887, Married Mary Shupe, 1891, of Washington
                                                            County
    Children: Gertrude, Married J. W. Wooldridge
                Marye, Ma·ried Horace Shirey
                Evelyn
                L. L., Jr., 1929
                Riley Jay, 1933

STRATTON, ALBON M., 1814-1875, Married Sarah Ann Woodson, 1813-1894
    Children: Thomas J., 1843-1918, Married Mary E. Harris
                Sterling C., 1851-1944, Married Lena Myers of Hollins
                James M., 1847-1870
                Gellette W., 1855-1862
                Agnes A., 1841-1933, Married John O. Thornhill

STRATTON, CHESLEY MELVIN, 1858-1937, Married Virginia Willie Drinkard,
                                                            1863-1937
    Children: Chesley Melvin, Jr., 1887, Married Eula Carson, 1890
                Aubrey Hunter, 1889, Married Dorothy Holt of Lynchburg
                Mary Winifred, 1891, Married Clarence Price of Lynchburg
                                Second husband: Seldon Bruce Gilliam
                                                of Buckingham
                Ethelbert Douglas , 1893, Married Mary Lucy Taylor, 1902
                Bessie, 1896, Married D. A. Christian
                Sarah Mildred, 1898, Married J. H. Elder
                Charlie LeGrand, 1904-1937

STRATTON, CHESLEY MELVIN, (continued)
Alice Virginia, 1907, Married Guy A. Jacobs

STRATTON, CHESLEY M., JR., 1887, Married Eula Carson, 1890
Father: Chesley Melvin Stratton   Mother: Virginia Willie Drinkard
Children: Louise, Married C. F. P. Crawley
             Fay, 1921, Married Dick Ramsey Thomas of Mississippi

STRATTON, ETHELBERT DOUGLAS, 1893, Married Mary Lucy Taylor, 1902
Father: Chesley Melvin Stratton   Mother: Virginia Willie Drinkard
Children: James D., 1927
             Jean Clare, 1929
             Carroll Taylor, 1931
             Jack Henderson, 1935

STRATTON, SR., E. M., 1863-1942, Married Bruce Robertson, 1870-1933
Father: Peter Lee Stratton   Mother: Elizabeth Woodson LeGrand
Children: P. Brent, 1892, Married Jessie Stuart Steves
             W. Robert, 1895, Married Helen Scruggs
             Elva
             Ruth, Married Mr. Cheatham
             E. M., Jr.

STRATTON, JAMES ALBERT, 1866-1945, Married Bessie LeGrand, 1871
Father: Peter Lee Stratton   Mother: Elizabeth Woodson LeGrand
Children: Frances Walker, 1907, Married Dr. T. E. Shaffer of Penn.

STRATTON, JOHN WESLEY, 1850-1931, Married Elizabeth Johnson, 1864

STRATTON, P. BRENT, 1892, Married Jessie Stuart Steves of Colorado, 1892
Father: Ethelbert Marshall Stratton   Mother: Bruce Robertson
Children: Margaret Bruce, 1925

STRATTON, PETER LEE, 1827-1910, Married Elizabeth Woodson LeGrand,
                                                           1832-1911
Children: Ethelbert Marshall, 1863-1942, Married Bruce Robertson,
                                                           1870-1933
             James Albert, 1866-1945, Married Bessie LeGrand, 1871
             Dela Hunter, 1871
             Henry Hartwell, 1873

STRATTON, THOMAS CORBAN, 1872, Married Elizabeth Burnett
Father: Thomas J. Stratton   Mother: Mary E. Harris
Children: Mary Lena
             Thomas James
             Sterling Rolfe
             Cornelia Gills
             Hubert Thornhill

STRATTON, THOMAS J., 1843-1918, Married Mary E. Harris, 1843-1917
   Father: Albon M. Stratton   Mother: Sarah Ann Woodson
    Children: James Ernest, 1869-1927, Married Nannie L. Jennings, 1885
               John Album, 1871
               Thomas Corban, 1872, Married Elizabeth Burnett
               Frank Woodson, 1874, Married Pearl Taylor
               Walter Harris, 1876, Married Edna Lenora Kirk
               Sarah E., 1878, Married W. R. Scott of Bedford

STRATTON, WILBER PETER, 1853-1928, Married Mollie Sue Anderson, 1858-193
    Children: Marvin, Married Miss Bondurant
              ------, Married W. R. Seay of Lynchburg

STRATTON, W. ROBERT, 1895, Married Helen Scruggs, 1905
   Father: Ethelbert Marshall Stratton   Mother: Bruce Robertson

STRONG, W. D., 1905, Married Maude Martin, 1905-1944
    Children: Ella J., 1935
               Linda Lee, 1941
                       Second wife: Willie Ann Martin, 1893

SWAN, ALEX STEPHEN, 1832-1909, Married Ella W. Jenkins, 1852-1933
    Children: William A., 1873, Married Allie W. Wilkerson
               Hugh B., 1874, Married Lizzie McCue of Bluefield
               Ella Ouida, 1879, Married J. H. McCue, 1867-1936
                           Second husband: N. S. Topping, 1866
               Mary Elizabeth, 1876-1876
               Ida, 1882-1929, Married Edgar F. Covington, 1874-1942
               Jennie, 1885, Married Ray Young of Prince Edward
               Estelle, 1888, Married C. C. Rosser
               Colyer, 1891, Married Gurna Parks

SWAN, WILLIAM A., 1873, Married Allie W. Wilkerson of Prince Edward
   Father: Alex Stephen Swan   Mother: Ella W. Jenkins
    Children: Hattie Frances, 1901-1901
               Ruth, 1903, Married Mr. Brockwell of Newport News
               W. A., Jr., 1905
               Helen, 1907-1907
               Louella, 1910-1911
               Gladys, 1915, Married Robert McClenney

SWEENEY, JOSEPH A., 1842-1863

TAYLOR, EDWARD, 1807-1889, Married Mary A. E. Mathews, 1812-1877
    Children: Albert Raine, 1837-1860
               Nannie Sue, 1839-1897, Married George Routen
               Richard Oglesby, 1841-1841
               Edward M., 1842
               William Benjamin, 1843, Married Adaline Crews
               Sarah Elizabeth, 1848-1875
               Zachery, 1849- Married Virgie Woodson, 1852-1931
               Thomas Milton, 1851-1931, Married Ann Harding, died 1931·
               Samuel Patteson, 1853-1927, Married Sallie C. Drinkard
               James Baster, 1855- Married Maude Vaughan of Powhatan
                         Second wife: Lula Jones of Bedford

TAYLOR, EDWARD MATHEWS, 1842-1906, Married Mary J. Stratton, died 1923
Children: William Stratton, 1873, Married Fannie Sears, 1876-1943
Mary Lizzie, 1875-1890
John Daniel, 1880, Married Daisy Myers
Raymond Mathews, 1882-1902

TAYLOR, EMMETT, 1868-1947, Married Lulie B. Peers, 1870
Children: Curtis, 1895, Married Beatrice Holdridge of California

TAYLOR, E. P., 1897, Married Irma Chenault, 1905

TAYLOR, GEORGE WERT, Married Susie Josephine Moore
Second wife: Gladys Emory Martin

TAYLOR, SAMUEL PATTESON, 1853-1927, Married Sallie C. Drinkard, 1856-
1941
Father: Edward Taylor   Mother: Mary A. E. Mathews
Children: Jeane, 1880, Married A. S. Hester of Lynchburg
Grace, 1882-1943, Married W. H. Hawkins
M. Ethel, 1884, Married Vaughan Taylor
Charles E., 1885, Married Irma Kann of Illinois
Maggie A., 1887, Married J. R. Cardwell of Campbell
Samuel M., 1890
Sallie B., 1890
George William, 1893
Fannie Sue
Elizabeth M., 1895
Olive Leigh, 1897, Married Mr. Cardwell of Campbell

TAYLOR, WILLIAM ERIC, 1906-1942, Married Anna Virginia Hunter, 1908

TAYLOR, WILLIAM STRATTON, 1873, Married Fannie Sears, 1876-1943
Father: Edward Mathews Taylor   Mother: Mary J. Stratton, died 1923
Children: Raymond Sears, 1905, Married Frances Redd
John Paul, 1907, Married Grace Price
Hazel Ann, 1911, Married Charles B. Cole

TAYLOR, ZACHERY, 1849-Married Virgie Woodson, 1852-1931
Father: Edward Taylor   Mother: Mary A. E. Mathews
Children: Lula B., 1876, Married Will Carson, 1871-1917
Second husband: William H. Morgan, 1861-
1934
Norman, 1878-1925
Fannie P., 1889, Married Joseph Oscar Baker

TANNER, HARRY A., Married Susie Baldwin, 1888

TANNER, NATHAN H., 1856-1934, Married Mattie J. Davidson, 1868-1943
Children: Thomas Houston, 1907, Married Hula M. Cunningham, 1903

TANNER, THOMAS HOUSTON, 1907, Married Hula M. Cunningham, 1903
Father: Nathan H. Tanner   Mother: Mattie J. Davidson
Children: Richard H., 1930
Frank C., 1933

TEGETHOFF, E. D., 1898, Married Edythe Kyle of Philadelphia, 1913
        Moved to Appomattox in the year of 1943.
        Richard, 1931
        Edmund, 1935
        Ronald, 1937
        Edith Virginia, 1947

TERRY, HENRY THEODRIC, 1873, Married Mary A. Abbitt, 1885
    Children: Nathaniel Chatham, 1913, Married Nannie Ruth Cooper
                Mary West, 1911, Married P. A. Robinson
                Joseph B., Married Mary E. Featherston
                Henry Theodric, Jr., 1917
                George Abbitt, 1920
                Sallie Love, 1924, Married B. A. Chandler
                Virginia Elizabeth, 1928
                Ann Bolling, 1930

TERRY, JOSEPH B., Married Mary Elizabeth Featherston
    Father: Henry Theodric Terry   Mother: Mary Ann Abbitt
    Children: Joseph B., Jr., 1946

THOMAS, REV. ALSON, 1816-1902, Married Virginia Whitehead, 1933-1917
    Children: Louisa, 1851, Married Edward Coleman
                Mittie, Married Tom Patteson
                Mildred, Married W. C. Perrow
                Berta, 1861, Married Abbitt Horsley
                A. F., 1862-1945, Married Virgie Dickerson
                Kate, 1865, Married Richard Bruce
                R. L., 1868, Married Lennie LeFew, 1866-1930
                Warner, 1872, Married Miss Peters
                Lillie, 1875-1929, Married Harry Dowdy

THOMAS, DANIEL T., 1899, Married Pauline Wharton, 1905, of Campbell

THOMAS, R. L., 1868, Married Lennie LeFew, 1866-1930
    Father: Rev. Alson Thomas   Mother: Virginia Whitehead
    Children: Aubrey McCoy, 1890
                Almira, 1893, Married John Durham
                Vernard Dickerson, 1896, Married Georgia Doss
                Edward Lee, 1897, Married Della Carter
                Lillie Bell, 1901, Married V. Terry
                Walter Elbert North, 1903, Married Elsie Guill
                Russell Carter, 1906, Married Ann Doss

THOMPSON, EDWARD, Married Louise Dickerson
    Children: Buddy Ray

THOMPSON, PERCY LEWIS, 1915, Married Elizabeth Ann Robertson, 1915
    Children: Oma Lewis, 1940

THORNHILL, ALBERT, 1819-1886, Married Lucinda Lowry, 1825-1907 of
                                            Bedford
Father: Thomas "Tanner"   Mother: Agnes Patterson
Children: Thomas J., 1849-1931
             Rev. Luther Rice, 1851-1931, Married Maddie Christian
                                      1850-1897
                              Second wife: Bettie Moody
             Charles W., 1855-1938
             Mary Agnes, 1858-1947, Married D. A. Christian
             Albert Beauregard, 1861-1928, Married Kate Smith, died 1923
             Fannie, Married E. C. James

THORNHILL, JAMES A., 1852-1926, Married Mattie Jenkins, 1860-1917
   Father: William Thornhill   Mother: Jeanette Steger
   Children: Janette, Married John A. Rooker, 1882, of Roanoke
             William J., 1884- Married Harriet Sargeant of Buckingham
             Obie, 1886
             Mary F., 1885-1886
             Allen, 1901-1932

THORNHILL, JESSE, 1763-1837, Married Elizabeth Stevens, 1766-1845
   Children: Thomas, 1785, Married Agnes Patteson
             Susannah, 1787, Married William Duiguid
             Elizabeth, 1789, Married Sam Davidson
             Jemima, 1791
             Lucy, 1793, Married James Agee
             William, 1796, Married Miss Walton
                          Second wife: Jeanette Steger
             Samuel, 1800
             Joshua, 1803, Married Judith Reveley
             Jesse, 1805, Married Mary Doss
             John, 1807, Married Miss Harvey
                        Second wife: Miss Brent
             Polly, 1809, Married William Gough

THORNHILL, II, JESSE, Married Mary Carson Doss
   Children: Joshua Taylor, 1839-1906, Married Sarah Stratton
                              Second wife: Lucy Gough
                              Third wife: Roberta Stratton
             Jesse Stevens, 1843-1920, Married Senah Frances LeGrand,
                                    1844-1887
             Robert Hall, 1845-1931, Married Fetna Eleanor Webb, 1852-
                                          1889
                              Second wife: Cornelia Pugh
                              Third wife: Amand Sue Drinkard

THORNHILL, JESSE STEVENS, 1843-1920, Married Senah Frances LeGrand,
                                      1844-1887
   Father: Jesse Thornhill, II   Mother: Mary Carson Doss
   Children: Ethelbert LeGrand, 1869-1920, Married Roberta Rohr
             Mary Lellie, 1870-1935
             Lucy Cornelia, 1872-1904
             Jesse Blanche, 1874-1934
             Charles Overstreet, 1876-1939

THORNHILL, JESSE STEVENS, (continued)
            Emeline LeGrand, 1878
            Janie G. Maben, 1880-1932, Married Aubrey Harvey

THORNHILL, JOHN H., 1852-1939, Married Mildred Garrette, 1855-1938
      Children: Wilson Walker, 1876, Married Lillie Spiggle, 1872-1937
                   Robert D., 1877, Married Maude Stewart of Lynchburg
                   Alfred, 1878-1920
                   Whiteley
                   Leonard Meredith, 1891, Married Lula Estelle Harris, 1897
                   John Leslie, 1886, Married Effie Wingfield of Charlotte
                   Pearl, Married Branch Harris
                   Vinston, Married Grace Mathews of Lynchburg
                   Fitzhugh Lee, 1885-1945, Married Miss Gunter

THORNHILL, JOHN LESLIE, 1886, Married Effie Wingfield of Charlotte
      Father: John H. Thornhill   Mother: Mildred Garrette

THORNHILL, JOSHUS TAYLOR, 1839-1906, Married Sarah Stratton
      Father: Jesse Thornhill, II   Mother: Mary Carson Doss
                            Second wife: Lucy Gough of Amherst
                            Third wife: Roberta Stratton
      Children: Emily
                  Burrell

THORNHILL, LEONARD MEREDITH, 1891, Married Lula Estelle Harris, 1897
      Father: John H. Thornhill   Mother: Mildred Garrette
      Children: David Leonard, 1918, Married Elizabeth Trent, 1919
                  James Alfred, 1922, Married Pauline Trent, 1924
                  Raymond Henry, 1926
                  Lula Margaret, 1927
                  Sallie Mildred, 1928
                  Sylvia June, 1931

THORNHILL, REV. LUTHER RICE, 1851-1931, Married Madline Patteson
                                        Christian, 1850-1898
      Father: Albert Thornhill   Mother: Lucinda Lowery
      Children: Aubrey Jeter, 1876-1930, Married Alice Jeter of Richmond
                            Second wife: Annie B. Carlton of
                                        Roanoke
                  Lucy Abigail
                  Dr. William Albert, died 1929, Married Jennie E. Button of
                                        Culpeper
                  Madelene, Married Ernest Long of Orange
                  Annie Collier, Married Lester L. Sargent of Washington, D.C.

THORNHILL, ROBERT HALL, 1845-1931, Married Fetna Eleanor Webb, 1852-
                                                            1889
      Children: Merrie Webb, 1867-1880
                  Joshua Taylor, 1871, Married Bessie Staples of Campbell
                  Janie Watkins, 1874
                  George Overstreet, 1876
                  Lizzie, 1879
                  Annie Mosley, 1883-1925, Married J. Osborne Davidson
                            Second wife: Cornelia Pugh

THORNHILL, ROBERT HALL, (continued)
Children: Robert Hall, II, 1896, Married Elsie Carson
                       Third wife of R.H., Amand Sué Drinkard

THORNHILL, II, ROBERT HALL, 1896, Married Elsie Carson
    Father: Robert Hall Thornhill   Mother: Cornelia Pugh
    Children: Martha Watkins, 1925
                    Elsie Carson, 1929

THORNHILL, SAMUEL AUSTIN, 1838-1908, Married Hatcher Patteson, 1842-1905
    Children: Benjamin P., 1866-1933, Married Alice Murrell of Lynchburg
                    Maude, Married McGuffey Woodson
                    Robert, 1873-1940, Married Fannie Thornhill of Lynchburg
                    Annie, 1876, Married Robert Thornhill of Lynchburg

THORNHILL, SAMUEL NORTH, 1903, Married Lois Lawhorn, 1901, of Nelson
    Father: Wilson Walker Thornhill   Mother: Lillie Spiggle
    Children: Laura May, 1933

THORNHILL, THOMAS "TANNER", 1785-1847, Married Agnes Patteson, 1788-
                                                                                                1878
    Children: Samuel, 1811-1876, Married Susan Thornhill, died 1844
                                Second wife: Agnes Jane Thornhill, died
                                                                                        1852
                                Third wife: Margaret McCracken, died
                                                                                        1919
                    Nancy, died, 1831, Married John Stevens of Buckingham
                    Harriet, 1817-1841, Married Mr. Spiller
                    Mary Elizabeth, 1825-1852, Married Peter Phelps of Bedford
                    Gemima Catherine, 1810-1882, Married Rev. John Cawthorn
                    Charles Burke, 1813-1950
                    Nelson, 1814, Married Elizabeth Thornhill
                    Albert, 1819-1886, Married Lucinda Lowry
                    Elvira A., 1820-1857, Married Samuel Cawthorn
                    Jesse, 1822-1857
                    Thomas Edward, 1827- died in infancy
                    Susan Pauline, 1832-1857, Married Lonnie Cousins

THORNHILL, WILLIAM, 1796-1857, Married Miss Walton
                                            Second wife: Jeanette Steger, 1812-1900
    Father: Jesse Thornhill   Mother: Elizabeth Stevens
    Children: Margaret, Married Alex White
                    Fannie, Married Robert Atkinson
                    William A., 1836-1899, Married Ellen Virginia Jones, 1836-
                                                                                                1911
                    Samuel A., Married Hatcher Patteson
                    Harriet, Married John R. Snoddy
                    Mary Susan, Married D. M. Anderson
                    J. T. E., 1850-1919, Married Lula Wilber
                    James Alfred, 1852-1926, Married Mattie Jenkins, 1860-1907

THORNHILL, WILLIAM ANTHONY, 1836-1899, Married Ellen Virginia Jones,
1836-1911
    Father: William Thornhill   Mother: Janette Steger
    Children: William David, 1861-1917, Married Page Watts of Charlottes-
ville
            Dora, 1866
            Maggie A., 1869
            Dr. George Tudor, 1872-1944, Married Elsie Fout
            Warren Ashby, 1875, Married Mary Elizabeth Featherston,
1876
            Dr. Edwin O., 1878-1911

THORNTON, FRANCIS BAKER, Married Mary Susan Armstead of Charlotte

THORNTON, FRANCIS H., Married Virginia Frances Gilliam, 1840-1871
    Children: Frank Floyd, Married Allie Dutton of Crewe
            Lacy Wert, 1866-1939, Married Flora E. Meadows
            Lewis, 1868
THORNTON, LACY WERT, 1866-1939, Married Flora E. Meadows
    Father: Francis H. Thornton   Mother: Virginia Frances Gilliam
    Children: Robert Lacy, 1894
            Edward
            Frank
            Wert
            Alice, Married Roland Carson of Richmond
            Virginia

THORNTON, SAMUEL M., 1873-1945, Married Mazie McDearmon, 1873
    No Children

THORNTON, WILLIAM D., Married Emma Walker Franklin
    Children: Harry F.
            Herbert Lacy
            Bessie
            Allie, Married Dr. F. H. Lukin
            Mattie
            Wilsie
            Flossie, Married W. F. Martin
            Robert Franklin

THROCKMORTON, LUTHER WRIGHT, Married Ola Lee Abbitt
    Children: Nan

THORPE, BERNARD, 1878-1940, Married Julia Nowlin, 1877
    Children: Marion Palmer, 1900
            Edith Virginia, 1905, Married Byron J. Kirkman of Idaho

THORPE, F. G., 1844-1919, Married Miss Carter of Nelson
                   Second wife: Mollie Susan Paris, 1870

TIBBS, JACOB, Married Nancy Jane Walker LeGrand
    Children: Tipton, Married Ocie Mason
                Berta, Married E. G. Hix
                Eva, Married E. G. Hix
                James
                Ned Archer, Married Bettie Hix
                      Second wife: Lucy Overton
                Callie, Married James Childress of Christiansburg
                Nancy Jane, Married Auelius Abbitt
                Will

TINSLEY, BENJAMIN TOLBOT, 1813-1880, Married Emiline Sydney Trent,
                                            1824-1892
    Children: Mollie, 1844, Married E. T. Kindred
                William Henry, 1849-1931, Married Helen Johnston of Salem
                Minnie Holland, 1851-1943, Married William Taylor of
                                    Roanoke

TOLLEY, J. H., 1889, Married Annie Price, 1899
    Father: L. C. Tolley   Mother: Ola Farrar
    Children: Edith, 1923, Married Lewis A. Lane, 1924
                Peggie, 1928

TOLLEY, L. CALLY, 1864-1943, Married Ola Farrar, 1874
    Children: J. H., 1889, Married Annie Price, 1899

TORRENCE, A. E., Married Mary Agnes Coleman
    Children: Olivia, Married W. D. Woodson
                John, 1868, Married Mollie Lucado, 1874-1944
                Ida, 1876, Married F. A. O'Brien
                Ira, 1877, Married Annie Gilliam
                      Second wife: Miss Reid of Bedford
                Arthur, 1879-1943, Married Fannie Cawthorn
                Sarah, 1880, Married Charlie Agee
                Dr. George, 1881
                Samuel Early, 1878-1939, Married Lucy Chenault
                Berkley, 1883
                Hallie, 1884, Married Robert W. Morris
                Jesse L., Married Lavelette Torrence

TORRENCE, C. LEWIS, 1875, Married Lula Lillie
    Father: P. A. Torrence   Mother: Fannie Bagby
    Children: Geneva, 1897, Married George R. Abbitt
                Dewey, 1899, Married Miss Penning of West Virginia
                Holland, 1901, Married Miss Meadows of West Virginia
                Frances, 1903, Married J. L. Buford of Bedford
                      Second wife: Mrs. Nunnelly
    Children: Charles Lewis, Jr., 1928

TORRENCE, DAVID EUGENE, 1881, Married Hattie A. Drinkard, 1883
    Children: Frances
                Alfred Drinkard, 1918
                John Wellington, 1921
                Charles David, 1925
                Frank Allen, 1926

TORRENCE, ELLIOTT, Married Myrtice Lorraine Hamilton, 1918
    Father: J. L. Torrence   Mother: Annie Lavelette Torrence

TORRENCE, HENRY CLAY, 1844-1925, Married Louisa Watts Rosser
    Children: Leslie, 1869-1940, Married Gertie Inge, 1876
                Wirt Henry, Married Bettie Bryant
                Oscar Russell, Married Gladys Moore
                Walker, 1866, Married B. L. Jordan
                Ola, Married J. W. Patteson
                Sallie B., 1876-1947, Married T. U. Conner
                Allie, 1869-1940, Married P. J. Shepherd

TORRENCE, JAMES R., 1883-1944, Married Frances P. Cawthorn
    Children: Alfred W., 1909

TORRENCE, O. R., 1891, Married Gladys Moore, 1899
    Father: Henry Clay Torrence   Mother: Louisa Watts Rosser
    Children: Nellie, 1919, Married W. R. Jobe, Jr.
                Louise, 1921, Married Hugh W. Brown

TORRENCE, PLEASANT A., 1841- Married Fannie Bagby, 1847
    Children: Willie, 1867, Married Mattie Garrison
                Mary L., 1869, Married Lewis Napoleon Patteson
                Joseph, 1871-1882
                Jim, 1873-1889
                C. Lewis, 1875, Married Lula Lillie of West Virginia
                Emmett, 1877-1944, Married Nicholas Gordon
                Maude, 1879, Married Oscar Haga
                Bessie, 1881, Married Roland Haga

TORRENCE, SAMUEL EARLY, 1878-1939, Married Lucy Ellen Chenault, 1879
    Father: A. E. Torrence   Mother: Mary Agnes Coleman
    Children: Ruby Myrtle, 1903, Married J. Artie Gilliam
        Twins   (Gracie Lyle, 1905, Married J. R. Thomas of Lynchburg
                (Lacy Early, 1905, Married E. M. Wells of Hopewell
                Mary Vertener, 1908, Married J. Newman of Hopewell
                Garland Edward, 1909, Married R. E. Mintor
                Fannie Louise, 1914, Married J. M. Foster of Farmville
                Lorene, Married James Richardson
                Bertha, Married Eddie Dickerson

TORRENCE, W. H., Married Rosa B. Bryant, 1879

TORRENCE, WILLIAM LESLIE, 1868-1940, Married Gertrude Inge, 1872
Children: Alma C., 1893-1918
             Annie Lavelette, 1894, Married J. L. Torrence
             Edna E., 1896, Married Tommy Covington
             Ora S., 1898, Married R. H. Coleman
             Reva, 1906, Married Otis C. Smith of Halifax
             Mary Edith, 1908, Married Burnett Gilliam
             David Raymond, 1912, Married Elgin Gilliam
             William Leslie, Jr., 1914, Married Hazel M. McFadden
             Eula Gertrude, 1916, Married Waveley Gilliam

TRENT, SR., THOMAS, 1757-1820, Married Elizabeth Edwards, 1752-1831
Children: Henry, 1784, Married Phoebe Walton
             Capt. Thomas, Jr., 1786-1861, Married Martha Holland
             Mary, 1788-1857, Married Elliott Thomas
             William, 1790, Married Elizabeth Webb
             Elizabeth, 1792, Married Mr. Webb
             Nancy, 1795, Married Thomas Walton

TRENT, JR., THOMAS, 1786-1861, Married Martha A. Watts
                              Second wife: Martha Holland, 1801-1850
Children: Alexander, 1797, Married Mary Hix
             James Walker, 1819-1822
             William Henry, 1832-1906, Married Mary Johns
             Ella Walker, 1836- Married Joseph Barrett
             Mary Elizabeth, Married Col. Henry Flood
             Martha Walker, 1827-1907, Married N. H. Ragland
             Emeline Sydney, 1824-1892, Married Ben Tinsley

TRENT, THOMAS HENRY, 1890, Married Bessie Gilbert, 1898
Children: Thomas Alvin, 1919-1945, Married Irene Lucado, 1920
             Robert Edward, 1925
             Ethel Eloise, 1927
             Joel A., 1938

TRENT, WILLIAM JACKSON, 1860-1940, Married Pearl Pamplin Pankey, 1872
Children: Mildred Jackson, 1902, Married Justin L. Burkey, 1898-1938
             Elizabeth Pamplin, 1904, Married John E. Fox
             William Jackson, Jr., 1907, Married Bernice Montgomery,
                                                        1916, of Detroit
             Mary Virginia, 1910

TRENT, JR., WILLIAM JACKSON, Married Bernice Montgomery
Father: William Jackson Trent   Mother: Pearl Pamplin Pankey
Children: Mary Elizabeth, 1935
             William Jackson, III, 1944

TUGGLE, HENRY, Married Martha Puckett

TUGGLE, THOMAS W., 1852- Married Rosa Lee Ingrim, 1872-1938
    Children: Joseph C., 1891-1919
                Winnifred, 1893, Married A. J. Monger of Rockingham
                Blanche Ray, 1894, Married Clinton Steele of Campbell
                Nellar E., 1897-1916
                Thelma J., 1890, Married Fred Blanton of Roanoke
                           Second husband: Reace Kearnes of North
                                          Carolina
                Milton N., 1902
                Henry J., 1904, Married Miss Askew of Canada
                Mable Alice, 1909

TURNER, JAMES NELSON, 1856-1905, Married Emma Walker Bell, 1855-1934
    Children: W. A., 1878-1940, Married Lillie Woody of Nelson
                Maude Virginia, 1880-1910, Married William Raborg of
                                  Richmond
                James Walker, 1885-1945, Married Nettie B. Cash of Nelson
                Lucy Jane, 1887-1931, Married Houston Cash of Nelson
                Mary Pearl, 1890, Married Jeremiah Wood of Nelson
                Annie Watkins, 1892, Married T. L. Anderson of Albemarle
                Hal Flood, 1896-1909
                Thomas Elma, 1896-1942, Married Mattie Hammersley, 1897
                Norman, 1896-1896
                Nannie Bell, 1899, Married James Garrette of Nelson
                Edward Jones, 1883-1945, Married Mattie Louise Omohundro
                                of Buckingham

TURNER, THOMAS R., 1870, Married Annie P. Wood, 1870

TWEEDY, CHARLES ROSSER, 1915, Married Bettie Sue Moore, 1916
    Father: John A. Tweedy   Mother: Ruth Cawthorn
    Children: Charles Allen, 1938

TWEEDY, JOHN ALLEN, 1885, Married Ruth Virginia Cawthorn, 1893
    Father: Joseph Walton Tweedy   Mother: Lucy Ann Barnard
    Children: Charlie Rosser, 1915, Married Bettie C. Moore, 1915
                Catherine C., 1917, Married Robert McQueen of Smythe
                John Allen, Jr., 1921
                Lewis C., 1923
                Bettie Sue, 1931
                James Melvin, 1936

TWEEDY, JOSEPH WALTON, 1849-1906, Married Lucy Ann Barnard, 1853-1935
    Children: John Allen, 1885, Married Ruth Virginia Cawthorn, 1893
                Walton
                Annie, Married Robert Cawthorn
                          Second husband: J. W. Covington
                Mary Sears, Married Jennings O'Brien

TWYMAN, DR. D. N., 1877-1940, Married Phoebe Shaw, 1883-1913
    Children: Frederick
                Henry
                Virginia
                      Second wife: Miss Hobson

VEST, JAMES, Married Emma Viar
    Children: Willie, Married Miss Leftwich of Bedford
                 Cora, 1869-1939, Married George W. Robertson
                 Dave
                 Joe
                 Elsie, 1881, Married R. Dowdy of Lynchburg
                 James

VIER, WILLIAM B.,
    Children: Willie, died, 1921
                 Mattie
                 Ossie, 1886

WAGERS, NED A., 1895-1943, Married Russell Mae Ferguson
    Children: Hilda Dale, 1921, Married G. H. Wilson of Florida
                 Helen Virginia, 1924, Married Norris E. Diddle of Mass.

WALKER, BENJAMIN PATTERSON, Married Mary Jane Branch
    Children: Susan Winifred, Married Henry Flood Bocock
                 Heath, Married Joseph Abbitt.
                 2nd. wife of Benjamin Patterson Walker, Maria Boyd
    Children: Maria
                 Kate
                 Dan

WALKER, ISAAC, 1810-1839, Married Sarah Branch, died, 1904
    Children: Samuel Branch, 1834-1906, Married Mollie Venable, 1837-1913

WALKER, JAMES A., 1835-1914, Married Sallie Paul Jones, 1834-1901
    Father: John Walker   Mother: Martha Stovall Penn
    Children: David Jones, 1860-1921, Married Permalia McMillan
                 Mary Alice, 1866-1940
                 Anna Elizabeth, 1868-1944, Married John Wallace
                 James Paul, 1871, Married Nannie Dove Hurt, 1876
                 Frank Roland, 1873, Married Ida Maybee of Nelson
                 Herbert Bass, 1878-1934, Married Maggie Bowles of Nelson

WALKER, JOHN, Married Martha Stovall Penn, 1801-1881
    Children: Mary C., 1831
                 James A., 1835-1914, Married Sallie Paul Jones, 1834-1901
                 Martha E., 1832

WALKER, JOHN MERRIWEATHER, Married Susan Christian
    Children: Samuel Jennings, 1809-1866, Married Martha Ann Walton,
                                                            1812-1888
                 Isaac, 1810-1939, Married Sarah Elizabeth Branch
                 Benjamin, Married Jane Branch
                        Second wife: Sally Byrd Thompkins

WALKER, SAMUEL BRANCH, 1834-1906, Married Mollie Venable, 1837-1913
    Father: Isaac Walker   Mother: Sarah Branch
    Children: Isaac, 1860-1862

WALKER, SAMUEL J., 1809-1866, Married Martha Ann Walton, 1812-1888
    Father: John Merriweather Walker   Mother: Susan Christian
    Children: John William, 1831-1832
                Benjamin Walton, 1832-1906, Married Ariana Sims of Texas
                Isaac Winston, 1834-1884, Married Kate Doswell Taliaferro
                Harvey Christian, 1835-1861
                Maria Elizabeth, 1837-1903, Married W. H. Jones
                William Henry Harrison, 1840-1903
                Edmund Winston, 1842-1916, Married Jennie Massie of Kentucky
                Sue C., 1844-1923, Married Henry D. LeGrande
                Mary Virginia, 1846-1906, Married B. W. Babcock
                Sarah Frances, 1849-1912, Married Col. R. W. Withers of
                                               Campbell
                Samuel J., 1851-1914, Married Lucy Massie
                Nannie Lee, 1854-1906, Married William R. Elliott of Kentucky

WALLER, J. W., 1903, Married Fannie Mae McLendon, 1911, of South Carolina
    Children: Loretta Ann, 1933

WALTON, DALLAS EUGENE, 1887, Married Jamie F. Moss, 1878-1914
    Father: E. A. Walton   Mother: Kate Jones
                Second wife: Ruth Harris of Nelson, 1896

WALTON, EUGENE ADOLPHUS, 1850-1921, Married Katherine Jones, 1862-1931
    Father: John William Walton   Mother: Mary Vawter
    Children: William J., 1885, Married Frances Harvey
                Walker Scott, 1891, Married Nellie Davis of Buckingham
                Dallas Eugene, 1887, Married Jamie Moss
                        Second wife: Ruth Harris
                John, Married Miss Davis
                Zan, Married Miss Harris
                Lela, Married D. M. Harris
                Evie, Married Mr. Harris
                Mary, Married Carrington Bolton
                Bessie, Married Frank Payne

WALTON, JOHN WILLIAM, 1821-1889, Married Mary Vawter, 1829-1887
    Children: Eugene Adolphus, 1850-1921, Married Katherine Jones, 1862-
                                                    1931
                Bettie, Married George Dallas Abbitt
                Annie Eliza, Married Mr. Mitchell

WALTON, THOMAS E., 1830-1882, Married Martha Woodson, 1832-1920
    Children: Thomas A., Married Virginia Purdum
                Mattie E., Married Ed. Purdum
                George, 1867, Married Emily Purdum
                Annie, 1871, Married Robert A. Staples
                Ella, 1874, Married R. F. Jamerson
                Carrie, 1876, Married J. D. Moses

WALTON, WALKER SCOTT, 1891, Married Nellie Davis of Buckingham
    Father: E. A. Walton   Mother: Katherine Jones
    Children: Winston Davis, 1931
               Josephine Walker, 1932
               Shirley Mitchell, 1934

WALTON, WILLIAM J., 1885, Married Frances Harvey, 1890
    Father: E. A. Walton   Mother: Kate Jones
    Children: Eugenia, 1921
               Louise, 1928
               William Jones, 1929
               Mildred Frances, 1916
               Katherine, Married George Carson

WARRINER, WILLIAM EDWARD, 1883, Married Mattie A. Evans, 1886
    Children: Ernest Edison, 1906
               Carrie Elanie, 1910, Married J. T. Gibson of Washington D.C.
               Roy Witt, 1913
               Mary L., 1920, Married W. H. Smith of Alexandria
               Linda Louise, 1927

WATKINS, JOEL, 1861, Married Sallie Marshall
    Father: William Watkins   Mother: Susan Jane Dillard
    Children: Katherine
               William Jones, 1897
               John Marshall, 1900, Married Adele Hutchinson
               Joel, Jr., 1903, Married Catherine Armstrong

WATKINS, WILLIAM, 1819-1899, Married Susan Jane Dillard, 1832-1928
    Children: Joel, 1861, Married Sallie Marshall

WATSON, HERMAN, Married Bettie Sue Riley

WATSON, THOMAS R., 1885, Married Bettie Seay of Buckingham, 1892

WEAKLEY, ATWELL, Married Eddie Colyer Abbitt, 1893

WEBB, ALBERT, Married Miss Jennings

WEBB, HENRY, 1849-1899, Married Susan Lewis, 1850-1929
    Children: Van, 1886, Married Peggy Wooldridge
               Stella, 1888, Married S. W. Caterson
               Nannie, 1890
               John R., 1896, Married Miss Glenn of Prince Edward

WEBB, JOHN THOMAS, Married Miss Wilkerson
    Children: One daughter Married Mr. Pugh
               Two sons, neither married

WEBB, JOHN WILLIAM, 1861-1943, Married Fetner Webb
                            Second wife: Lelia Walker Ferguson,
                                        1876-1944
        Children: John Walker, 1903
                    Richard Meade, 1904, Married Bettie Agnes Morris, 1900
                    Carrie, 1910
                    Thelma, Married J. E. Martin
                    Henry Delaware, 1912, Married Margarite Krenitzky
                    William Archer, 1915
                    Martin Luther, 1917
                    Robert Everett, 1919

WEBB, MONROE, Married Ruby Otway Jenkins

WEBB, NATHAN, Married Polly Strange

WEBB, SAMUEL, 1846- , Married Sallie Ann Coleman, 1846
        Children: Ella, Married W. T. Coleman
                    Anna B., 1871, Married Patrick Stacks
                                Second husband: William Caterson
                    James, 1877
                    Charles, 1879

WEBB, SYDNOR, 1833-1897, Married Cassie Dickerson
        Children: George E., 1867, Married Mamie Elam of Prince Edward
                    James A., 1869-1939, Married Mamie Beasley, 1896
                    John Henry, 1869-1890
                    Mary Alice, 1871-1873
                    Mildred, 1873-1943, Married P. W. Coleman
                    Lizzie H., 1875, Married Russell Thomas of Prince Edward
                    Cassie, 1876, Married Joel W. Coleman

WEBBER, SARAH G., 1803-1946

WEBBER, RUTH, 1766-1845

WELLS, ALONZO, 1824-1920, Married Sarah E. Phelps, 1850-1913
        Children: Geneva, 1876, Married Joseph Dixon of Buckingham
                    Addie L., 1878, Married John Cunningham of Buckingham
                    Whitcomb A., 1879, Married Early Jane Phelps, 1885
                    Tempie, 1881, Married Bill Mills of Newport News
                    Bessie J., 1882, Married Sam Cunningham of Buckingham
                    Effie J., 1885, Married J. R. Cash of Lynchburg
                    Ethel Othelia, Married Sam Moore

WELLS, OTHA LUTHER, 1918, Married Allyne Harding, 1922
        Father: Whitcomb A. Wells   Mother: Early Jane Phelps
        Children: Otha Luther, Jr., 1939
                    Eldridge Leon, 1941
                    C. Gay, 1944

WELLS, ROYAL W., 1910, Married Louise A. Phelps, 1912
    Father: Whitcomb A. Wells   Mother: Early Jane Phelps
    Children: Daphine Virginia, 1934
              Loretta Gardner, 1938
              Royal W., Jr., 1944

WELLS, WHITCOMB A., 1879, Married Early Jane Phelps, 1885
    Father: Alonzo Wells   Mother: Sarah E. Phelps
    Children: Richard A., 1907-1909
              Royal W., 1910, Married Louise Phelps, 1912
              Olive J., 1915, Married Doris Sprivey of Newport News
              Walter Eugene, 1917, Married Miss Burks of Buckingham
              Other L., 1918, Married Allene Harding
              Richard P., 1923, Married Ada Coleman
              Howard W., 1925-1927

WHEELER, ALEXANDER CHRISTIAN, 1850-1926, Married Annie Eliza Layne,
                                                             1860-1916
    Father: Andrew Wheeler   Mother: Henrietta Agee
    Children: Annie, Married R. J. Paulette

WHEELER, ANDREW STRATTON, Married Henrietta Agee
    Children: Sue, Married Mr. Patteson
              William, 1836-
              Bettie, 1941-
              Radford H., 1843-1925
              Lelia T., 1844-1922
              Pattie
              Christian, Married Eliza Layne
              Gertrude, Married Mr. Paulett
              Clara, 1851- Married Tom Steger of Buckingham
              Ella, 1858-
              Andrew
              Ann

WHEELER, B. L., 1875-1941, Married Cora Lee Bondurant, 1876
    Children: Joe, Married Virginia Noel of Roanoke
              B. L., Jr., Married Esta 'Pugh of Charlotte
              Max, Married Elizabeth Inge of Campbell
              John B., Married Hessie Jordan of Campbell
              Irby B. Wheeler, Married Miss Alvis

WHEELER, IRBY BANKS, 1899, Married Eloise Alvis, 1904
    Father: B. L. Wheeler   Mother: Cora Lee Bondurant
    Children: Ben David, 1924
              Robert Irby, 1926
              William Allen, 1930
              Betsy Lee, 1933
              Bertha Louise, 1935

WHEELER, R. S., 1873-1936, Married Ruth Moore, 1895
    Children: Frances Marvin, 1922-1923
              R. S., Jr., 1923-1925
              Mary Ann, 1926

WHITAKER, ALICE W., 1855-1900

WHITAKER, CORA, 1854-1940

WHITAKER, JAMES, 1842- Married Miss Beale

WHITAKER, JOHN WILLIAM, 1845-1926, Married Elvira Susan Furbush, 1849-
1900

WHITAKER, ROBERT D., 1847-1933

WHITE, ALEX., Married Margurite Thornhill
    Father: Andrew White   Mother: Margaret Ferguson
    Children: Roberta, Married Pleas Preston of Lynchburg

WHITE, ANDREW, Married Margaret Ferguson
    Children: John F., born about 1815, died about 1880
              William A., 1818-1900, Married Miss Mundy
              Robert
              Alex., Married Margurite Thornhill
              Peter J., 1825-1879, Married Fannie Ruffner, 1837-1928
              A. A., 1836

WHITE, JOHN W., 1840-1901, Married Susan Peers, 1830-1893
    Children: Myrtle Lee, 1869, Married Nathan D. Marshall
              Mary Virginia, 1864-1900
              Henry T., 1880

WHITE, PETER J., 1825-1879, Married Fannie Ruffner, 1837-1928
    Father: Andrew White   Mother: Margaret Ferguson
    Children: Margaret, 1856-1944, Married Dr. Camm of Lynchburg
              Emma Tell, 1858, Married Dr. Dillard of Lynchburg
              Andrew P., 1861-1925, Married Lizzie Abbitt, 1870

WHITEHEAD, J. L., 1890, Married Maude Page, 1897
    Children: Elizabeth, 1914-1932
              James, 1915, Married Christine Robertson
              Evelyn, 1917, Married Carlton Harris
              Virginia, 1919, Married Lloyd Doss
              Louise, 1921, Married Lee Mays

WHITTEN, JOSEPH TINSLEY, 1861, Married Elizabeth Wright of Amherst,
1863-1939
    Children: Irene, 1885, Married Will Price of Campbell
              Joseph Tinsley, Jr., 1887, Married Mattie Leat
              Henley Clarance, 1883, Married Mrs. Hamilton of Lynchburg
              Forest, 1901, Married Miss Garrett of Lynchburg
              Willie, 1910
              Laura, 1903, Married Mr. Daniel of Campbell

WILBUN, R. E., 1906, Married Hazel Mason of Campbell
    Children: Ryland, 1940
              Gerald, 1943
              Chas. Edward, 1947

WILKERSON, CLARENCE ELMO, 1891, Married Nannie Sue Bingham, 1893
Children: George Earl, 1912, Married Agnes Page, 1919
             John Archer, 1913, Married Thelma Fisher of Halifax
             Clarence Eddie, 1916
             Hubert Lester, 1922
             Florence Huldah, 1924, Married Clyde Reynolds

WILKES, JOHN, 1913

WILKES, LACY MORTON, 1879, Married Alma May Wooldridge
Children: Mabel Christine, 1924

WILSON, JAMES BLAIR, 1880, Married Stella Watkins Abbitt, 1886
Children: Ellen McCorkle, 1912, Married E. D. McClure of Rockbridge

WILLIAMS, TRIGG, 1888- Married Essie Smith
Children: Dollie, 1927

WILLIAMSON, ELBERT LEE, 1925, Married Ruby Rogers
Father: William Lee Williamson   Mother: Ruth Marsh
Children: Elbert LeRoy, 1943
             Brenda Gale, 1947

WILLIAMSON, MERVWYN WILTON, 1921, Married Rhoda Lott
Father: William Lee Williamson   Mother: Ruth Marsh
Children: Mervwyn Wilton, Jr., 1944

WILLIAMSON, WILLIAM HENRY, 1854-1946, Married Selinda Gordon, 1849-1930
Children: H. Harrison, 1887-1947, Married Golden Wooten
             William Lee, 1889, Married Ruth Marsh, 1894
             James
             Nora, Married Robert Wooten

WILLIAMSON, WILLIAM LEE, 1889, Married Ruth Marsh, 1894
Father: William Henry Williamson   Mother: Selinda Gordon
Children: Mervwyn Wilton, 1921, Married Rhoda Lott of Texas
             Audrey Morris, 1923, Married Everett Phelps
             Elbert Lee, 1925, Married Ruby Rogers
             Verta Lonell, 1928
             Melva Gordon, 1933
             William Henry, 1934

WILMER, GEORGE WASHINGTON, Married Vernona Bell, 1861-1932

WINGFIELD, ALEXANDER S., 1852-1920, Married Ella Callahan, 1860-1908
Children: Norman A., died 1903
             Robert Alexander, 1898
             Pearl, died, 1940, Married Mr. Franklin
             Mary E., died 1946, Married Mr. Perdue
             Mattie W., Married Harry Totty
             Ella V., Married Mr. McFadden
             Sallie B., Married Bernard Ferguson

WINGFIELD, C. ANDREW, 1870, Married Janie Godsey, 1881
    Father: Charles A. Wingfield   Mother: Mary Wingfield
    Children: Agnes, 1898- Married B. Bobbit of Petersburg
                  Julian J., Married Zelia Jones
                  Pat, Married Miss Wingo
                  Mattie, Married Mr. Belgium of Petersburg
                  Geneva, Married John Wilson
                  Nellie, Married Henry Harvey
                  Herman
                  Bradley, Married Hazel Moore
                  Twyman, Married Miss Guffey of Halifax
                  Myrtle, Married Ernest Smith
                  Lester, Married Flossie Goodrich

WINGFIELD, CHARLES A., Married Mary Wingfield
    Children: Signora, Married Mr. Loornot of Richmond
                  Bettie, Married John Williams
                  Bell, Married Paul Goin
                  Vick
                  Peter, 1860-1944
                  Walter, 1862-1946
                  C. Andrew, 1870, Married Janie Godsey, 1881

WINGFIELD, CHARLES HENRY, 1844-1918, Married Sara Frances Callahan,
                                                  1852-1924

WINGFIELD, JAMES JULIAN, 1900, Married Zelia Page Jones, 1908
    Father: Andrew Wingfield   Mother: Janie Godsey
    Children: Richard Lewis, 1928
                  Joyce Bobrie, 1930
                  Betty Jane, 1932
                  James Ray, 1934
                  Frederick Charles, 1943

WINGFIELD, JOHN WILLIAM, 1841-1933, Married Laura White of Bedford

WOOD, DAVID PHARR, 1894-1917

WOOD, ROBERT FRANKLIN, 1891-1922

WOODALL, W. S., Married Dorothy Marsh, 1904

WOODSON, REV. DRURY, Married Miss Bruce of Prince Edward

WOODSON, EDWIN R., 1842-1891, Married Miss Hill
                            Second wife: Miss Franklin, 1851-1915
    Children: Ruby, 1878, Married Edward B. Price of New Jersey
                  Pearle, 1880, Married C. B. Cross
                  Mathews

WOODSON, JACOB, 1905, Married Nannie Austin, 1914
    Father: Thomas S. Woodson   Mother: Nora Austin
    Children: Phoebe, 1935
               Mary G., 1936

WOODSON, JACOB O., 1834-1922, Married Lucy Jane Carnefix, 1831-1912
    Children: William D., Married Olivia Torrence
               Thomas E., 1870-1930, Married Nora Austin, 1877

WOODSON, JAMES A., 1841-1904, Married Bettie Gertrude Harris, 1845-1889
    Children: Lula Gertrude, 1881-1891
               James Norvell, 1882, Married Mattie R. Wright
               John Holcomb, 1884-1946, Married Miss James
               Thomas Cleveland, 1885- Married Annie Faulkner
               Ernest Alfred, 1887-1919
               Laura Elsie, 1889-1890

WOODSON, J. C., 1853-1930, Married Fannie Binford of Campbell
                            Second wife: Bennie Gibson of Buckingham
                            Third wife: Lilly Scott of Bedford

WOODSON, NANCY, 1821-1906

WOODSON, THOMAS EDWARD, 1913, Married Edna Seay, 1916
    Father: Thomas S. Woodson   Mother: Nora Austin
    Children: Margie, 1935

WOODSON, THOMAS S., 1870-1930, Married Nora Austin, 1877
    Father: Jacob O. Woodson   Mother: Lucy Jane Carnefix
    Children: William A., 1901, Married Bernice Bagby, 1897
               Mandy, 1902
               Janie, 1903
               Jacob, 1905, Married Nannie Austin, 1914
               Mattie, 1908, Married Gallier Austin
               Lena, 1910, Married Norvel Bagby
               Thomas E., 1913, Married Edna Seay, 1916

WOODSON, WILLIAM A., 1901, Married Bernice Bagby, 1897, of Buckingham
    Father: Thomas S. Woodson   Mother: Nora Austin
    Children: Katie, 1925
               William C., 1935

WOODSON, WILLIE D., 1867-1939, Married Olivia Torrence, 1870
    Father: Jacob O. Woodson   Mother: Lucy Jane Carnefix
    Children: Lucy W., 1891, Married Ernest Ferguson
               Maggie, 1893, Married Barton S. Reid of Kentucky
               Harry T., 1895-1928, Married Gladys Bingham
               Cassie A., 1897, Married Dr. H. O. Miranda of Brazil
               Hattie L., 1901, Married John W. Hope of Hampton
               Cornelia, 1899
               Mary A., 1906
               Orville
               Kermit, 1910, Married Mr. G. K. Grady of North Carolina
               Willie Dillard, 1913, Married Florence Slaughter of Richmond
               Leone E., 1903, Married Henry Dodd of Amherst

WOODSON, WILLIAM McGUFFIE, 1857-1917, Married Maude Thornhill, 1868-
1913

WOODSON, WILLIE WIRT, 1877, Married Ada Cheatham, 1877-1923
                       Second wife: Olivia Rush, 1896

WOODY, CARRINGTON

WOODY, MOLLY

WOOLDRIDGE, ARCHER S., 1850, Married Anna C. Wooldridge, 1849
    Father: Presley R. Wooldridge   Mother: Nancy E. Wooldridge
    Children: Bertha Viola, 1877, Married James Abner Martin
                  Maggie Bell, 1879-1903
                  Frank Leslie, 1882, Married Mary Willie Moultrie
                  Susie E., 1885-1898

WOOLDRIDGE, CARL R., 1925, Married Illa Harding, 1916

WOOLDRIDGE, DABNEY ELLIS, 1813-1894, Married Appolonia Gordon, 1816-
1888
    Father: William Wooldridge   Mother: Catherine Kelly
    Children: Henrietta W., 1839- Married Henry Cheatham
                  Matilda H., 1841, Married B. F. Jennings
                  Ethelbert A., 1843-1865
                  Victoria J., 1845, Married Tucker Evans
                  Adeliade C., 1847, Married Sidnor Farrar
                  Anna C., 1849, Married Archer S. Wooldridge
                  Rosa B., 1852, Married Jehue Godsey
                  Onelia E., 1855, Married Joseph Martin
                  Richard, Married Fannie Kelly

WOOLDRIDGE, DANIEL, 1823-1907, Married Lucy Martin, 1874
    Children: Patrick Henry, died 1922, Married Fannie Wright
                  Daniel, Jr., Married Willie Wright
                  Tom, Married Sallie Fore
                  Nannie, Married Robert Wooldridge
                        Second husband: James Almond
                  Lucy Ann, Married Major Cumby

WOOLDRIDGE, FLOYD, 1885-1944, Married Vashti Davis, 1884-1945
    Children: Ursula, 1908, Married Otis Davis
                  Randall, 1911, Married Weselene Williams
                  Ruby L., 1913, Married J. K. Hamilton
                  Larry F., 1915, Married Kathleen Evans

WOOLDRIDGE, HUMPHREY LEE, 1885, Married Florence Martin, 1885
    Children: Robert, 1905-1937, Married Elsie Shaner of Concord
                  Vivian, 1907, Married O. C. Coffman of Green Bay
                  Woodrow, 1914
                  Eddie, 1916, Married Margaret Hudson of Clarksville
                  Kathrine, 1919, Married Hall Clark of Meherrin
                  Frank Dwight, 1925

WOOLDRIDGE, JETER WITT, 1913, Married Gertrude Stewart, 1914

WOOLDRIDGE, JOSIAH BENJAMIN, Married Polly Giles
    Children: Emma, 1858, Married Allie B. Nowlin
               Ellis N., 1961, Married Ida Inge
               Walter, 1865, Married Lucy Inge
               Nannie, Married W. C. Nowlin
               Willie, Married Len Mitchell
               Addie, Married Charlie Hamilton
               Walker, Married Flecia Perdue

WOOLDRIDGE, LARRY F., 1915, Married Kathleen Evans
    Father: Floyd Wooldridge   Mother: Vashti Davis
    Children: Cecil, 1940
               Peggy, 1941

WOOLDRIDGE, NATHAN, 1870-1940, Married Alma Davis, 1873-1928
    Children: Edna, 1914, Married Tucker Evans
                       Second husband: Harry Williams
               James, Married Emma Jennings

WOOLDRIDGE, NORMAN ELLIS, 1890, Married Orpha Whitney Babcock, 1903
    Children: Eleanor, 1931
               Daniel Ellis, 1926, Married Madeline Ann Torchia

WOOLDRIDGE, PRESLEY R., Married Nancy E. Wooldridge, 1829-1901
    Children: Willie, died young
               Presley R., Jr., 1854-1908, Married Mary O'Conner
               Archer Smith, 1850, Married Anna C. Wooldridge
               Dabney E., Married Opie Crawley
               G. Walker, 1858, Married Nettie Witt
               Emma E., 1860, Married John Edward Martin May

WOOLDRIDGE, RANDALL, 1911, Married Weselene Williams
    Father: Floyd Wooldridge   Mother: Vashti Davis
    Children: Barbara Ann, 1939

WOOLDRIDGE, SAM MOORE, 1845-1925, Married Ella F. Pugh, died 1939

WOOLDRIDGE, THOMAS J., 1818-1862, Married Elizabeth M. Pugh, 1819-1892
    Children: Samuel M., 1845-1925, Married Ella Frances Pugh, 1861-1939

WOOLDRIDGE, SAMUEL M., Married Ella Frances Pugh, 1861-1939
    Children: John Thomas, 1885
               Travis Taylor, 1891, Married Inese Pugh
       Twins   (Susan Estelle, 1895
                (George Wiley, 1895
               Annie Abbitt, 1900, Married James Daniel Cawthorn
               Samuel Pugh, 1886-1893

WOOLDRIDGE, WALKER, Married Flecia Perdue
    Father: Josiah Benjamin Wooldridge   Mother: Polly Giles
    Children: Earl
               Alex
               Aubrey

WOOLDRIDGE, WALTER, 1865, Married Lucy Inge
    Father: Josiah Benjamin Wooldridge   Mother: Polly Giles
    Children: Alex., Married Miss McCall of Lynchburg
                Berkley
                Odelle
                Eva, Married Clarence Thomas
                Jimmie, Married Eva Gray

WOOLDRIDGE, WILLIAM, 1767-1857, Married Catherine Kelly, 1789-1878
    Children: Dabney Ellis, 1813-1894, Married Applonia Gordon
                Nancy Elizabeth, 1829-1901, Married Presley R. Wooldridge
                Jane, 1822-1898
                Betsy
                Harker

WOOLDRIDGE, WILLIAM EDWARD, 1858-1915, Married Virginia A. Farrar,
                                            1848-1916
    Children: Thomas Willie, 1882, Married C. A. Warren
                Addie Lena, 1884, Married Luke Ferguson
                Nannie Sue, 1887, Married John William Ransone

WOOLDRIDGE, W. W. (MOODY), 1875-1947, Married Elvira Frances Marshall,
                                            1890
    Children: Berdie, 1902-1923, Married Penick Harvey

WOOLFOLK, W. F., 1895, Married Emma M. Hancock, 1897
    Children: W. F., Jr., 1928

WOOTEN, JACK, 1854-1918, Married Bettie Inge, 1868
    Children: Robert, 1885, Married Nora Williamson, 1882
                Golden, Married H. H. Williamson

WOOTEN, ROBERT, 1885, Married Nora Williamson, 1882
    Father: Jack Wooten   Mother: Bettie Inge
    Children: Gertrude, 1911, Married Claude Jennings
                Williamson

WRIGHT, THOMAS H., 1860-1945, Married Annie Johnson, 1870-1904
    Children: Raleigh, 1887
                Emmett, 1885-1936, Married Pocahontas Scruggs, 1890
                Myrtle, 1892, Married Hubert Scruggs
                Lottie, 1896, Married Sandford Rider of Orange
                William, 1900, Married Lucy Franklin of Campbell
                Mattie, 1902
                Mamie, 1904, Married Joe Franklin of Campbell
                Ruth, 1906-1925, Married Wallace Bondurant

WRIGHT, WILLIAM, Married Susian Turner

YOUNG, ELLA

YOUNG, JOHN A., 1888, Married Edna Inge, 1896

YOUNG, LARRIE A., 1903, Married Nellie Byrd Harvey Cole, 1906

www.ingramcontent.com/pod-product-compliance
Lightning Source LLC
Chambersburg PA
CBHW071853270326
41929CB00013B/2217